The publisher gratefully acknowledges the generous support of the following:

The Authors Imprint Endowment Fund
of the University of California Press Foundation,
which was established to support exceptional
scholarship by first-time authors

The Asian Studies Endowment Fund
of the University of California Press Foundation

The Anne G. Lipow Endowment Fund
for Social Justice and Human Rights
of the University of California Press Foundation,
which was established by Stephen M. Silberstein

The Director's Circle of the University of California Press
Foundation, whose members are:

Clarence and Jacqueline Avant
Nancy and Roger Boas
Lloyd Cotsen
Richard E. Damm and Sara Duryea Damm
John and Jo De Luca
Harriett and Richard Gold
Betty Hine and Holly Suich
Marilyn Lee and Harvey Schneider
Thomas and Barbara Metcalf
Robert J. Nelson and Monica C. Heredia
Margaret Pillsbury
Lucinda Reinold

The Darjeeling Distinction

CALIFORNIA STUDIES IN FOOD AND CULTURE

Darra Goldstein, Editor

The Darjeeling Distinction

*Labor and Justice on
Fair-Trade Tea Plantations in India*

Sarah Besky

UNIVERSITY OF CALIFORNIA PRESS

Berkeley   Los Angeles   London

University of California Press, one of the most distinguished university presses in the United States, enriches lives around the world by advancing scholarship in the humanities, social sciences, and natural sciences. Its activities are supported by the UC Press Foundation and by philanthropic contributions from individuals and institutions. For more information, visit www.ucpress.edu.

University of California Press
Berkeley and Los Angeles, California

University of California Press, Ltd.
London, England

Library of Congress Cataloging-in-Publication Data

Besky, Sarah.
  The Darjeeling distinction: labor and justice on fair trade tea tlantations in India / Sarah Besky.
      p.   cm. — (California studies in food and culture ; 47)
  Includes bibliographical references and index.
  ISBN 978-0-520-27738-0 (cloth, alk. paper) — ISBN 978-0-520-27739-7 (pbk., alk. paper)
  1. Tea trade—India—Darjeeling (District)   2. Tea plantations—India—Darjeeling (District)   3. Competition, Unfair—India—Darjeeling (District).   I. Title.
HD9198.I43 D3733   2013
338.1'7372095414—dc23   2013021968

Manufactured in the United States of America

22   21   20   19   18   17   16   15   14   13
10   9   8   7   6   5   4   3   2   1

In keeping with its commitment to support environmentally responsible and sustainable printing practices, UC Press has printed this book on Cascades Enviro 100, a 100% post consumer waste, recycled, de-inked fiber. FSC recycled certified and processed chlorine free. It is acid free, Ecologo certified, and manufactured by BioGas energy.

For the tea workers of Darjeeling

CONTENTS

ILLUSTRATIONS

MAPS

FIGURES

ACKNOWLEDGMENTS

This book would not have been possible without the help and support of numerous people and institutions. I was fortunate to receive funding for my field research from the American Institute of Indian Studies (2008–9), Fulbright Hays Doctoral Dissertation Research Abroad Program (2007–8), the Graduate School at the University of Wisconsin-Madison (2009), and the Land Tenure Center at the University of Wisconsin-Madison (2009–10). My fieldwork would not have been as productive without the support of multiple Foreign Language Area Studies (FLAS) Fellowships in Nepali, Hindi, and Tibetan from the Center for South Asian Studies (2005–7), as well as predissertation fieldwork funding from the Center for Global Studies (2006) and the Graduate School (2009), all at the University of Wisconsin-Madison. The writing of this book was supported by an Andrew W. Mellon / American Council of Learned Societies Dissertation Completion Fellowship (2011–12) and a Michigan Society of Fellows Postdoctoral Fellowship (2012–present).

I owe a great debt of gratitude to my graduate advisor at the University of Wisconsin-Madison, Kirin Narayan. Kirin painstakingly read drafts of this and many other pieces of writing, but more importantly, she taught me how to narrate the lives of others in a rich and respectful way. My mentors and dissertation committee members Jane Collins, Katherine Ewing, Jill Harrison, Paul Nadasdy, and Claire Wendland all provided comments and critiques that helped usher this project from dissertation to book.

Over the life of this research, I have greatly appreciated conversations with Sandy Brown, Nicholas D'Avella, Gina Drew, Phillip Lutgendorf, Laura-Anne Minkoff-Zern, Jonathan Padwe, Peter Rosenblum, Ashwini Sukthankar, Paige West, and Bradley Wilson. In Wisconsin, a number of friends and colleagues shaped my thinking about tea, food studies, India, and political ecology: Chris Butler, Chelsea Chapman, Jake Fleming, Jim Hoesterey, Erika Robb Larkins, Chris Limburg, Larry Nesper, Natalie Porter, Mary Rader, Susan Rottman, Lillian Hsiao-Ling Su, Noah Theriault, and Denise Wiyaka. I owe Abigail Neely a great debt of gratitude for so carefully reading every page of this manuscript in its final stages. I am also grateful to the organizers and participants in the SociETAS Seminar in the Department of Community and Environmental Sociology, where I was able to test early versions of the arguments herein. Finally, the Center for Culture, History, and the Environment provided a vibrant intellectual community while I wrote up my dissertation.

The Department of Anthropology at the University of Michigan has been a warm and stimulating intellectual environment. My special thanks to Stuart Kirsch for reading multiple drafts of the material presented within, as well as the students in his graduate-level environmental anthropology class for reading an early draft of chapter 2. Krisztina Fehérváry, Tom Fricke, Matthew Hull, Webb Keane, Erik Mueggler, Eric Plemons, Elizabeth F. S. Roberts, and other participants in the Socio-Cultural Workshop all carefully read and commented on an early draft of chapter 5.

The Michigan Society of Fellows has created a one-of-a-kind interdisciplinary community. Thank you to Donald Lopez and Linda Turner as well as the junior and senior fellows for pushing me to think of ways to communicate across disciplinary boundaries. I would like to extend particular appreciation to Lydia Barnett, Elise Lipkowitz, and Damola Osinulu for reading and commenting on chapter 1, and to Clare Croft and Eric Plemons for their readings of chapter 2. Laura, Randolph, and Astrid Miles provided much-needed outdoor diversions; and Erik, Sheela, and Napa Linstrum sheltered me and my extended family during the final stages of writing. Also at Michigan, the Center for South Asian Studies and the School of Natural Resources and Environment made great intellectual second homes. I am particularly grateful to Rebecca Hardin, who inspired me to think more expansively about gender and the moral economy.

I gave lectures on sections of this book at Bowdoin College (2011); the Columbia University School of Law (2012); and the National Museum of Ethnology in Osaka, Japan (2012). I also presented pieces of this book in various stages at a number of conferences. A special thanks is due to the participants and audience members at: the Annual Conference on South Asia (2007); Central States Anthropological Society Meeting (2007); the Dimensions of Political Ecology Conference (DOPE) at the University of Kentucky (2011, 2012); the Workshop on the History of Environment, Agriculture, Technology, and Science (WHEATS) (2010), with thanks to Ashley Carse, Jess Gilbert, and Matt Turner for their helpful comments; the Roy Rappaport Prize Panel at the Annual Meeting of the American Anthropological Association (2010), with particular thanks to Lisa Gezon, Laura Ogden,

Laura Zanotti, and Rebecca Hardin for reading some of the first writings on this project; and the Association for Nepal and Himalayan Studies Meeting (2011), with particular thanks to Tina Harris, Debarati Sen, Sara Shneiderman, Mark Turin, and Mélanie Vandenhelsken for a lively discussion of the Darjeeling-Sikkim Himalayas.

Other interdisciplinary conversations have shaped this book. Thank you to Mike Goodman and Christine Barnes, organizers of the 2012 "FoodMediaPolitics" sessions at the Association of American Geographers (AAG) Annual Meetings. And thank you to the organizers of the 2013 AAG panel "Value Chains, Neoliberal Regulation, and Global Restructuring," Jennifer Bair and Marion Werner. My conversations with geographers over the years have helped me think more critically about the concepts of landscape, place, and circulation. Though I was unable to attend the conference, Peter Vandergeest and Derek Hall kindly delivered my paper at "Certifying Asian Food: International Expectations, Domestic Priorities, Nationalist Discourses" at the 2012 Association for Asian Studies Conference. The critiques of the discussant, Adam Sneyd, were particularly insightful. Finally, I thank Jill Didur and Jayeeta Sharma and the attendants at "Foodways: Diasporic Dinners, Transnational Tables, and Culinary Connections," at the Annual Conference of the Centre for Diaspora and Transnational Studies, University of Toronto.

Three wonderful panels at the American Anthropological Association (AAA) Annual Meetings helped me think through much of this book. Sarah Lyon, who organized "What's Fair: Environmental and Social Justice through Markets," at the 2007 AAA meetings allowed me to present a paper that became chapter 4. An early version of it was published in an edited volume that came out of that panel, *Fair Trade and Social Justice: Global Ethnographies* (edited by Sarah Lyon and Mark Moberg [New York: New York University Press, 2010]). At the 2010 AAA meetings, I was pushed to think about the complexities of circulation and the production of environmental commodities. Thank you to Molly Doane and Paige West for organizing the panel, "Natural Circuits: The Political Ecology of Environmental Commodities," on which I presented a draft of chapter 5, and to June Nash and Jane Collins for their comments. Lastly, I wish to recognize my co-organizer on the panel "People Plants and Practice: Garden Variety Investigations of Domesticated Nature" at the 2011 AAA meetings, Jonathan Padwe. With the help of Jonathan, our discussant Virginia Nazarea, and the other panelists, I was able to discuss a draft of chapter 3 and think with the idea of the "garden."

I trace the roots of this project back to an undergraduate class at Connecticut College, Authenticity in Art and Culture, taught by Chris Steiner. Chris, I thank you for showing me where anthropological inquiry could go. I would also like to thank Sarah Queen and the beloved Harold Juli for their encouragement.

Part of the writing of this book was conducted while I was a Visiting Scholar at Franklin and Marshall College (2011–12). In Lancaster, Pennsylvania, I would like to thank Tania Ahmad and Roberta Strickler for their friendship and support. My research assistant, Hang Pham, did an excellent job; and Victoria Galanty, Ellanna Benabou, and Mia Damiano also provided research assistance.

Over the final months of writing this book, I thrived on correspondences with James Sinclair, the great-great grandson of one of the first tea planters in Darjeeling. I have relished hearing his stories and look forward to hearing many more. James kindly provided two of the photographs in this book. The first (figure 8) is a beautiful image of an old postcard of Chowrasta. The second (figure 10) is picture of his tea planter father at Steinthal Tea Estate in Darjeeling. I am grateful to James for allowing me to use these images in this book. I would also like to thank the phenomenal photographer and tea merchant, Benoy Thapa, owner of Thunderbolt Tea, for allowing me to use his photograph for the book jacket.

In Darjeeling, I wish to extend the biggest *dhanyabad* to the tea-plucking women with whom I shared many days and afternoons. Without their warmth and openness, this project would not have been possible. I refrain from naming these workers here. I also refrain from naming the planters, plantation owners, and GJMM activists who were kind enough to talk with me. B.G., R.S., U.R., V.P., N.C., S.S., P.S., and G.S. were crucial to my work in Darjeeling. The University of North Bengal in Siliguri, the Centre for Studies in Social Sciences in Kolkata, and my CSSS supervisor Bodhisattva Kar, provided institutional support for this project. My time in India would not have been nearly as productive and enjoyable without the assistance of the Fulbright Commission in Delhi and the American Institute of Indian Studies, particularly Subir Sarkar. For guidance and perspective in Darjeeling, I must extend a special thank you to Ranen Dutta and Khemraj Sharma. My fieldwork benefitted from the support of the Indian Tea Association and Darjeeling Tea Association in Darjeeling and Kolkata, especially Kaushik Basu, Monojit Das Gupta, and Sandip Mukerjee, as well as Aninditta Ray of the Tea Board of India.

I continue to find inspiration in my colleagues working in Darjeeling, in particular Keera Allendorf, Ida Benedetto, Siddhartha Gyaltsen, Rhys Fookler, Barbara Gerke, Thomas Shor, C. Townsend Middleton, Nayomi Sajan, and Debarati Sen. I would also like to extend a very special thanks to Mary Boland, Niraj Lama (now the owners of Happy Earth Tea in Rochester, New York), Tara, and Rory-Dorje for friendships and conversation in the field. The International Trust for Traditional Medicine (ITTM) in Kalimpong and Glenary's provided crucial writing sanctuary. To Aama and Pala: thank you for always being there with tea, biscuits, and a wonderful story.

Some text in this book appeared earlier in the following form: "The Labor of *Terroir* and the *Terroir* of Labor: Geographical Indication on Darjeeling Tea Plantations," *Agriculture and Human Values* (forthcoming); "Colonial Pasts and Fair Trade Futures: Changing Modes of Production and Regulation on Darjeeling Tea Plantations," in *Fair Trade and Social Justice: Global Ethnographies*, ed. Sarah Lyon and Mark Moberg, 97–122 (New York: New York University Press, 2010); "Can a Plantation Be Fair? Paradoxes and Possibilities in Fair Trade Darjeeling Tea Certification." *Anthropology of Work Review* 29(1) (2008): 1–9. Thank you to *Agriculture and Human Values* for allowing me to republish selections of my article.

At the University of California Press, I would like to thank the editor of the California Studies in Food and Culture Series, Darra Goldstein, for encouraging this book in its nascent stages. Thank you too to my editor, Kate Marshall, for her helpful feedback and kind assistance through various stages of this book's life. Andrew Frisardi provided careful copyediting on the manuscript. I am grateful to Sarah Lyon, Phillip Lutgendorf, and an anonymous reviewer for their helpful comments for revisions. Cindy Fulton carefully guided this book to completion. Thérèse Shere meticulously compiled the index.

Thank you to my parents, Andrea and Edward Besky, and to Susan and Alex Nading for their support. Finally, I am most deeply grateful to Alex Nading, whose love and encouragement propelled this project and supports all my other endeavors. Kitty, Sidney, and Floyd provided crucial emotional support and healthy distractions during many hours of writing.

NOTES ON ORTHOGRAPHY AND USAGE

English, Tibetan, Hindi, and Bengali words are folded in to the Darjeeling dialect of Nepali; it is distinctly different from the Nepali spoken in Nepal. All translations and transliterations of Nepali in the text follow Ralph Lilley Turner's (1997 [1931]) *Comparative Entomological Dictionary of the Nepali Language.* For words that do not appear in the Turner dictionary, I consulted Ruth Laila Schmidt's *Practical Dictionary of Modern Nepali* (1993), as well as Mahendra Caturvedi and B. N. Tiwari's *Practical Hindi-English Dictionary* (1970), for spelling guidance. In the case of words that do not appear in any of these dictionaries (as many Darjeeling words do not), I have transliterated them to best reflect their pronunciation.

In my transliterations of Nepali and other South Asian languages, I have striven for readability over technical precision. In cases where Nepali words are commonly used in English (e.g., bazaar, Nepali, coolie), they are not italicized or rendered with diacritics. Place names, organizations, and personal names are also not rendered in italics or with diacritics. English words used in Nepali appear in italics and are phonetically written out (e.g. *industri* for "industry"). Similarly, *Chowrasta* and *Chowk Bazaar* are used in their popular spellings (substituting *chau* with *chow*). The word *Nepali* is used to describe both people and language. *Calcutta* is used for the colonial city, while *Kolkata* is used for the contemporary city, in congruence with the city's official renaming in 2001. Other words translated and transliterated from Tibetan, Hindi, or Bengali are noted in the text.

A quick guide to commonly used letters with diacritical marks: The letter *ā* is pronounced like the vowel sound in *cat*. The letter *ī* is pronounced like the vowel sound in *tea*. And the letter *ū* is pronounced like the vowel sound in *food*. For ease of pronunciation, the letter *ś* is rendered as *sh*. Instead of *c* and *ch,* I use *ch* and *chh* to better reflect pronunciation. Vowels with a tilde (e.g., *ã*) indicate nasalization.

Plurals of Nepali words have an unitalicized *s* at the end of them. A select few words I wish to emphasize have the Nepali plural marker and postposition -*haru* at the end of them.

In general, all personal names and plantation names in this book are pseud-onyms. The exceptions are well-known public figures (i.e., Madan Tamang, Sub-hash Ghisingh, and Bimal Gurung), and two plantations briefly mentioned in the text (Aloobari and Steinthal), neither of which were included in my field study. Given that they are readily searchable, I also use the real names of plantations profiled in media reports I quote in chapter 3.

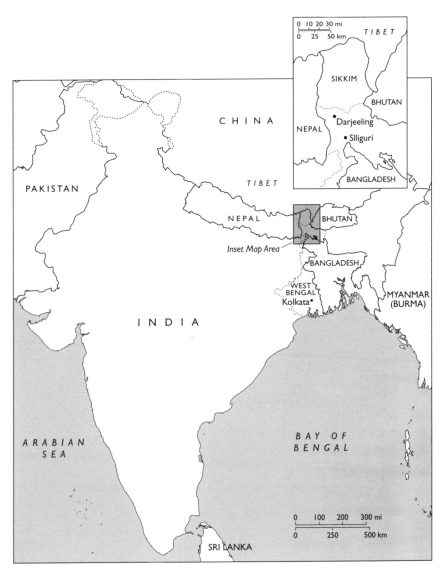

MAP 1. Map of India, with inset of Darjeeling district.

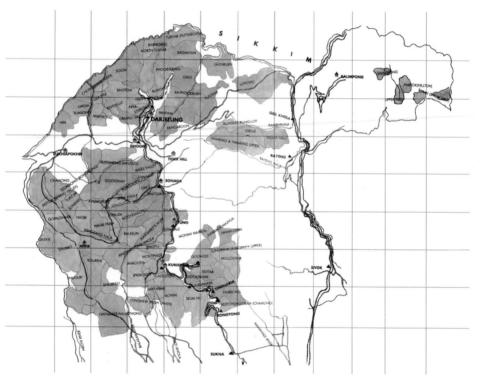

MAP 2. Map of Darjeeling, with plantations shaded. Courtesy Tea Board of India.

Introduction

Reinventing the Plantation for the Twenty-first Century

Darjeeling town, perched on one of the highest ridges in the northernmost part of West Bengal, is connected to the rest of India by a rough and bumpy road that begins in the dusty market town of Siliguri. At Siliguri, the railroad from West Bengal's capital, Kolkata, gives way to a narrow gauge, steam locomotive known locally as the "Toy Train," which carries tourists up the ridge on a smoky six-hour journey to Darjeeling. By car, the journey from Siliguri to Darjeeling takes just three to four hours, traversing through the foggy forests and tea plantations that fall off the road and plummet into the valleys below. Cars zig and zag back and forth up the mountain, weaving in and out of the path of the Toy Train, and passing a few villages precariously clinging to the sheer hillsides. Dense forests of *duppi* (*Cryptomeria japonica*) trees hug the road in a moist evergreen shade. They are planted in military-like formation—perfectly spaced, with impeccable posture—their armlike branches presenting bulbous clumps of needles straight up toward the sky.

The drive is mesmerizing (and for many, nauseating), and the landscape is striking. The tea plantations are immediately recognizable. Green and orderly like the *duppi*, the fields of tea go on for miles over and around the undulating landscape. But Darjeeling's is a beauty of a manufactured kind: the product of over 150 years of extensive capitalist extraction. The vivid greenness of colonially rooted tea plantations and *duppi* forests obscures the acute environmental and social effects of a long history of monoculture and marginalization. Long brown streaks left by landslides on the verdant slopes are reminders of the precariousness of people and plants here. These scars evoke questions about the sustainability of the entire place. This is the landscape of the twenty-first-century plantation.

This book tells a story about the social life of some of the world's most expensive and sought after tea. Darjeeling's tea laborers, planters,[1] and townspeople all know that Darjeeling and its tea are famous all over the world. Some trace the distinction of Darjeeling and its signature product to the misty mountain climate or the loamy soils; others talk about the work ethic of the laborers; and others mention the importance of the region's general *vāstu* (meaning "property" or "place," in Hindu spiritual geography).[2] Whatever the reason, since colonial times, Darjeeling tea has been associated with luxury and refinement, and the Darjeeling region has been a romantic "outside" within India: a cool, mountainous complement to the plains, and a home to exotic Nepali-speaking tea pluckers, recruited by British plantation owners beginning in the 1850s to staff what came to be known as "tea gardens." This book narrates how Darjeeling tea workers' ideas about value, plantation life, and social justice emerge through their encounters with tea's colonial legacy. It shows how these ideas have been reshaped by strategies to reinvent Darjeeling tea for twenty-first-century consumers seeking not only escape and refinement, but also, through "fair trade" and other agricultural certification schemes, a sense of social solidarity in their daily cup.

Today, Darjeeling is a district of the Indian state of West Bengal.[3] The descendants of the Nepali migrant laborers recruited to work on British plantations constitute its majority, with migrants from across India, Tibet, and beyond making up the remainder of the population. The Darjeeling district sits in the northernmost part of West Bengal, pinned in by international borders with Nepal, Bangladesh, and Bhutan (Chinese-occupied Tibet sits just to the north, above the small Indian state of Sikkim). In this unique and ecologically vulnerable mountain landscape on the periphery of modern India—populated by Nepali-speaking tea laborers, elite Indian planters, a multicultural mélange of immigrants, and the Anglo-Indian descendants of the British Raj—transnational movements for ethical trade have converged with a colonially derived system of tea production and a heated postcolonial discourse about economic and social rights. Over the past 150 years, consumers and marketers have given Darjeeling tea a specific territorial distinction as a luxury beverage. It is "the Champagne of teas." At the same time, Indian Nepali, or "Gorkha," laborers on tea plantations have developed a geographically and historically distinct identity, ideas of social justice, and feelings about the value of Darjeeling as both a product *and* a homeland.

In this book, I trace the ascendancy, decline, and revitalization of Darjeeling tea—born in British colonial India, transformed through Indian independence, and thriving today as a globally recognized crop. Consumption of this delicate, expensive brew has long been a marker of class distinction. Since the earliest days of British colonial production, Darjeeling has been exceptional because of its delicacy and because, unlike other teas, it has *not* normally been consumed with milk or sugar. Darjeeling tea tends to be light in color, and its flavor tends to be smoky and slightly floral. (Indeed, the controlled vocabulary professional tea tasters and graders use to describe Darjeeling—with vivid adjectives like cheesy, biscuity, and knobbly—is reminiscent of the words sommeliers use to describe fine wine.)

Ideas about place tie labor firmly to distinguished commodities like Darjeeling tea. As an anthropological study of a luxury beverage, this book is also about the relationship of taste and value to place, of labor to product, and of production to consumption. It tacks back and forth among stories about a *place* (Darjeeling); about *labor* (how tea is produced there); and about *meaning* (what makes tea—and Darjeeling in particular—special to tea drinkers and tea pluckers). This book melds a social ecology of tea, a study of the intimate relationships between laborers and the Darjeeling landscape, with a "food system perspective." As geographer Julie Guthman explains, taking a food system perspective entails "incorporating the entire array of ideas, institutions, and policies that affect how food is produced, distributed, and consumed."[4] An ethnography that adopts a food system perspective must look not only at production and circulation, but also at the spaces in between that make production and circulation possible and meaningful. To do so, it is important to be clear about the material conditions under which Darjeeling tea is produced. It is significant not only to this book, but to an understanding of Indian tea's place in the global food system more broadly, that the vast majority of tea grown in the world, from Kenya to Sri Lanka to Indonesia to India (with the notable exception of China and Japan) is produced *on plantations*. And plantations are landscapes of empire, governed by processes of colonial consumption, production, and expansion. While plantation agriculture still predominates in India and much of the postcolonial world, we know little about how plantation workers themselves understand the plantation as a social and ecological form. This book is an attempt to answer that question.

THE EMPIRE OF TEA

Records show that tea was cultivated and drunk as early as the fourth century B.C.E. in Taoist monasteries in China, where it was plucked locally from tall trees and processed by hand rolling the leaves against a screen perched over a fire.[5] Tea consumption spread through China and into Japan in the late sixth century C.E. As in China, in Japan it was cultivated largely in monastic gardens to rejuvenate and purify the minds and bodies of mediating monks.[6] Over the centuries, tea cultivation and consumption spread beyond monastic contexts in China and Japan, as wider publics began drinking it with an eye to improving health and mental acuity. Despite being native to the Eastern Himalayas, tea was not cultivated on the Indian side of the range until the 1830s, and not adapted as an everyday drink in India until decades later.[7]

Exploration and trade throughout the seventeenth century introduced Portuguese, Dutch, and British sailors to the exotic materials of the Far East, such as spices, silk, and tea.[8] The Dutch East India Company began trading Chinese tea in the 1600s, and the British East India Company soon followed. Traders quickly realized that tea, like coffee and cocoa, gives the drinker a little kick. As a result, tea, like these other drinkable stimulants, was initially marketed as a pharmacological product. Though tea has long been considered the "national beverage" of England, in the early eighteenth century, there was little tea consumed there. Coffee and cocoa were initially more popular beverages, and these remained favored in the court and elite English social spheres. But by early nineteenth century, tea had become a commonplace beverage in households across social classes in Britain.

Tea consumption spread into the British public through the proliferation of London coffeehouses in the early eighteenth century. In coffeehouses, coffee and tea consumption became a central component of *male* social life. But in 1717, Thomas Twining, owner of the male-dominated Tom's Coffee House, opened the Golden Lyon retail teashop. At the Golden Lyon, *women* could purchase teas and the newest tea accoutrements—locking tea chests, tea pots, porcelain cups and saucers—for at-home tea parties.[9] In the mid-eighteenth century, the patterns and spaces of English tea consumption began to shift.[10] Tea moved from the coffeehouse to domestic space. The home "tea gardens" that sprang up across London in the eighteenth century were spaces of feminized, middle-class tea consumption.[11] By the 1750s, tea was well on its way to being the quintessential British drink.

To source a growing demand for tea by both British men and women, the East India Company exchanged silver for tea with Chinese merchants. Trade with China, however, had reached a peak by the mid-1700s. The East India Company could not offload any more silver bullion, despite the fact that demand for tea was still growing. The acquisition of territory in Bengal in the 1760s changed this and would eventually revolutionize the tea trade. Mughal rulers controlled much of the Indian subcontinent and provided favorable and eventually duty-free terms on which the East India Company could trade jute, indigo, spices, and other exotics. The Company collected taxes from those in the annexed territory and used the revenue to invest in Indian textiles, which were then exported to Canton, the only port in China in which foreigners were allowed to trade. The proceeds from the sales of Indian-made goods were reinvested in tea. This connection allowed Chinese tea to circulate back to England at an increasing rate.

In the late eighteenth century, as demand for Chinese tea increased in Britain, so did Chinese demand for opium. But opium was not legally traded in China. To stoke demand and supply opium in Canton, the British East India Company began expansive cultivation of opium in newly acquisitioned lands in Bengal. Private merchants transported and sold the opium to corrupt officials in China. British merchants were paid in silver, and this silver was sold back to the East India Company in London. That silver was then sent *back* to Canton to pay for tea. The East India Company maintained that its officials were not themselves participating in—or even condoning—the opium trade with China, but British East India Company opium production increased exponentially between the 1760s and the 1830s. Despite all attempts by Chinese government officials to control the trade and consumption of opium, circulation intensified. This trade surge culminated in the Chinese government's seizure and burning of one year's worth of opium and the imprisonment of both British and Chinese agents involved in the trade of that stash. After this, Britain declared war on China. During the First Opium War (1839–42), the British navy pummeled Chinese forces and coerced the Chinese into severe concessions. Among these were the cession of Hong Kong to the English Crown, the creation of several other "open ports," the paying of reparations, and the acceptance of British supervision in customs. After the Second Opium War (1856–60), Chinese addiction to opium soared, as did domestic cultivation in China. By the end of the century, China was supplying the bulk of its own opium demand, and British opium cultivation dwindled.[12]

In the mid-nineteenth century, Britain sat in the center of two trading spheres— one to the east, which included India, China, and points in between, and one to the west, which enveloped Africa and the West Indies. The eastern trading sphere circulated tea, textiles, opium, and silver. The western trading sphere circulated sugar and people. British and American traders purchased human beings in Africa and shipped them to the West Indies. There, enslaved Africans cultivated sugar on British plantations. That sugar was then sent back to London, where it found its way into, among other places, teacups.

Anthropologist and pioneering food system scholar Sidney Mintz described this second trading sphere in his history of sugar, *Sweetness and Power*. Mintz traces the way in which, between the seventeenth and nineteenth centuries, the consumption of tea and sugar shifted from an exclusive practice of elites to an essential necessity of the growing industrial British working class. The circulation of slaves, silver, sugar, and tea created a drink that fueled the Industrial Revolution.[13] The popularity of tea came thanks in part to the rise of sugar, which became the uniting ingredient in what Mintz calls the British "tea complex."[14] This not only included sugary hot tea, but also cakes, pastries, and the accouterments of "tea-time."[15] Tea's position as "food," then, remained dependent upon sugar. Like coffee and cocoa, tea's taste is bitter and its health benefits debatable.[16] Chinese drinkers did not take their tea with sugar; sweetening tea was a unique British practice. As I mentioned above, Darjeeling tea remains the lone Indian tea that is favorably compared to Chinese tea, and it is the only other variety routinely consumed around the world without milk or sugar.

After the First Opium War, East India Company officers began discussions on how to cultivate tea in recently annexed territories in northeastern and northwestern

India to supply the growing demand back home.[17] Beginning in the 1830s, British settlers began experimenting with tea cultivation in these mountainous regions. Within fifty years, and with the help of the introduction of coal-fired tea-processing machinery, these settlers had created an industry so vast and efficient that much of British demand could be sourced from the British Empire itself. Over the rest of the nineteenth century, British colonial tea plantation production spread from the Himalayan foothills to South India, East Africa, and Sri Lanka.

With the development of the sugar trade, the darker, maltier, more tannic black tea grown in India on British-run plantations overtook Chinese green tea in popularity in Britain (and sugar became ever more desired to complement it). A new form of consumption was born. Tea was a nonalcoholic drink people could enjoy at home. It was cheaper and much easier to prepare than coffee or cocoa. All they had to do was boil water and pour it over some dried leaves. Certainly, the look of that ritual appeared different across the British classes—from porcelain pots to dented metal cups. The boiled water, too, as anthropologist Alan MacFarlane suggests, was revolutionary to the public health of Britain.[18] Yet the productive driver of this popularity lay in the plantations of Britain's colonies in South Asia and East Africa.

WHAT IS A PLANTATION?

The social science literature on agriculture and labor in the food system remains dominated by U.S. case studies, examining the experiences of laborers as well as how agribusiness forms perpetuate themselves. Food system scholars rarely, if ever, apply the term *plantation* to Euro-American agribusiness, for obvious reasons. The word plantation evokes painful and uncomfortable memories about the American South. Industrial farms—even the massive corporate fields found in the Central Valley of California or the Great Plains—are not plantations. Still, the plantation, born of colonial control and resource extraction, is thriving today in a global market that incorporates—albeit unequally—former colonies in Asia, Africa, and Latin America. Commodity crop production on plantations still fuels consumption in the former imperial metropolises. In the market, after all, power tilts to large-scale producers who can turn out low-cost products. Both plantations and industrial farms can deliver such products, but as a rich vein of anthropological work has shown, the plantation is distinct socially and historically from the industrial farm.[19]

We can make productive comparisons between different kinds of large-farm systems. The plantation certainly contains elements of a seemingly bygone era of bonded or sharecropping labor, but it also reminds us of the capitalist industrial agricultural system that brings us strawberries in December, in that it features large-scale production of single crops in an ecologically intensive and sociologically hierarchical manner. But plantations also contain elements of "peasant" agriculture.[20] "Peasant" agricultural systems, characterized by small farmers working land often owned by a large holder and growing crops for subsistence as well as for large estates, have also been of longstanding interest to anthropologists and other social scientists.[21]

Plantations share with feudal peasant systems a unique form of labor organization and remittance. James Scott explains that the numerous definitions of "the peasantry" share two elements in common: (1) a peasant is a "rural cultivator whose production is oriented largely toward family consumption . . . this defines his central economic goal"; and (2) a peasant "is part of a larger society (including nonpeasant elites and the state) that makes claims upon him and this, in a sense, defines his potential human antagonists (or collaborators) in attaining that goal."[22] Darjeeling tea laborers are not growing food primarily for their families' consumption, but it is important to highlight that unlike industrial farm workers, plantation laborers, even in contemporary Darjeeling, are not "hired" in an "open" labor market. Most plantation laborers are permanent, life-long members of the plantation workforce. They not only work on plantations but live on them as well, in villages owned by tea companies. While not bonded in the same sense as colonial plantation workers—what British colonialists called "coolies"—contemporary tea workers are still subjugated by a system of indebtedness, reciprocity, and social reproduction that keeps them tied to the land. In Darjeeling, plantation jobs are not acquired through a market, but passed from person to person, often through kinship networks.

Industrial farm workers, on the other hand, generally receive wages, not in kind benefits or forms of nonmonetary compensation (e.g., housing, rations, health care, and schooling).[23] Though they work on farms whose scale mirrors that of industrial agribusiness, Darjeeling tea plantation laborers, like peasants, do receive a significant amount of their income in kind, through relationships with plantation owners and management. Though Darjeeling tea laborers, unlike classic peasant farmers, do not grow their own food, most do see themselves as working with the goal of basic familial subsistence. As part of their compensation, Darjeeling tea workers receive land for cultivation, housing, food rations, medical facilities, schooling, firewood, and other necessities. These nonmonetary forms of compensation promote the subsistence of workers and their families.[24]

Tea plantations, then, are large landholdings where laborers produce commodity crops for global consumption. But unlike large industrial farms in the United States or Europe, plantations depend for their success on the continued bondage of laborers to land. Wages on plantations are too low to support independent livelihoods. Plantation families depend on food rations, housing, and other nonmonetary forms of compensation. These forms of compensation provide long-term social stability for plantation workers, their families, and their villages. In workers' eyes, the abundance of rations is directly linked to the success of the tea trade. The plantation, in other words, ties workers to place in ways that give them both a deep sense of connection and a unique experience of exploitation—an experience perhaps less familiar and seemingly more anachronistic than that of migrant wage laborers in the farms of the First World. The process of tea production, to which I now turn, depends upon the persistence of the plantation form.

TEA: FROM FIELD TO CUP

Whether or not it comes labeled as "fair trade" or with a geographical distinction that links it to a place (Darjeeling, Assam, Sri Lanka), most of the tea we see today, broken up into our tea bags or packaged into beautiful tins, is produced in a similar fashion. It must be plucked from its bush, withered, fermented, rolled, dried, sorted, tasted, packaged, and finally shipped off to its retailers and consumers. This process spans days and involves the labor of thousands of people, most of whom are women.

"Tea" comes from the brewing of leaves of a select few varieties of the camellia plant in hot water. Camellia are a genus of flowering plant in the family *Theaceae,* and, even though they are native to eastern and southern Asia, they have traveled across the globe, finding homes in the backyard gardens of the West. One variety of camellia is even the state flower of Alabama. The most renowned camellia is *Camellia sinensis,* or the China variety of tea. *Camellia sinsensis* has a lesser-known cousin, *Camellia assamensis,* the Assam variety of tea, indigenous to Northeast India. Historians and anthropologists believe that human consumption of tea made from camellia began somewhere on the slopes of the Eastern Himalayas near Darjeeling—in contemporary Southwest China, Burma, and Northeast India.[25]

Green and wiry, tea bushes will grow into trees if left unattended. Even though, like all camellias, tea bushes are capable of producing beautiful white and yellow flowers, tea's value and taste—regardless of its location of cultivation—comes from its leaves. The plant is pruned and groomed into a flat-top bush, so that cultivators can pluck the youngest shoots—two leaves and a bud—for processing (see fig. 1).

While the topography and climate of tea plantations across India and the postcolonial world differ, tea cultivation and processing on these plantations looks much like it does in Darjeeling. Tea cultivation starts in sweeping green fields that span hundreds of feet in altitude. Women workers traverse these hillsides combing the bushes for delicate sprigs. In Darjeeling, women pluck tea six days a week, from seven o'clock in the morning to four in the afternoon, with a brief lunch break in the middle of the day.

Fine teas like Darjeeling are valuable in part because this field work is done by hand. In Darjeeling, workers do not use machines for harvesting tea, and given the need to pick only two small leaves and a bud, excluding stems and drier, coarser,

FIGURE 1. *Dui patti ek suero*: "two leaves and a bud." Plantation laborers look for this young sprig of tea while plucking. Photo by author.

larger leaves, delicacy is a must. Freshly plucked green leaf is transported to an on-plantation processing factory, either by tractor or by porters. In the factory, it undergoes multiple phases of processing to produce the fragrant twists of tea sold in shops as "loose leaf." While women make up the majority of the field labor force, men, often the husbands or brothers of field laborers, dominate the factories (see figs. 2 and 3).

In the factory, tea passes through four processes before it is packed for shipping. First, tea is *withered*, which involves placing the green leaves onto long elevated troughs with mesh bottoms. Under the troughs is a mechanism for circulating hot air. This process removes most of the moisture from the leaves (fig. 4).

Second, male laborers place the withered leaves on large racks where they *ferment,* or more accurately, oxidize. When exposed to the air, like a peeled avocado or cut apple that sits out on the counter, green tea leaves turn brown, signifying the breakdown of the leaves' chlorophyll and the release of their residual tannins. There is some room for variation in the fermentation process. Different degrees of fermentation yield different tastes, or "styles" of tea. The teas we know as "green" and "white" are unfermented, "oolongs" are semi-fermented, and "black" teas are

FIGURE 2. Female tea workers plucking tea under the watchful eye of their male supervisor. Photo by author.

FIGURE 3. Male field supervisors collecting leaf to bring up to the factory. Photo by author.

FIGURE 4. Tea withering in specially designed troughs in a tea factory. The process of withering removes the excess moisture from the tea leaves. Photo by author.

fully fermented. Within this green-oolong-black spectrum, there is a great deal of variety in taste and appearance.

Third, the fermented but still damp leaves are put into a *rolling* machine. Usually, the withering and fermentation processes take place on the upper floor of a tea factory. To initiate the rolling process, tea slides down a chute from the upper floor. Around and around and around, the tea leaves are pressed and rolled in antique British-era contraptions that look like metallic grain mills. Imagine taking a damp leaf and compressing and turning it between your palms, making the flat surface into a twisted sprig. The rolling machine is a steel, coal-fired version of this process. By hand or by machine, the pressure and friction release oils and essences in the leaves. The machine also rolls the once full leaves into cylindrical twists (fig. 5).

Fourth, the leaves are *dried,* or "fired," in a different machine. This device, also of colonial vintage, is something like an oven with a built-in conveyor belt. It essentially bakes the tea to remove the last bit of moisture. Firing gives the twisted leaves their dry, brittle finish. This step enables Darjeeling and other teas to sit for months without losing their flavor, as long as they are stored in a dry place. Rolled and dried, Darjeeling teas can endure the long trip to markets abroad, packaged in

FIGURE 5. Rolling machine in a tea factory. Tea is placed in the rolling machine after fermentation to twist tea leaves into their characteristic shape. Photo by author.

boxes made from the soft wood of the *duppi* tree, that other iconic British botanical import.

Today, Darjeeling tea is either shipped directly to buyers abroad or is sold at auction in Kolkata, the old colonial port and contemporary capital of the state of West Bengal. At auction (and through direct sales, though these figures are not made public), the prices of tea fluctuate dramatically throughout the year because of what people in the tea business refer to as "flushes." There are four flushes, or seasons, of Darjeeling tea: *first flush* (mid-March to mid-April), *second flush* (mid-April to May), *monsoon flush* (June to August), and *autumn flush* (September to November). Darjeeling's first and second flushes are among the most prized and some of the highest-priced teas in the world. A Darjeeling plantation makes all its annual money before the start of the monsoon at the end of May, when the heavy rains start and the quality of the leaf changes, becoming bigger and more fibrous. There are several grades of leaf tea, all yielding different prices, from STGFOP (Super Fine Tippy Golden Flowery Orange Pekoe), FTGFOP (Fine Tippy Golden Flowery Orange Pekoe), TGFOP (Tippy Golden Flowery Orange Pekoe), GFOP (Golden Flowery Orange Pekoe), FOP (Flowery Orange Pekoe), to OP (Orange

Pekoe), broken leaf BOP (Broken Orange Pekoe), and "fannings" (tea typically found in tea bags and in many cases swept up from the factory floor).[26]

In 2010, women field workers received sixty-three rupees (just over a dollar) for each day's work.[27] Workers use most of this money to supplement their biweekly food rations (four kilograms of wheat flour and two kilograms of rice every fifteen days). Plantation village households are relatively small. Women workers generally live with husbands, unmarried children, and possibly a set of elder parents. Unlike in other parts of South Asia, in which women join patrilineal "joint families" headed by their husbands and their parents, Darjeeling women tea pluckers tend to live in nuclear families. Still, earnings are low, and staple foods are particularly expensive high in the hills. In fact, everything is more expensive in Darjeeling. Tea bushes occupy almost all of the district's arable land, which means that most food has to be trucked to Darjeeling from Siliguri, some four hours downhill. During the time of my fieldwork, a kilogram of lentils (*dāl*) cost twenty rupees, a kilogram of tomatoes cost thirty to forty rupees, a kilogram of potatoes twenty to thirty rupees, and a bunch of mustard greens ten rupees. The sixty-three rupees and the biweekly rations need to support four to five people. Even for public schools, women and men have to pay for their children's uniforms, books, paper, and fees.

In a day, a worker might pick anywhere between one and six kilograms of tea. It takes about three kilograms of green leaf to make one kilogram of processed tea. Women in Darjeeling are keenly aware of the irony that they produce some of the world's most expensive tea yet get paid a miniscule fraction of what this tea fetches abroad. They also express frustration with the swaths of fields of verdant green bushes that produce nothing edible. At the same time, most workers are voracious consumers of broken-leaf Darjeeling tea, which they receive in rations and buy in the local market. In the fields, they consume tea in the form of *kālo chiyā* ("black tea," pronounced *chee*-yaa), leaves steeped with a generous amount of sugar, and *nunko chiyā* ("salt tea"), leaves steeped with salt. The only consumers of *phikā chiyā* ("bland" or "unseasoned tea," i.e., served with no milk or sugar) are the chronically ill or diabetic. At home, workers usually drink a *chiyā* prepared with sugar as well as milk. Tea provides a vehicle for salt, sugar, and calorie delivery, albeit in a "complex" decidedly unlike that which Sidney Mintz envisioned for middle-class Britain.

Depending on the season of harvest, a plantation can make anywhere from five to five hundred dollars per kilogram for leaf grade teas at the Kolkata auction. Often, the finest, most expensive grades of tea, particularly from the first and second flushes, never make it to auction; instead, they are sold directly to buyers abroad. But Darjeeling planters, even though they are ambivalent about the rise of such "direct buying" relationships, many of which are fuelled by the fair-trade market, know that the international tea market, and the burgeoning U.S. tea market in particular, is dominated by tea bags. Though they are dismissive of Americans' penchant for drinking Darjeeling out of tea bags, planters' ability to sell low grades for tea bags both for the international and domestic market is providing a financial boon to the industry.

THE TWENTY-FIRST-CENTURY PLANTATION

During the colonial era, there was a built-in market for Darjeeling and other empire-grown teas. British companies controlled all aspects of production and marketing. After Indian independence in 1947, British companies slowly divested themselves of Indian manufacturing, selling their Darjeeling tea plantations to elite Indians, who quickly found that they did not have the kind of capital British corporations did to maintain the plantations. When British companies left India, they turned to remaining British colonies in Kenya and Sri Lanka to supply their domestic demand. The tight relationship between tea production in India and consumption in England was severed. In 1973, it was further broken up when the government of India passed the Foreign Exchange Regulation Act (FERA), which prohibited profits made in India to be repatriated to Britain and mandated that companies in India be majority Indian-held.[28] Since the demand for Indian tea was supplied by tea producers in former British colonies in East Africa, a new class of tea planters in Darjeeling found themselves with a surplus of tea and fewer people to buy it.

In this bleak market, Indian-run Darjeeling plantations found new markets in the Soviet Union. As the USSR developed, so did Soviet demands for Darjeeling tea. "The Soviets," many planters told me, recounting the tumultuous last few decades in Darjeeling tea production, "would buy anything" as long as it made a cup of black tea.[29] The breakup of the Soviet Union in 1991 ruptured this trade network. The district spiraled into a decade of decreasing yields, closed gardens, and starvation deaths, more severe than they had experienced in the downturn immediately following independence and FERA.

Despite this, Darjeeling, as a place, remained evocative of a distinct luxury and refinement. The colonially rooted Darjeeling tea plantation endured after independence, and with the help of new international ethical trade initiatives, particularly fair trade, the system is now thriving. Many contemporary teas—Darjeeling most prominent among them—are now labeled "fair trade," "sustainable," *terroir,* and "organic." These terms infuse senses of social justice and solidarity with the luxury distinction so long associated with Darjeeling and its tea. Since the late 1990s and early years of the new century and the entrance of international agricultural certifications like fair trade into the picture, Darjeeling's tea industry has witnessed a resurgence: plantations that closed after the fall of the Soviet Union have reopened, Darjeeling tea is fetching higher prices, and tourists have even begun coming to plantations to learn more about how the famous tea is produced.

Fair-trade, organic, and shade-grown labels guide our purchasing and attest to the conditions of production of the products they adorn: conditions that we believe are *better* as the result of our purchases. In this book, I question the extent to which workers reap the rewards of Darjeeling tea's market revival and distinction through consumer-driven systems. The most prominent of these is fair trade. Fair-trade packaging, in particular, claims that purchasing such products supports "small farmers," who have access to higher monetary yields for their crops and democratically decide how these revenues are distributed.

"Fair-trade plantation" may seem like an oxymoron, as plantation workers are not small farmers. They are laborers who, like peasants, live and work on land they do not own. In the late 1990s, however, tea plantations in Darjeeling became the first plantations in the world to receive fair-trade certification. Hope was high among certifying agencies that fair trade would alleviate the inequities of postcolonial tea production. Despite these hopes, Darjeeling's plantation laborers, who produce some of the world's most expensive tea, remain some of the tea industry's worst-paid workers.

This book situates fair trade amid two other moves to bring the Darjeeling tea plantation into a twenty-first-century market for geographically distinguished and ethically sourced food, and to bring the Darjeeling region into a twenty-first-century multiethnic Indian democracy. The first, World Trade Organization Geographical Indication status, or GI—a distinction Darjeeling shares with famous place and food names like Scotch, Champagne, and Roquefort—uses international law to limit the number of plantations that can call their tea "Darjeeling" and to establish the tea grown there as the intellectual property of the government of India. The second, the Gorkhaland agitation, is a longstanding movement to form an Indian state separate from West Bengal, which would include Darjeeling, its tea plantations, and its majority of Indian Nepalis, or "Gorkhas." These three movements—fair trade, Geographical Indication, and Gorkhaland—are all strategies for reinventing the colonially rooted Darjeeling plantation in an era of increased consumer consciousness about the social and environmental conditions of food production. I argue that each of the strategies for plantation revitalization—fair trade, GI, and Gorkhaland—attempt to make plantation life "better" by situating the plantation within what I call a "Third World agrarian imaginary."[30] In essence, each is an effort to undo the injustices of the colonial past, yet each only partially addresses the concerns of plantation workers themselves.

In his analysis of "distinction," Pierre Bourdieu described the economic and social relationships between embodied and sensory taste, aesthetics, and the logics of the market.[31] Bourdieu was largely interested in the consumption of luxury commodities, and his study helped spur a considerable literature on "the social life of things," the circulation of commodities, and the selling of goods linked to particular places, cultures, and lifestyles.[32] For Bourdieu, "taste" exists in a mutually constitutive relationship to systems of production, whereby changes in the consumptive field induce changes in the productive field, and vice versa.[33] Following this insight, I suggest that workers play an active role in the distinction of Darjeeling—both as a tea and as a place. Darjeeling's distinction within the global tea trade, which stretches from former colonial possessions in East Africa to Indonesia, stems from British colonial notions about the relationships between flavor, environment, and value.

This book bridges cultural anthropology with food system studies. One intellectual focus of food system studies, an interdisciplinary field dominated by sociologists and geographers, is the way in which people reconcile social values (i.e., justice, sustainability) and market values (i.e., price, luxury).[34] In the sense that I adopt it here, "value" emerges both from economic exchange relations, in which price and utility are at the forefront, and from a shifting set of moral ideas about the relationships between economic actors and between people and the things they consume, produce, and sell.[35]

Karl Marx called attention to such fluidity in notions of value. For Marx, commodity markets require quantitative commensurability. Commodities acquire an "exchange value," measured in monetary price. The reduction of commodities to exchange values makes the "qualitative" worth of those things, their practical value, or their "use value," of lesser economic importance. Use value is not a given quality, however; rather it emerges in specific social contexts. The subsuming of use value to exchange value was, for Marx, key to the abstraction of human labor from things. As Marx argued, notions of quantitative and qualitative value both obscure the role of labor in production.

Contemporary theorists of value have extended this idea to examine not only the interplay between quantitative and qualitative value but also the forms of labor that reproduce these assessments. Doing so, they have called closer attention to social context: the moral ideas that guide people in their relationships to the things they produce. Drawing on the sociologist Georg Simmel's *Philosophy of Money*, Arjun Appadurai notes that the market economy "consists not only in exchanging values but in the exchange of values."[36] Appadurai coined the phrase *regimes of value* to describe the way in which social and political context shapes, as Simmel puts it, the desires of consumers and producers and the terms of their exchanges.[37] Attention to regimes of value shows how exchange is embedded "in more encompassing systems of value production," systems of moral ideas, political consciousness, and ethnic or class identities, in which, as anthropologist Fred Myers writes, "value ... must be sustained or reproduced through the complex work of production."[38] As Myers suggests, the contrast between "qualitative" value (moral, meaning-laden, "encompassing") and "quantitative" value (economic, utilitarian, price-related) "may underlie significant dynamics within structures of social action."[39] Building on this insight, the present book pays particular attention to the role of geographically and historically specific productive practices—in particular, how Darjeeling tea workers understand their work and the plantation—in bringing moral and market values into proximity.

For workers, labor, management, *and* the agro-environment are bound together in what I call a "tripartite moral economy." E. P. Thompson developed the concept of the moral economy in his study of bread riots in eighteenth-century England. The riots took place across the country because the public saw in rising bread prices a violation of moral relations between the poor and the wealthy. As Thompson writes: "[The riots were] legitimized by the assumptions of an older moral economy, which taught the immorality of any unfair method of forcing up the price of provisions by profiteering upon the necessities of the people."[40] Massive-scale protests, he explains, "indicate an extraordinarily deep-rooted pattern of behavior and belief." These mass actions were made possible by imaginaries of social relationships in the past. James Scott extends the concept of moral economy to rural life among Southeast Asian rice farmers.[41] Scott describes precapitalist relationships between peasants and landholding elites as rooted in a "subsistence ethic," by which peasants, who lived at the brink of survival, could rely on the elites for their basic needs. Scott explains that these relationships broke down at the hand of capitalist market forces, and as a result, peasants could justify resisting and revolting against the elites. Urban or rural, the reciprocal basis of a moral economy is similar. There are certain economic and social conditions that the public agrees upon as acceptable. When these conditions deteriorate, however, riots, shirking work, or other forms of resistance ensue. Crucially, Thompson and Scott highlight that we often do not understand moral economic relationships until they break down.[42]

Market-driven programs like fair trade and GI, propelled by universal notions of what social justice means, and the Gorkhaland movement, driven by sense that plantation justice might come from geopolitical sovereignty, each present challenges to Darjeeling's moral economy. If fair trade, GI, and Gorkhaland create a market for justice, then ideas of justice themselves must respond to the realities of production and to tea workers' ideas of what makes working conditions tolerable. Despite attempts by fair-trade certifiers, tea marketers, and politicians to sanitize it through appeals to justice, moral economic understandings of the plantation remain central to the culture of tea production and to the ways in which tea workers envision its future.

WHAT IS A GORKHA?

Outside of India, Darjeeling is probably best known for its tea, but within India, the region is at least as well known as the de facto homeland of Indian Nepalis, or Gorkhas. Just as it would be impossible to think of Darjeeling without thinking of tea, it would be difficult to understand Darjeeling tea without understanding the unique history of the Gorkhas and their decades-long struggle for political autonomy in the region, the Gorkhaland movement. Indeed, if one asked a tea worker about her identity, she would likely respond, "Nepali" or "Gorkha." In Darjeeling, the terms Nepali and Gorkha are interchangeable.

But Gorkha identity, as I show in this book, is about more than just a name. Indian Nepalis' struggle for a separate Indian state stems in part from their understanding of themselves as a unique social group. Gorkha identity has its roots in three processes, which I describe in more detail over the forthcoming chapters. The first is a history of colonial service, including most notably tea plantation work and military service under the British Empire. The second is the postcolonial formation of class consciousness among Indian agricultural laborers, which began during the struggle for independence in the 1930s and brought Indian Nepalis firmly into the political life of the new, multiethnic Indian democracy. The third is a series of social movements, spearheaded by Indian Nepali elites, to establish Gorkhas as an Indian ethnic group.

The words Gorkha and Nepali became synonymous in India thanks to a particular linguistic interpretation of Nepali political structure. The Kingdom of Nepal, established by the Shah dynasty, had its base in the Gorkha district, northwest of present-day Kathmandu. During the eighteenth and nineteenth century, British explorers, traders, and military men came to know their Nepali interlocutors as "Gurkhas," a slight Anglicization of Gorkha. Impressed with the resolve of the Shah dynasty's army, the British began recruiting Nepali soldiers into special Gurkha regiments. When they established tea plantations in Darjeeling, then a sparsely populated region, in the mid-nineteenth century, they recruited people from Tibeto-Burman ethnic groups in Nepal's eastern hills to build and work them, homogenizing them as Gurkhas. Over time, soldiers, servants, and tea workers, most of whom hailed from Tibeto-Burman speaking groups, began speaking Nepali, the Indo-Aryan language that was used to unite Nepal.

By the turn of the twentieth century, these Nepali soldiers and servants, together with Tibetan and indigenous residents of Darjeeling, began forming social and political associations, representing themselves alternately as Nepalis, as Hillmen, and as Gorkhas. The first call for administrative recognition of Gorkhas was officially lodged by the Hillmen's Association in 1907.[43] After Indian independence in 1947, Gorkha politicians continued to petition state and central governments for recognition and autonomy.

Those calls failed, and the Darjeeling district became a part of the Indian state of West Bengal. As ethnic minorities in their own state, and as members of a group known for its loyalty to the British military, the Gorkhas remained marginalized. For decades after independence, leaders of the Nepali Bhasha Andolan (Nepali Language Movement) fought a parallel battle for language recognition on both state and local stages. In 1961, Nepali became an official language of the Darjeeling district. Amid a series of high profile attacks on Nepalis elsewhere in India, the 1980s saw a rise in Nepali political action in Darjeeling.[44] In 1980, Subhash Ghisingh, the child of a tea plantation, and his Gorkha National Liberation Front (GNLF), initiated a new movement to push for the autonomy of the Darjeeling district from the state of West Bengal and the formation of a separate state within India. This movement culminated in the first Gorkhaland agitation, a violent conflict that pitted GNLF activists against both the West Bengal government and India's Central Reserve Police. Memories of the first Gorkhaland agitation, which lasted just two years, between 1986 and 1988, were still vivid among Darjeeling residents I met during my fieldwork. Nearly everyone knew a person who had been killed in the violence that marked those years, and tea plantation workers were no different. Stories of rapes, disappearances, and beheadings, as well as burned plantation bungalows, villages, and factories, were commonplace. The second Gorkhaland agitation, led by the Gorkha Janmukti Morcha (GJMM) began in late 2007 and forms the background to this book.[45] This second coming of the movement never reached the furious pitch of the first, but the legacy of death and destruction continued to loom over life in the district. Gorkha life and identity, then, were shaped by the violence of war, both imperial and insurgent, as well as by the more subtle rhythms of plantation labor.

CONTENDING VISIONS OF JUSTICE

How should we understand the relationship between justice and the market? Certainly, justice and its pursuit remain central to the mobilization of political movements, the articulation of inequality in the face of corporate expansion, the evaluation of development projects, experiences of marginalization, and expressions of law. Yet justice is an elusive concept. Indeed, the concept of justice is perhaps most often invoked when actors perceive its absence: injustice. Anthropologists and other social scientists frequently qualify the term. The literatures on food justice, environmental justice, and economic justice, to name a few, have grown tremendously in recent years.[46] The predominance of these qualifiers raises the question of how (and indeed whether) anthropologists might theorize in general about justice. One way to do this, I argue, is to examine how different sets of actors *do* justice.

Ideas of justice (explicitly articulated or not) undergird all of the phenomena with which I am engaged in this book. An emphasis on how proponents of GI, fair trade, and Gorkhaland do justice links the question of what people who see themselves as involved in these movements for justice desire to the question of what actions they take. Discourses of justice serve not only as critiques of current political, economic, or environmental circumstances, but also as enactments of visions for the future and of the conditions necessary for social change. These critiques and enactments not only depend upon visions of what counts as justice but also upon what counts as injustice.

The concept of justice, as Anna Tsing has argued, presents itself as a "universal": an idea that "inspires expansion—both for the powerful and the powerless."[47]

Using Tsing's observation as a starting point, I suggest that justice entails not only envisioning the world as it ought to be but also imagining (though not necessarily directly engaging with) the world as it already is. In my explorations of Geographical Indication, fair trade, and the Gorkhaland movement, I am driven by questions of power and powerlessness. My argument is that putting ideas of justice into action requires imaginatively framing *injustice*. Power lies in the ability to mobilize imaginaries of injustice as much as in proffering visions of justice.

Notions of justice and injustice in the market must, of necessity, engage with conditions of production, yet under commodity capitalism, as Marx pointed out in *Capital,* those relations are obscured.[48] Commodities mask the (unjust) conditions of their own production. Appeals to justice in the market, therefore, all entail claims to "unmask" these conditions: to expose their shortcomings and make them better. Yet claims to justice in the market—short of Marx's own revolutionary theory—do not fundamentally question market capitalism. When appeals to justice in the market arise, then, they present visions of productive conditions that are partial and largely imaginary. Justice is a trade of ideal types. I suggest that discourses of injustice, too, depend on ideals and imaginaries. We can begin to trace the act of doing justice anthropologically by studying whose imaginaries of injustice gain political traction, and why.

In Darjeeling, movements for justice invariably depend upon imaginaries of tea plantation landscapes, labor, and life. Since the founding of tea plantations in the region over 150 years ago, the plantation has been imagined as a space for moral action, from colonial environmental and social "improvements" in the nineteenth century, to labor-management struggles in the early and middle twentieth century, to fair trade, GI, and subnationalism in the late twentieth and early twenty-first centuries. The reinvention of the plantation in the twenty-first century, in fact, is largely an imaginary project: an attempt to make the plantation into something other than the paradigmatic space of colonial and postcolonial capitalist agricultural production that it obviously is. Imagining justice in Darjeeling requires creatively imagining injustice as something that can be overcome *within the context of the plantation itself.* GI, fair trade, and Gorkhaland each attempt to do this.

In most frameworks that pertain to the market, justice is about the distribution of social and economic goods, as well as rights to access those goods.[49] I suggest, drawing on tea workers' engagements with the plantation system as well as with the national and regional political and social contexts of those engagements, that justice entails more than just distribution, access, and rights. I argue that for Darjeeling tea workers, justice also entails a capacity to critique the conditions of production and their contexts and to visualize ways in which people might transcend those conditions.

Fair trade, GI, and the Gorkhaland movement are not merely economic recovery strategies. They are each a means of importing abstract ideas of economic, juridical, and geopolitical justice into the global food market.[50] During my fieldwork, these parallel visions of justice only partially succeeded in enacting social change. Fair trade, GI, and Gorkhaland each ultimately left unquestioned the foundational organization of the plantation and the basic conditions of plantation labor (part industrial farm work, and part peasant labor). Instead, proponents of fair trade attempted to wedge the plantation into a market dominated by cooperative goods, while proponents of GI inserted the plantation in a market for traditional, artisanal, or craft foods. The 2007–11 Gorkhaland agitation, which claimed to represent the interests of Nepali-speaking tea workers, perhaps had more reason than fair trade or GI to question the plantation system, but instead, it, too, largely left unchallenged the tea industry's principal mode of production. Each, then, attempted to put tea workers "in the market" for the purposes of achieving different kinds of justice. If there is a market for justice, however, then some ideas (i.e., those of owners, consumers, and powerful politicians) will dominate while others (i.e., those of workers) will be suppressed.

JUSTICE AS PROPERTY: GEOGRAPHICAL INDICATION

Darjeeling's distinction as a good tea comes from its associations with a pleasant *taste* and a restful *place*.[51] The town of Darjeeling, surrounded by some eighty-seven plantations, was established early in the British colonization of India, initially as a sanitarium for convalescing soldiers to recover in the cool mountain airs. The refuge quickly grew and developed into a "hill station" and the summer capital of British India. Regarded for its recuperative airs and misty mornings, Darjeeling has long existed in Indian and Western imaginaries as a place of purity, an accessible Shangri-la.

Unlike coffee, tea is a rather geographically undifferentiated market. Consumers frequently drink teas from Malawi, Java, Bangladesh, or Cambodia, but these teas are rarely distinguished as such. Tea from across the globe is instead commonly blended into varietals, such as "Earl Grey," "English Breakfast," and "Russian Caravan," which can be sourced from any tea-growing region or grade. These teas, blended from broken leaf and dust grades, make up the bulk of the international market. There is little demand within India for Darjeeling tea, as the price is exponentially higher than the price of tea produced in Assam, the Dooars, or other Indian tea-producing regions. These cheaper, extralocal teas are actually preferred by Darjeeling tea workers and town residents. As I was told by many Darjeeling residents, Darjeeling tea was far too expensive, and *bland*. Tea workers frequently reminded me that Darjeeling tea was grown for foreign consumption. Foreigners, they explained, liked *halkā chiyā* ("light tea") like Darjeeling.[52]

Geographical Indication status, an international intellectual legal distinction, protects the use of the word *Darjeeling*. The emergence of geographically distinguished craft food production has been described primarily from the perspective of consumption. Consumers, it seems, are demanding some differentiation in a global food system in which food "comes from a global everywhere, yet from nowhere that [consumers] know in particular. The distance from which their food comes represents their separation from the knowledge of how and by whom what they consume is produced, processed, and transported."[53] In consuming Champagne over sparkling wine, Roquefort over blue cheese, and Darjeeling over generic English Breakfast, buyers can see themselves as supporting "traditional" forms of food production even as they imbibe luxury distinction based on place. Distinction and rarity have a price. GI products are more expensive precisely because they come from somewhere in particular and because they must travel across to globe from that place to make it into consumers' cups.

In broad terms, a "Geographical Indication" is any material or linguistic symbol used to establish that a product comes from a particular location. Contemporary GI laws, fashioned by the World Trade Organization (WTO), descended from national laws aimed at curtailing the imitation or falsification of products whose values were linked to place of origin and traditional forms of production. Though it has undergone several transformations throughout the twentieth century, one of the first systems for the protection of the geographical indication of food products is the French *appellation d'origine côntrolée* (AOC), first codified in 1905. Food items that meet AOC regulations that verify that they are made in a particular geographical location (one that confers a distinct *terroir*, or "taste of place") can have a French government-issued stamp on them. AOC regulations have governed French wines and cheeses for over one hundred years.[54] Such regulations existed in several countries by the middle of the twentieth century, and in 1958, the Lisbon Agreement extended "appellation of origin" protection to products from several countries.

Under the Geographical Indications Act of 1999, Darjeeling tea became the first of India's now 150 registered GIs.[55] This legislation endowed the Tea Board, and by extension the government of India, with "ownership" over the words *Darjeeling* and *Darjeeling tea* as well as the Darjeeling tea logo of a tea plucking woman in profile holding two leaves and a bud (fig. 6).[56] This domestic legislation enabled Darjeeling tea to be protected under the 1994 WTO Trade Related Aspects of Intellectual Property Rights, or TRIPS, Agreement.[57] Under TRIPS, producers of Roquefort and Comté cheeses are protected from cheese makers in other regions using these place distinctions to sell their cheese. TRIPS also enables corporations like Monsanto to patent biological life—turning genetic material into intellectual property.[58] Much as Monsanto can patent and "own" genetically modified plant varieties such as pest-resistant Bt cotton, the Tea Board of India, the government regulator of the tea industry, "owns" Darjeeling tea. The 1999 Indian GI act recast the name "Darjeeling" and its logo as certified trademarks (CTMs) regulated by the Tea Board of India (fig. 7).

FIGURE 6. Darjeeling tea logo. Photo credit: Tea Board of India.

FIGURE 7. Certified trademark (CTM) billboard at the entrance to a tea plantation. As the billboard reads, the mark is conferred by the Tea Board of India. Photo by author.

Under TRIPS, both Bt seeds and boutique tea are considered the "intellectual property" of their corporate owners. WTO-enforced GI status aims at thwarting the blending of Darjeeling tea with other teas and marketing the blend as Darjeeling. The Darjeeling Tea Association believes that this juridical protection and promotion has given struggling plantations a better market for their tea.[59] GI presents a vision of justice for Darjeeling tea plantations that hinges on private property rights that are guaranteed by law.[60] GI's vision of justice, then, was predicated on the "natural" connection between tea laborers and tea plantations, underwritten by their belonging within the Indian state. Under Darjeeling's GI, the tea and the name Darjeeling were the intellectual property of the Tea Board of India, and hence the nation. By protecting this property, GI advocates claimed, the market would provide more robust benefits to all people involved in the tea industry, as well as to consumers desirous of a "pure" product. These benefits, according to Tea Board officials, could be inherited by future generations of both producers and consumers.

JUSTICE AS FAIRNESS: FAIR TRADE

Certifications such as fair trade, organic, Rainforest Alliance, and shade-grown are granted by international nonstate agencies to agricultural producers who (1) comply with a set of prescribed standards; (2) submit to regular checks on standard compliance; and (3) pay administration fees to an international body to cover the overhead of certification. Certifications are also granted to retailers of fair-trade products. So to trade or produce a fair-trade product, a seller must be certified. Fair trade responds to what its advocates see as the uneven or unfair distribution of agricultural profits in the free market by developing new standards of production and ethics of circulation. Fair-trade institutions adopt a universal definition of "fairness," based on perceived moral relations between consumers and producers, which ensure better economic compensation for farm products. When farmers receive higher monetary yields for their products, fair-trade advocates claim, the system of global agricultural production becomes "fair."

The fair-trade movement began on Latin American coffee cooperatives, but over time, international certifiers like Fairtrade Labelling Organizations International (FLO) developed a set of what they call "hired labor" standards to incorporate noncooperative farmers.[61] Since the late 1990s, FLO has been certifying tea plantations in India. When I began the research for this book, FLO had expanded plantation certification to include not only tea plantations, but also banana and flower plantations as well as factory-made products like sport balls and dried fruit.[62]

Ethnographies of fair trade have focused predominantly on cooperative coffee in Latin America.[63] Scholars of fair trade have shown how fair trade presents an alternative to neoliberal economic policies, as fair-trade certification enables producers to sell to certified retailers at a predetermined price—a price set outside of the free market.[64] Rooted in neoclassical economics, neoliberalism upholds the free market—a market that is free of obstacles to trade like national government policies, and a market that privileges the power of private interests over publicly held institutions. This privileging of private interests over public interests, and of individual over kin, political, or other group identities, is known to fair-trade scholars as a "disembedding" of production from its social context. Fair trade seeks to "re-embed" the market in society, hedging against the community fracture and economic risk that attend free markets.[65] Paradoxically, however, even as fair-trade certification acts as a protective measure against the volatility of the neoliberal market, it extends the neoliberal economic emphasis on nongovernmental regulation and individual empowerment.[66] Like neoliberal reforms, fair trade often explicitly aims to circumvent or remove state barriers (labor laws, nationalized industries) so that individuals can better participate in the global market. In the case of tea production, the individual market participants imagined by fair trade range from consumers to tea workers themselves.

To situate fair trade on Darjeeling tea plantations, it is important to explain a few concepts in fair-trade certification. The implementation of fair trade hinges on (1) *minimum prices* and (2) *premiums*. These quantitative figures are different and serve complementary purposes. FLO, the international governing body for fair-trade certification, sets minimum prices, ideally higher than the going market value, for a product.[67] The fair-trade premium is an extra bit of money set by FLO for a given product (an extra that, like the minimum price, differs across regions and grades of the same product). The premium is paid on top of the minimum price. This additional premium for fair-trade products is supposed to be paid separately to the cooperative or plantation, so that the producer community can democratically decide how best to distribute it. Aside from the obvious differences in land tenure, the way in which the fair-trade premium is distributed is perhaps the most obvious way that fair trade functions differently on plantations. On coffee cooperatives, cooperative members decide themselves how to spend the fair-trade premium, but on tea plantations, a "Joint Body," composed of management and workers, distributes the premium.[68] The distribution is not left to plantation laborers themselves.

Fair-trade prices and premiums, which are folded into the exchange value of certified products, render a conceptual economic link between producers and consumers. But on Indian tea plantations, the "producers" include not just workers but also plantation owners. Given the vast power differential between these two groups, fair trade in practice allows owners, not workers, to access new markets. Fair trade heralds what its proponents call "direct trade" as a keystone to success. According to Fair Trade USA, this means that "importers purchase from

Fair Trade producer groups as directly as possible to eliminate unnecessary middlemen and empower farmers to develop the business capacity necessary to compete in the global marketplace." Tellingly, coffee roasters—particularly high end coffee roasters like Intelligentsia, Counter Culture Coffee, and Stumptown Coffee Roasters—wishing to work outside of mainstream fair-trade certification or be "fairer than fair trade"—also evoke the language of "direct trade" to attest to the transparent and humane conditions of coffee production.[69]

For coffee—the iconic fair-trade product—these direct trade relationships enable producers and buyers to circumvent intermediaries, or "*coyotes*," and presumably make a higher price—the minimum price—because producers do not need to pay the intermediaries to shepherd green coffee to market. Sociologist Daniel Jaffee explains this relationship: "Fair traders work to make the trading chain both shorter and fairer—that is, return a large share of the consumer's purchase directly to farmers (often called producers) or laborers who grew the coffee or picked the bananas. In practical terms, the fair-trade system accomplishes this objective by cutting out many of the intermediaries or middlemen, such as exporters, importers, and brokers, who typically take a cut at each step along the route from tree, field, or farm to the coffee shop or grocery shelf."[70] In Darjeeling, fair-trade advocates describe the decline of the tea industry as an economic problem (farmers without income) with an economic solution (price minimums and premiums). Instead of questioning wage relationships or land rights, fair trade's corrective to plantation production is to provide money to plantation owners and select representatives of the workers, who might invest in development projects or provide loans to entrepreneurial plantation workers who might want to invest in livestock or stores.

The extension of fair trade onto plantations became newly relevant in 2012, after Fair Trade USA (formerly called Transfair USA), the largest third-party certifier of fair-trade products in the United States, announced that it would withdraw from FLO and become an independent certifying organization. Fair Trade USA seeks to double the volume of fair-trade-certified goods imported into the United States by 2015. To do so, Fair Trade USA plans to expand the number of hectares under and producers for fair-trade products. Fair Trade USA aims to meet this goal by *extending* fair-trade certification to *more plantations* across the postcolonial world.

Fair Trade USA has adopted a new motto, "Fair for All," describing itself as "more inclusive for more impact." The Fair Trade USA Web page elaborates:

> Today Fair Trade standards simultaneously and successfully support both cooperative members as well as *small farmers unable to access the support of a cooperative* in the categories of tea, flowers, and bananas, but not coffee, sugar, or cocoa. As a model that seeks to alleviate poverty and empower farming communities, this inconsistency and systematic exclusion with the Fair Trade system is no longer acceptable.

To create a more just and consistent Fair Trade model, Fair Trade USA will *adapt existing international fair trade standards from tea, bananas, and flowers,* and apply them first to coffee and then to additional categories over time.

We must innovate responsibly, including more people without negatively impacting out current partners in the Fair Trade system. . . .

We will continue to set common rigorous standards for all industry partners as we work to provide consumers with a broad selection of Fair Trade products that allow them to make their small everyday purchases matter.[71]

Fair Trade USA's decision to certify more plantations has sparked a lively debate within the fair-trade community. But why would there be backlash against Fair Trade USA's breakoff and the inclusion of more people in the movement? Isn't more fair trade better than less? After all, tea, bananas, and cut-flower plantations have long been integrated into FLO certification. The backlash was centered on Fair Trade USA's movement to certify coffee plantations. The most vociferous corporate opponent of the Fair Trade USA break off is Equal Exchange, a Massachusetts-based company, which markets its own brand of fair-trade products with the slogan, "Small Farmers, Big Change."[72] Equal Exchange saw the move to certify large plantations as a sign of moral degradation within the fair-trade system.[73] Equal Exchange argued that Fair Trade USA had a financial interest in expanding certification, which would allow them to deal with big industrial ventures, who would pay an exponentially higher amount of money to fair trade in overhead (e.g., in certification fees). The inclusion of coffee plantations would also, Equal Exchange argued, envelop companies like Nestlé, Folgers, Starbucks, and Dunkin Donuts and enable them to market a higher percentage of their coffees as fair-trade certified. In an interview with the *New York Times,* Dean Cycon, the owner of Dean's Beans, another Massachusetts-based coffee roasting company, said, "Starbucks, Green Mountain, and other coffee companies will be able to become 100 percent fair trade not because they have changed their business practices one iota, but because Fair Trade USA has changed the rules of the game."[74] Amid the controversy over the certification of fair-trade *coffee* plantations, no one—for or against the idea—has asked whether certification of tea plantations, in many ways the prototype for this move, has made a meaningful change. Filling this gap, I argue that the inclusion of Darjeeling plantations in the fair-trade market has not only not brought workers any closer to justice, it has actually undermined non-market mechanisms for ensuring workers' well-being.

JUSTICE AS SOVEREIGNTY: THE GORKHALAND MOVEMENT

Fair trade and Geographical Indication are planter-driven strategies to sell more tea. For Darjeeling tea workers, on the other hand, justice on the tea plantation and for its laboring masses is inseparable from discussions of "Gorkhaland." The leaders of the Gorkhaland movement criticized West Bengal politicians for neglecting their constituents in the Darjeeling hills. In public rallies, politicians spoke about the lack of development and increased environmental degradation experienced by Darjeeling residents at the hands of West Bengal, but they often did so by comparing the present to a less austere colonial past. By couching the West Bengal state government as more oppressive than the British one, they established a framework for political independence and control over the Darjeeling landscape. They called for the recognition of the "rights" of Gorkhas to sovereignty over the Darjeeling district. In some moments, they traced these rights to colonial times, when Nepali migrants clear-cut forests for tea fields, moved and broke rocks for roads, and fashioned felled trees into a railroad to transport Darjeeling tea to the plains. In this narrative, Nepali laborers and British imperialists were both settlers in the hill station of Darjeeling. They co-developed its landscape and turned it from a forested "wasteland" (Darjeeling's colonial administrative category until 1910) into a productive tea district. After independence and the Partition of India, the newly formed Indian state of West Bengal took control of the district, leaving Nepalis demographically and politically marginalized. In other moments, however, leaders claimed that the Gorkha presence in the hills predated the coming of the British and the founding of plantations and that Darjeeling had never been part of Bengal. In these moments, they made claims to Darjeeling that were based upon timeless, primordial connections to the land.

The leaders of the Gorkhaland agitation maintained that the money made from tea production stayed in Kolkata and did not travel "back up the mountain" to Darjeeling. Gorkhaland activists blamed West Bengal politicians for the lack of reinvestment in the marginal lands in the north of their state. Darjeeling tea workers involved in the movement used the concept of "justice" (often inserting the English word into Nepali-language conversations) to reference a future in which workers would control the land under tea. According to both male and female workers, a Gorkha-run state government would better manage Darjeeling and its tea plantations, but it would not eliminate them. Most workers were familiar with the unique property arrangement that governed tea plantations. Plantation owners and companies did not own the land under their bungalows, factories, and tea fields. They leased it from the government of West Bengal, on long-term contracts that spanned to the days before independence. Thus, laborers were particularly interested in the *land* in "Gorkhaland." As one worker explained when I asked her how a separate Indian Nepali state would lead to "justice," "the *whole land* becomes ours." For tea laborers, political identity, as well as senses of belonging in the Darjeeling landscape, were forged through tea plantation work and histories of labor and commodity production. Labor on plantations was a pretext for senses of belonging. Most importantly, laborers could not envision the revitalization of the plantation without also envisioning a restructuring of the relationship between the region and the state.

But the 2007–11 Gorkhaland movement took the existence of "big businesses" and the plantation itself as givens. Notions of property rights—somewhat similar to those proffered in GI—were paramount in the Gorkhaland movement. In the movement, however, property rights were cast in the language of indigeneity, citizenship, and geopolitical sovereignty. The vision of justice promoted in Gorkhaland was predicated on the assumption that Gorkhas, as the residents of Darjeeling, deserved to reap the benefits of the region's industries, principally tea. Importantly, the Gorkhaland movement was a *sub*nationalist struggle. It was a separatist movement that, paradoxically, asserted Gorkhas' belonging within the nation-state. Like GI, it asserted territorial distinction as a way of forging connection. While this model for justice worked to some extent in the context of GI, it ultimately failed for Gorkhaland, partly because its leaders and most ardent supporters—most of whom were *not* tea pluckers—remained ambivalent about the place of tea plantations in the making of a sovereign Gorkha community. It failed because it could not adequately reckon with the history that brought the community into being. Gorkhaland, like GI and fair trade, rested on a Third World imaginary of primordial belonging in a natural landscape.

THE THIRD WORLD AGRARIAN IMAGINARY

Fair trade, GI, and the Gorkhaland movement, while seemingly disparate, share a few important things in common. Each seeks to bring nonmarket values (ideas about justice, or "the right thing to do") into proximity with market values, or, in the language of food system studies, meanings into proximity with material relations. Still, what seems most glaring about all these movements is that none of them, despite their appeals to justice, critically questions the plantation system itself. Indeed, all of them pointedly work *within* the plantation system. Fair trade, GI, and Gorkhaland are thus linked by something other than justice: a way of seeing Darjeeling's agro-environment and a noneconomic way of giving it value. I call this way of seeing a "Third World agrarian imaginary."

I adapt the concept of the Third World agrarian imaginary from Julie Guthman's identification of an "agrarian imaginary" that shrouds contemporary organic agriculture in the United States. Guthman's *Agrarian Dreams* describes the lives of laborers under industrial production. She argues that despite being perceived as "farming in nature's image," alternative agriculture schemes such as organic farming are wrapped up in the processes of industrial agriculture its consumers see it challenging.[75] Despite the sociopolitical salience of the owner-operated "family" farm, organic agriculture in the United States (like organic tea production in Darjeeling) is highly industrialized and depends on ethnically marked and marginalized laborers (Latino labor in the United States, Nepali labor in Darjeeling).[76] The roots of the agrarian imaginary can be seen in the writings of Thomas Jefferson and more contemporary back-to-the-landers. In *Notes on the State of Virginia*, Jefferson writes: "Those who labor in the earth are the chosen people of God . . . whose breasts he has made his particular deposit for substantial and genuine virtue. . . . Corruption of morals in the mass cultivator is a phenomenon of which no age nor nation has furnished an example."[77] Modern consumers of organic food share Jefferson's pastoral, arcadian vision, in which working the land for oneself and one's own kin is an inherently redemptive exercise. For Guthman, organic food's value rests in part on this imaginary.[78] The imaginary implies moral rectitude. Organic food is righteous to eat, and presumably, righteous to make.[79]

The Third World agrarian imaginary transfers this redemptive narrative to postcolonies. The Third World agrarian imaginary is not only an image of farming as an original, ecologically balanced form of connection between people and place but also a set of ideas about the relationship between people and nature—particularly about the relationship between women and nature.[80] The Third World agrarian imaginary helps fair-trade, GI, and Gorkhaland advocates explain why things are bad in Darjeeling *and* frame the path and tools to make things better. This agrarian imaginary posits a potential for redemption—a return to a fictionalized distant past from which plantation societies have (unjustly) diverged.

GI uses law to undergird one of the central elements of the Third World agrarian imaginary. In GI discourse, the plantation becomes a "tea garden:" a site of "natural" agricultural heritage. A brochure distributed by the Tea Board of India and the Darjeeling Tea Association as part of Darjeeling's GI marketing campaign and sent to potential buyers of tea depicts "life on the gardens": "It's an idyllic existence close to nature's heartbeat. That's what makes this tea so unique. The tea pluckers sing of the tiny saplings which bend in the wind as they work. A melody of greenness surrounded by blue skies and the sparkle of mountain dews. And tied to the circle of life, the tea bushes sustain themselves day in and out, season after season, though the years. Life on a plantation is a completely natural, refreshing state of being."[81] This passage appears next to a glossy picture of a beautiful Gorkha woman plucking tea amid a field of green.

In her ethnography of female tea laborers on a Dooars plantation, to the south of Darjeeling, Piya Chatterjee describes how popular tea brands like Brooke Bond and Celestial Seasonings sexualize female tea workers and fetishize their delicate hands.[82] Chatterjee notes the way in which the feminization of tea merges ideas of labor and leisure, as the soft hands of tea pluckers echo the soft touch of the genteel colonial female tea drinker, always an implied presence in contemporary, postcolonial tea marketing.[83] In Darjeeling's Third World agrarian imaginary, tea becomes naturally occurring—it is self-sustaining; tea is not the product of hundreds of years of colonial exploitation and postcolonial industrial agriculture. Through marketing, GI renders a complex historical, relationship between bushes, labor, and management into a single, fetishized, feminized element of mystical "nature." The imaginary that GI sells and legally codifies has transformed female laborers into "ecologically noble," ahistorical, and hyperfertile features of the landscape.[84]

Gorkhaland promotes a similar imaginary of indigenous, ecologically noble belonging, this time on a political stage in which the plantation is a primordial homeland for Indian Nepali tea workers, who comprise the majority of the district's population. Darjeeling and its plantations are of course recent historical constructions, built by European settlers in the mid-nineteenth century. Gorkhas, too, are recent historical constructions. The Gorkhaland movement's discourse of justice hinges on alternating assertions of historical and natural linkages between Gorkhas and the plantation land on which they work and live. For Gorkha tea laborers late in the first decade of the new century, labor identity—rooted in a relationship to the plantation landscape—is inseparable from ethnic identity. For Gorkha politicians, however, proving that Gorkhas are "natural" and indigenous to the region is a primary objective. Gorkhas' nostalgic affinity for the British is part of a complex mimetic strategy.[85] They use their social and historical relationships to the British to make their rights to the Darjeeling seem "natural" while at the same time appealing to popular Indian subnational discourses of indigenous rights.

The Third World imaginary also couches planters, as well as workers, as caring environmental stewards. Fair trade turns plantations not into "gardens" but into "farms," a more familiar and palatable image of big agriculture. Plantation owners and managers become "farmers," not unlike the friendly family farmers Guthman describes in her analysis of the U.S. agrarian imaginary. (This is not entirely surprising, since much of the fair-trade market is in the United States and Europe). The imaginary of the tea plantation as a family-run business seems incongruous, but for international fair-trade certifiers and tea buyers, a key element of Darjeeling tea's revitalization is affirmation of the presence of engaged, caring owners, who recast themselves as paternal stewards of both land and labor.

To this image of happy farmers, benevolent environmental stewards, and bucolic landscapes, this Third World agrarian imaginary adds familiar narratives about the failings of "Third World" states. It is perhaps this element of the Third World agrarian imaginary that fair trade, GI, and Gorkhaland emphasize most. In this way, the Third World agrarian imaginary provides a reference point for measuring injustice. Injustice arises from corruption, environmental degradation, and the oppression of marginalized people. In the imaginaries of GI, fair trade, and Gorkhaland, the tea plantation is both the site of such injustices and the locus for their undoing. Each movement imagines a new and better plantation, revitalized and redeemed by particular programs for justice.

A TRIPARTITE MORAL ECONOMY

The visions of justice and of plantation life in Darjeeling proffered by GI, fair trade, and Gorkhaland hinges on complex yet ultimately uncritical imaginaries of plantation life. None of them fully engages workers' perspectives on justice. For workers, justice is rooted in ideas of reciprocity between management, labor, and the agro-environment in which they all reside. Taken together, these ideas form a fourth formulation of justice, what I call a "tripartite moral economy." While a focus on moral economy might emphasize the binary relations between workers and management, or between labor and capital, in the ethnographic descriptions that follow, I reveal a tripartite relationship that includes workers, managers, *and* the agro-environment.

The workers I lived with, ate with, worked with, and interviewed were clear-eyed about the fact that they worked on plantations. Workers' visions of justice were intimately shaped by the reality of plantation life as a set of human and non-human relationships. My descriptions of the plantation tripartite moral economy build on James Scott's work on the "moral economy" of peasant societies in Southeast Asia. Scott frames the moral economy as peasants' "notation of economic justice and their working definition of exploitation—their view of which claims on their product were tolerable and which intolerable."[86] The simultaneous attention to justice and exploitation is important.

I observed, as did Scott of Southeast Asian peasant cultivators, that stability was central to workers' understandings of justice. Insurance of stability came in the form of social as well as technological arrangements.[87] We may be able to talk about justice, then, in more processual terms: as a measurement of how far current conditions can stray from a perceived norm of stability.[88] The equation of stability with justice could certainly be glossed as "false consciousness," the condition in which the oppressed disregard or blindly accept the conditions of their own exploitation, but, along with Scott, I argue that it is not. An appeal to false consciousness obfuscates and confuses an exploration of the meanings of agricultural labor. Scott notes:

> The concept of false consciousness overlooks the very real possibility that the actor's "problem" is not simply one of misperception. It overlooks the possibility that he may, in fact, have his own durable standards of equity and exploitation—standards that lead him to judgments about his situation that are quite different from those of an outside observer equipped with a deductive theory. To put it bluntly, the actor may have his own moral economy. If this is the case, the failure of his views to accord with those of theory is not due to his inability to see things clearly, but to his values. Of course, one may choose to call these values as form of false consciousness as well. But to the extent that they are rooted in the actor's existential needs, to the extent that they are resistant to efforts at "reeducation," to the extent that they continue to define the situation for him, it is they and not theory which serve as reliable guides to his sentiments and behavior.

If the analytical goal of a theory of exploitation is to reveal something about the perceptions of the exploited—about *their* sense of exploitation, *their* notion of justice, *their* anger—it must begin not with an abstract normative standard but with the values of the real actors. Such an approach must start phenomenologically at the bottom and ask what the peasants' or workers' definition of the situation is. When a peasant considers 20 percent of his harvest a reasonable rent and 40 percent an unjust rent, how does he arrive at this judgment? What criterion of fairness does he use? On this basis it should be possible to construct the operational moral economy of a subordinate class.[89]

Attention to workers' understandings of the plantation system and what conditions are tolerable (and intolerable) is important for at least three reasons.

First, it fills a major gap in the literature on food systems, in which the lives of plantation and large farm workers are rarely given as much space as those of small farmers, managers, activists, or consumers. Workers' visions of justice are based not on abstract metaphysical ideals of justice but on pragmatic concerns about the subsistence of their families and of the landscape. Their subsistence depend upon the engaged presence of management and the provision of nonmonetary resources, including housing, land, schools, and health care. This understanding of justice is unsatisfying to those who would hope to find more revolutionary visions among plantation laborers. But Scott argues, and I agree, that attention to workers' perspectives "offers a more reliable guide to the behavior than abstract standards which offer no conceptual link between the theory of exploitation and the feelings of the exploited."[90] As Scott goes on to claim, "the *manner* of exploitation may make all the difference in the world."[91] Plantation labor, in workers' eyes, offers some promise of sustaining people and plants over time, and fair trade, GI, and Gorkhaland, despite their claims to justice, ultimately provide little promise of improvement.

Second, the acknowledgment that plantation workers possess a unique vision of social justice based in large part upon nonmonetary benefits is at the same time a recognition that plantation labor, unlike other forms of industrial agricultural work, is not bought and sold on a free market. On plantations, labor is not an undifferentiated variable. Each job on a plantation has a connection to social, kinship, and linguistic ties spanning back to the colonial era. A plantation worker neither simply works "for the money" nor simply subsists at the whim of a large landholder. The plantation worker is something in between: a participant in both a global market and a vestigial legacy of colonial feudalism.

Finally, the tripartite moral economy, with its attention to relations between workers, management, and the agro-environment, acknowledges that in the context of plantations, where workers both work and live, meaningful relationships to nonhuman nature can and do emerge. They do not emerge, however, in the "natural," "balanced," primordial senses described by GI and Gorkhaland advocates.

Rather, the social relations between plantation workers and the plants they grow are results of a longstanding, shared history.

FIELDWORK ON AND OFF THE PLANTATION

This book is based on thirty-one months of fieldwork I conducted between June 2006 and July 2012. I worked on twelve different plantations in Darjeeling: those that were both fair-trade- and organic-certified, only organic-certified, and plantations that were conventional. I interviewed twenty plantation owners and managers as well as several officers of the Darjeeling Tea Association, the Indian Tea Association, and the Tea Board of India.[92] On my initial trip, in the summer of 2006, and early in my fieldwork in 2008, plantation managers and plantation owners enthusiastically sought me out. The secretary of the Darjeeling Tea Association was particularly excited about the (positive, market-based) ramifications of my research in Darjeeling.

A few days after I arrived in Darjeeling in June 2006, I received a phone call on my brand new mobile phone. Someone had told someone, who told someone else, who told the secretary of the Darjeeling Tea Association (DTA), that there was an American *keti* (girl) here to study Darjeeling tea. I went over to an enormous bungalow in town, complete with stuffed animal heads on the wall and doily-lined trays for tea and biscuits. The secretary and other DTA officers and planters wanted to know about organic and fair-trade certification: how to get it, how much people in the United States were willing to pay for it, and, perhaps most importantly, what the Darjeeling plantations that were successful at implementing these certifications were actually doing. Was it really that difficult? "The welfare structures of the tea industry are fabulous," the secretary would tell me. "We should all be certified as fair trade!" I was perplexed as to why they were asking *me* these questions, because I was approaching them for answers to precisely these same questions.

The Tea Board of India and the Indian Tea Association (ITA) in Kolkata (where I was based for several months in 2009) were supportive of my presence. They were long used to dealing with researchers, particularly from the numerous universities in Kolkata. I also conducted archival research at the National Library in Kolkata. This was both a productive and demoralizing experience. The catalog of tea-related holdings is immense, but many of these materials have rotted or gone missing (tea, chemistry, and computational mathematics are the most pilfered topics, one librarian told me). Doing archival work on plantations was similarly difficult. Many of the documents were taken back with British owners after independence, or more likely, these documents just rotted in the hot, moist airs of the tea factory.

I attended tea management classes at the Darjeeling Tea Management Training Centre and at North Bengal University, as well as in Kolkata at the Birla Company's own tea management school, a kind of "farm team" for new assistant managers for Birla plantations. (I was asked to leave the Birla Tea Management School in Kolkata after several weeks, as I was deemed "too distracting." I was not sure if this was the case for the students, or more likely the teacher, who pegged me as a "labor sympathizer" early on and reveled in starting rather heated *adda* [in Bengali, "debate" or "dialogue"] with me during class.)

Most days, however, I joined female plantation laborers in Darjeeling, plucking and pruning tea bushes, collecting cow dung for organic compost, and sharing lunch during the midday break. Each day, I usually brought *channa* to share, but on other days I was given more direct requests for certain kinds of biscuits from the German-style bakery in town. While I conducted more formal interviews with plantation managers, plantation owners, and tea officials from both private and public institutions, I did not take this strategy with workers. I found the day to be more interesting for me (and for them as well, many women told me) if I plucked tea. I learned about plucking, bush productivity, and environmental degradation from working alongside women on the plantations. And I learned about just how much work tea production demands, something that the women I worked with were quick to point out.

Arguably, it was because I was a Nepali-speaking *woman* (or to many, just a *keti*) that I was left alone by management and able to do this research. (I also approximate the general size and hair color of a Nepali woman from afar.) Many people with whom I discuss my research (including renowned anthropologists of Nepal) are surprised when I explain that I just "walked on" to the plantations and chatted with the women. The planters seemed aware of my presence, though I always assumed that the planters thought that it would be more trouble for them if they put up more active resistance to my presence than just passive disregard. On most plantations, despite the phone calls made on my behalf from powerful tea "uncles" (a generalized honorific for men of high status) and officials in town to plantation managers, I was rarely granted access to tea-processing factories. The factories, and the processing that went on within them, were "trade secrets." Other plantation managers were more lenient, or perhaps more willfully dismissive of my presence. Some plantations ran tourism projects that brought large foreign tour groups. Following these groups enabled me to see processing in detail. After staying several months at a one of these tourist plantations, I began renting an apartment on the ridge of Darjeeling, and on most days, I hiked down the mountainside to the plantations below. On other days, I attended Gorkhaland political rallies in town. This going between plantation and town helped me understand the disconnect in visions of justice.

In the chapters that follow, I show how abstract ideas of economic, juridical, and geopolitical justice and imposed Third World agrarian imaginaries intersected with local understandings of justice. First, however, I flesh out the origins of the

Darjeeling plantation and the tripartite moral economy. Next, I read the projects of GI, fair trade, and Gorkhaland ethnographically, through the lens of tea laborers' experiences with them. The contribution of this book is not to resolve the conundrum of justice to which I alluded earlier, but to show in phenomenological terms—terms set by workers themselves, rather than planters, policymakers, economists, or activists—how the plantation, a partly industrial and partly peasant agricultural form, operates in the global food system.

The next chapter describes the construction of the Darjeeling landscape into a British hill station, and the making of a productive plantation industry out of what colonial administrators deemed to be a "wasteland." Drawing from archival research conducted in Kolkata, this chapter describes the basis of Darjeeling's distinction from the perspective of environmental history. The chapter recounts the growth of Darjeeling and its tea industry, as well as a story of the construction of a colonial infrastructure that remains politically salient today. I use stories about the tea-producing infrastructure, as well as the wider colonial organization of the town and the region to tell the story of Darjeeling's development as a site of both industrial production and leisure.

In chapter 2, I describe the tripartite moral economy by focusing on what workers described as the rise of *bisnis* practices on plantations. *Bisnis* stood in contrast to *industri,* a historical time in which planters provided workers good "facilities" (*faciliti-haru*) a catchall term for welfare and nonmonetary compensation. The provision of *faciliti-haru* was central to a stable tripartite moral economy, in which planters provided welfare structures and allotted capital reinvestments for the plantation landscape and workers, in turn, took care of the plantation agro-environment. This agro-environment, however, was not wholly inanimate. The tripartite moral economy was undergirded by elaborate fictive and actual relationships of plantation kinship, between workers, managers, *and* tea plants. The tripartite moral economy forms the root of tea workers' ideas about social justice. It is a relational concept, based in understandings of affective connections among plantation residents and the natural environment.

Chapter 3 explores Darjeeling's Geographical Indication (GI) status, asking how an industrial crop like Darjeeling tea can be remade into a product with a distinct *terroir,* and how plantation labor can be recast by international regulations as "traditional knowledge." Darjeeling tea laborers (unlike migrant workers in other agricultural contexts) are too visible to be ignored in the Geographical Indication of Darjeeling; as a result, they have been integrated into ideas about the product's *terroir.* In glossy brochures and billboards as well as UN reports, both tea and tea laborers appear as "natural" inhabitants of the landscape. Through GI, Darjeeling tea and laborers' knowledge then became the national patrimony of India.

In chapter 4, I discuss fair-trade certification. This chapter describes how fair-trade certification has been employed, in workers' terms, as a strategy of *bisnis*—a way to make more money on decreasing yields and lesser-quality teas. I also explore how fair trade presents a contending vision of the plantation's tripartite moral economy that actually enables *bisnis*-like extractive practices, particularly those that degrade the environment and destabilize plantation villages.

In chapter 5, I pick back up on many of the themes discussed throughout the book to describe the Gorkhaland movement that I witnessed during my fieldwork. I discuss Gorkha workers' visions of the past and future of Darjeeling and its plantations. I also narrate their descriptions of their own place in the Indian nation-state. I explore the significance of labor and the environment to what it means to be Gorkha in contemporary India, showing how both the moral economic ideas I trace in chapter 2 and the ideas about geographic distinction I depict in chapter 3 combined in the most recent move for Indian Nepali subnational autonomy.

In the conclusion, I identify a common thread in the three movements for justice that I describe in chapters 3, 4, and 5, namely, that each sees itself as filling a kind of social or environmental or political void. I suggest that, despite the claims of politicians, fair traders, and tea planters, these movements actually gain their traction by creatively obscuring a deeply elaborated tripartite moral economy, thus ignoring the ways in which workers themselves understand their own exploitation. Ultimately, despite attempts to reinvent it, the plantation continues to give Darjeeling—the place, the product, and the idea—its distinction.

1

Darjeeling

Chowrasta, Darjeeling town's central plaza, is the hub of early morning activity. Up and down "The Mall," the paved circular walkway that leads in and out of Chowrasta, macaque monkeys and homeless dogs compete for scraps of food for their morning meal. Students from the Himalayan Mountaineering Institute jog and practice calisthenics, dressed in matching polyester tracksuits. On clear mornings, the plaza draws vista-seeking tourists, anxious for a view of Mount Kanchenjunga, the Himalayan peak to the north and the world's third highest mountain, and the deep verdant tea plantations in the valleys to the east and west. The Mall and its bent and broken colonial-era iron fencing creates a perimeter around the Mahakhal Temple, and most mornings find older Tibetan women and men performing *kora*, a walking meditation that takes the form of circumambulation around a sacred site, thumbing prayer beads and quietly meditating as they make their way along the path. The word *chowrasta* appears in many Indo-Aryan languages, and in each, it is best translated as "crossroads."[1] In Darjeeling, Chowrasta marks the convergence of several roads, each leading up into town along a ridge that runs north to south, roughly perpendicular to the Himalayas.

Seen from Chowrasta, the tea plantations that spread down the ridge to the east and west appear as a "natural," even beautiful foreground to the high Himalayas and the towering Kanchenjunga, a carpet of green below the blues and grays of the mountains. But the tea landscape, like Chowrasta, was formed through the confluence of multiple historical, political, and ecological factors. Scholars of the Himalayas have long acknowledged that this mountain region is a unique contact zone between Indo-Aryan and Tibeto-Burman influences,[2] but Chowrasta's bandstand, the paved strolling paths, and the homes that dot the roads leading out of the plaza are ever-present reminders of the colonial presence in this landscape. More importantly, the living landscape, from the tea bushes to the towering evergreen *duppi* trees, which were imported and planted by the British, constitutes a botanical contact zone.

Contemporary Darjeeling has emerged over, around, and within material (and lively) colonial infrastructures, from Chowrasta to the tea bushes in the valleys below. Darjeeling's potholed roads, dried-up water pipes, mildewed bungalows, overgrown *duppi*, and even its fields of tea bushes are what Ann Stoler calls "imperial ruins": material symbols of British colonialism for Darjeeling residents, from 'tea pluckers, to merchants, to planters.[3] In this chapter, I use the imperial ruins of Darjeeling as material conduits for stories about the development of Darjeeling and its plantations, and as deteriorating reminders of the role Nepalis, British imperialists, and the climate itself continue to play in the life of the place.

At first, it might seem strange to couch tea bushes and trees as "ruins," but seen as part of what Stoler calls an "ecology of remains," we can understand ruins as anything but static. Indeed, they are "visible and visceral senses in which the effects of empire are reactivated. . . . To think with the ruins of empire is to emphasize less the artifacts of empire as dead matter or remnants of a defunct regime than to attend to their reappropriations and strategic and active positioning within the politics of the present."[4] In other words, Darjeeling is a *living* and *lived-in* "imperial formation"—a landscape manufactured by both human and nonhuman actors and experienced as a set of material, symbolic, and social relationships.

In this chapter, I tell stories about how a few imperial ruins—statues, botanical gardens, tea bushes, and tea plantation factories—have become reappropriated and positioned in the present, using those stories to narrate key moments in Darjeeling's colonial past. Tea workers and townspeople often reminded me that the successes of the Darjeeling tea industry would never have been achieved without the British. To Darjeeling residents, this history of colonization has become visible in Darjeeling's landscape of imperial ruins, the social and material remains that Darjeeling residents were, in Stoler's words, "left with" after the colonial period.[5]

The term *landscape* has two important meanings. In one sense, a landscape is a static, looked-upon, talked-about material world. In a second sense, a landscape is a moving, dwelt-in world.[6] For anthropologists, ideas about and experiences of landscapes inform one another to produce "place."[7] Making place means making political, economic, or social use of the landscape's past, or perhaps even inventing or revising it. In the chapters that follow, I describe several forms of such place making. As Stoler argues, some imperial ruins "are stubbornly inhabited to make a political point, or requisitioned for a newly refurbished commodity life for tourist consumption."[8] Stoler's theories are grounded partly in her work amid the remains of Javanese sugar plantations, but her thoughts fit the ways in which Darjeeling's ruins are looked at and lived in.[9] Tourists do still come to the area looking for vistas of tea plantations and mountains, and Nepali political activists do couch themselves as struggling to inhabit the plantation and the entirety of the Darjeeling landscape on their own terms.

A landscape is also a living aggregation of plants, animals, people, and nonliving materials. The living and nonliving, human and nonhuman elements of a landscape come to structure one another. They, as philosophers Gilles Deleuze and Felix Guattari put it, "mutually become" together.[10] That the valleys of Darjeeling were suitable homes for a monoculture of tea is as much an ecological and climatological fact as an historical one. The soils, rainfall, and altitude do support tea bushes remarkably well. Once established in Darjeeling, tea managed to thrive. Seen as a living legacy of the imperial moment, tea also acts as a stubborn political reminder. Like other, more familiar kinds of ruins (buildings, monuments, roads), the flora and fauna of empire blended and meshed with previous ecological forms. Tea, like those "man-made" imperial structures, was what Stoler would call both a "ruin" and an agent of "ruination," an active reminder of colonial production and a continued force of colonial destruction.[11]

CLIMATE AND CONVALESCENCE

With the formation of the British East India Company in 1600, British trade in India grew steadily. Rural Bengal and urbanizing Calcutta became the center of the Company's Indian trade, and later, in 1858, after the dissolution of the Company and the incorporation of India into the British Empire, Calcutta became British India's imperial center.[12] With the development of trade and later Empire in British India, came increased incidences of disease. From imperial hospitals in the plains, surgeons took detailed morbidity and mortality statistics in an attempt to determine the relationship between climate and health. They kept records of temperature, rainfall, wind, and other conditions in order to figure out what influenced the death rate in their colonial territories.[13] The sweltering climate and dense settlements of the plains, particularly in the trading port and imperial center of Calcutta, were thought to be a breeding ground for malaria and other tropical diseases. A "change of climate" became a popular prescription for those ailing in the plains.

Wars with Nepal (1814–16) and Burma (1824–26 and 1852) quashed powerful and expanding kingdoms in close proximity to Bengal and brought these fertile mountainous lands into the subjugation of the East India Company. British settlers in India looked toward the recently annexed lands in the Himalayas separating the Indian subcontinent from the tea fields and trading ports of China to establish seasonal hillside homes. In the mountains, British settlers could escape from the heat and disease of the plains, but they would also be in striking distance of Tibet, which was closed to foreigners but presented a tantalizing source of trade.

In the mid-1820s, the East India Company set up an experimental settlement in Cherrapunji in recently annexed Assam, located in India's northeastern arm, in hopes of establishing a retreat for ailing troops to convalesce. The damp climate and misty rolling hills reminded soldiers and officers of the British countryside, but Cherrapunji turned out to be one of the wettest places in the world. The whole settlement literally washed down the hillside in one of the first rainy seasons.[14] The Company rebuilt Cherrapunji, but continued to look for something more permanent in the northwestern and northeastern Himalayas, close to regional centers in the Punjab and Calcutta.

After the Anglo-Nepal Wars, in 1828, the East India Company dispatched army officers to the Himalayan foothills around the Dorje-ling monastery (*dorje* meaning "thunderbolt," and *ling* meaning "place" in Tibetan). This time, they went in search of a high-altitude respite for convalescing British officials.[15] In 1829, Company lieutenant general George W. Lloyd, while arbitrating a border dispute between the kingdoms of Nepal and Sikkim, declared that the area of Dorje-ling was "well adapted for the purposes of a sanitarium."[16] In 1835, Lloyd negotiated with the Chogyal of Sikkim the annexation of a narrow strip of land, twenty-four miles long and five to six miles wide, hugging the ridge of the highest foothill in the region.[17] The Deed of Grant specifically cited the region's climate as a reason for the annexation: "The Governor General having expressed his desire for the possessions of the Hills of Darjeeling, on account of its cool climate, for the purpose of enabling servants of his Government, suffering from illness to avail themselves of its advantages. I, the Sikkimese Raja, out of the friendship for the said Governor General, hereby present Darjeeling to the East India Company."[18] "Darjeeling," whose name was adapted from the name of the original monastery, quickly developed into a bustling town.[19] For a decade after the signing of the Deed of Grant, the British paid a yearly allowance for the use of the Darjeeling ridge. But British-Sikkimese relationships deteriorated through the 1840s, as the British continued to press for the establishment of a trade route to Tibet, which required passing through Sikkim.[20]

After the East India Company acquired the Darjeeling ridge in 1835, British administrators, fearing that Darjeeling would become another Cherrapunji, settled on the ridge for nine months and took copious notes on the temperatures, rainfall, and other climatic factors. British East India Company officials deemed the ridge a favorable site for a sanitarium for British soldiers and officers suffering from tuberculosis, malaria, and other diseases, not only because of Darjeeling's climate, but also because they deemed the region to be "uninhabited."[21] Despite a population of nomadic Lepchas, the indigenous peoples of Darjeeling and Sikkim, Lloyd determined that "there are no villages in the Sikkim hills that I have ever seen, each man or family lives in the midst of his own cultivation, but there are collections of huts in a similar style with a quarter of a mile of each other, which scattered groups are sometimes for want of a better name called villages. . . . But I must explain that the Lepchas are migratory in their habits and quit the spot they have been cultivating at the expiration of the third year and take up a new location."[22] British officials characterized the Lepcha as happy, gentle, and candid people—unsuited for the manual labor required to build a hill station. According to the British officer L. A. Waddell, the Lepcha "represent(ed) the state of primitive man."[23] The Lepcha were thought to live closer to nature; they knew about the local flora and fauna and served as guides to the Himalayan interior.[24] Both nomadic Lepchas and the land under which they practiced swidden cultivation were conceptualized as "free."

The fact that Darjeeling was deemed to be "uninhabited" when the East India Company acquired it led British cartographers and administrators to categorize their new possessions as a "wasteland." As a wasteland, Darjeeling was marginally autonomous. Unlike elsewhere in colonial India, where local Rajas maintained (at least for a time) a marginal degree of control of the land inhabited and used by the British, or where outposts of provincial government controlled remote parts of the polity, the whole of the Darjeeling district was largely managed and controlled by British settlers and colonial officials.[25] In 1865, the British solidified the boundaries of the present-day Darjeeling district and the entirety became classified as a "nonregulated area."[26] The classification of "nonregulated" meant that the acts and regulations of the British Raj (and the Bengal presidency) did not automatically apply in the district, unless specifically extended. This categorization was generally applied to "less advanced" districts of the empire.[27]

Under this fluid administrative setup, Darjeeling became one of several colonial mountain refuges, or "hill stations." Early on in the imperial project, hill stations served primarily as sites of leisure and recuperation. As more and more military and civil servants built homes in mountain "wastelands," these communities grew.[28] Seen as clean and relatively empty, hill stations were sites of refuge for convalescing soldiers and British officers, and for the wives and children of civil servants. Even though they were "nonregulated," many hill stations were the seasonal capitals of imperial administrative centers. For example, Darjeeling was the summer alternative to Calcutta in Bengal, and Shimla served a similar purpose for Delhi and the Punjab. Hill stations were romantic and quaint European villages, unlike the rest of regimented India. Streets were lined with gabled gothic villas, Tudor cottages, gingerbread ornamentation, and Swiss chalets (quite unlike the standardized verandahed bungalows across the Indian plains), as well as a multitude of schools. Unlike elsewhere in India, which was largely dominated by men, as the British presence in India grew, hill stations became the homes of women and children.[29] The Darjeeling district became a site for the education of both English and Anglo-Indian children, often the progeny of tea planters. (Darjeeling remains home to several internationally renowned English-medium boarding schools.)[30] Hill stations were originally conceived as sites where the British could reproduce the social *and* environmental conditions of home.[31] Only later did they become industrial centers for the production of commodities central to imperial expansion and British daily life such as tea, rubber, and cinchona, the source of quinine, a malaria preventative.[32]

NEPALI STATUES ON AN ENGLISH BANDSTAND

Out of this wasteland, European settlers carved bungalows, gardens, reservoirs, churches, schools, and all of the other makings for the social reproduction of Britishness. The most iconic of these built environmental perturbations was Chowrasta, where settlers could gaze at Kanchenjunga and take afternoon strolls. Chowrasta was constructed during the heyday of hill station development. As an imperial ruin, Chowrasta is the symbolic center of British colonial control and the geographic center of the land that the British East India Company annexed from Sikkim. Chowrasta was once the site of afternoon concerts by the Darjeeling Police Band, a brass ensemble that would entertain British vacationers each afternoon (fig. 8).

At the north end of Chowrasta, where the bandstand once stood, there are two statutes, both commemorating Nepali culture heroes. The larger of the two statues is an imposing, gilded full-body image of Bhanubhakta Acharya (1814–68), the Nepali poet who translated the *Ramayana* from Sanskrit into Nepali, and who is widely considered to be the first poet to write in Nepali. The monument strikes pride in Darjeeling residents, as it is a reminder that Darjeeling—not Kathmandu— is the home of the Nepali Sahitya Sammelan (Nepali Literary Society), which was forced to operate outside of Nepal in exile because authors, poets, and artists like Bhanubhakta were persecuted by the monarchy for writing in vernacular Nepali, not Sanskrit.[33] Bhanubhakta looks south across the open plaza, dwarfing and partly occluding the view of a second monument, to his countryman and contemporary Jang Bahadur Rana (1814–77), a soldier and politician who facilitated Bhanubhakta's release from imprisonment. Jang Bahadur became Nepal's prime minister in 1846, after distinguishing himself in battle with the British and consolidating political control over the country.[34]

During the period of my fieldwork, and indeed throughout the postcolonial history of Darjeeling, these statues have been alternately venerated and desecrated by Darjeeling's pro-Gorkhaland activists. On one hand, the statues were sites of cultural and ethnic pride, to which Gorkha Janmukti Morcha (GJMM) politicians during my fieldwork would point during their weekend rallies at Chowrasta as monuments to "ancestors." On the other hand, these statues of *Nepali* heroes served as constant reminders that Gorkhas, while citizens of India, had ancestral roots outside of the country. In fact, the present Bhanubhakta statue is a reproduc-

FIGURE 8. Chowrasta in the 1920s. Photo courtesy of James Sinclair.

tion of the original, which was destroyed in 1991 by Gorkhaland subnationalist activists from the Gorkha National Liberation Front (GNLF), whose leaders disparaged him as a "foreign" poet.[35] The statues thus call attention to the complex relationship between Darjeeling Gorkhas and Nepal (fig. 9).

Both of these statues sit atop the remains of the English bandstand. The ruins-upon-ruins at the epicenter of this imperial formation remind us that there is a similarly messy stratigraphy of imperial development and domination embedded in the landscape. At the base is the fact that Darjeeling's potential as a hill station, rather than as a plantation district, drew the first major wave of Nepalis to the region to labor in sculpting a landscape in line with British ideals of leisure and the countryside.

Darjeeling has long been a site for trade and pilgrimage, particularly between Nepal and Tibet. Well before the British came to Darjeeling, trans-Himalayan traders passed through with pack animals stacked high with brick tea, jewelry, and foodstuffs. These travelers included the ancestors of contemporary Gorkhas, who came from the Himalayan foothills of what is now eastern Nepal. The story of the migration and permanent settlement from those foothills to what is now Darjeeling begins in the district of Gorkha, west of Kathmandu, in the mid-eighteenth

FIGURE 9. Bhanubhakta Acharya statue in Chowrasta. Photo by author.

century. Hindus, led by Prithivi Narayan Shah, from the House of Gorkha, conquered and annexed the fertile slopes east of Kathmandu, occupied by Rai, Limbu, Tamang, Gurung, and other Tibeto-Burman-speaking peoples. The subsequent consolidation of Nepal in the late eighteenth century created a kingdom that spread from the Kangra Valley in contemporary Himachal Pradesh to the Teesta River in contemporary Darjeeling.[36]

The Gorkha monarchy imposed a caste system on all of the people living in this territory, including Tibeto-Burman speaking ethnic groups who practiced Buddhist and animism. This Hindu-centric caste system was predicated on the purity and power of Brahmans and Chettris.[37] While the children of these high-caste Hindus were educated in Sanskrit medium schools, children from marginalized

Tibeto-Burman groups were forced to work the land.[38] After 1816, the Gorkha rulers encouraged their high-caste subjects to colonize the communal lands (*kipat*) of eastern peoples for rice-paddy cultivation and irrigation.[39] Marginalized Nepali minorities who lived there found themselves surrounded by wealthy Hindu settlers that considered them to be inferior in every sense. At first, high-caste Hindus settled in the fertile lowlands, but they quickly expanded into the foothills, pushing minorities even higher up the slopes, into more marginal areas.[40] Many eastern Nepalis, divested of their lands and forced to pay taxes, were conscripted into the Kingdom of Nepal's army.

Territorial rivalry between the Gorkha kingdom and the British East India Company arose over the East India Company's desire for an overland trade route to Tibet and motivated the Anglo-Nepal Wars from 1814 to 1816.[41] During the course of the wars, the British expressed respect for Nepali soldiers, whom they called "Gurkhas." British officer Sir Charles Metcalf said of the Gurkhas: "We have not met with an enemy who has decidedly shown greater bravery and greater steadiness [against] our troops."[42] At first, the British lost ground to Nepal's army, comprised largely of displaced farmers from the eastern hills. The British were forced to commit considerable resources to the war effort, and after two years of fighting, they eventually annexed present-day Darjeeling and all territory east of the Mechi River.[43] They also drastically reduced the kingdom's western possessions.[44] After the Anglo-Nepal Wars, the East India Company gave a parcel of the land annexed from Nepal, including contemporary Darjeeling, to the Kingdom of Sikkim in exchange for rights to cross Sikkimese land into Tibet.

To offset the loss of land, Nepal's monarchy pressed for further reclamation and agricultural intensification of lands in the eastern hills on the west side of the Mechi River, squeezing marginalized farmers even further. Beginning in the 1820s, often with the support of the central Nepal government, the East India Company recruited de-landed and otherwise marginalized Nepalis by the thousands to work as soldiers in specially formed "Gurkha" regiments,[45] as woodcutters in the forests and jungles between Darjeeling and Assam, and as road builders, food producers, and graziers. Lacking the resources to pay taxes and displaced by settlers from the west, many hill people from eastern Nepal eagerly emigrated to British India, often lured by promises of agricultural land. Emigration meant an escape from financial oppression, while resettlement promised opportunities for steady wage labor and reliable supply of grains, albeit within a new system of colonial oppression.

FROM "WASTELAND" TO "GARDEN"

Chowrasta remains one center of urban life in Darjeeling. To get to the other, the Chowk Bazaar, where Nepalis, Bhutias, Lepchas, and other non-Anglos were allowed to shop and socialize during the colonial era, you have to zigzag down

Nehru Road, one of the thoroughfares that intersect at Chowrasta. Moving down Nehru Road, you walk past Tibetan women hawking shawls and hand-knit wares for tourists on your left and old colonial shops, reappropriated as restaurants, chemists, and children's clothing stores, on your right. Following the iron fencing that lines the downhill side of the road, you drop down, down, and down some more, through a maze of concrete. The dramatic incline is the only thing that orients you on the descent, as sunlight and the horizon are blocked by towering multifamily homes. In the bustling Chowk Bazaar, jeeps full of tourists and travelers going to and from Siliguri zip down the Hill Cart Road, running north and south out of town. Past a liquor store and a couple of *pān* sellers, behind a towering building, and down a pot-holed footpath, sit the unassuming gates of Lloyd Botanical Gardens.

The Lloyd Botanical Gardens are a veritable Secret Garden, tucked in the middle of the overbuilt bazaar. Through the gates, the sky opens up to the south-facing downslope of the ridge, and sun shines down through the antique *duppi*. On the ground, however, the space is vacuous, dead, and haunted. Bare bushes mark the winding paths through the gardens, while the work of long-dead colonial gardeners is rendered in labyrinths of limp, leafless twigs, unidentifiable without the antique labels that accompany them. At the base of the gardens, in a splotchy grass pitch, sits the conservatory, a replica in miniature of the famous Kew Gardens' glassy centerpiece. Inside, the musty, thick air holds dainty Himalayan orchids and lilacs, resiliently clinging to their colors—and to life itself—in suspended animation. A mass grave of broken, moldy terracotta flowerpots stacks up outside the door. This gothic scene evokes a sepia image of bygone verdant vibrancy, when children played amid picnicking families, and colonial botanists propagated exotic plant varieties for capitalist exploitation.

E. C. Dozey's 1922 tourist guide describes the Lloyd Gardens this way:

> The garden is divided into two main parts, the upper or indigenous section, and the lower or exotic section. Many of the paths intersecting it are lined with the tea plant, the flowers of which are white with a pale yellow centre, reminding one of orange blossoms. The whole plot measuring 14 acres of land is neatly laid out, and contains specimens of nearly all our flora as well as many exotic plants, including the Australian Blue Gum tree (eucalyptus). There is a pavilion for use by picnic parties; while in the hot-house, which stands in the centre of the grounds, is a beautiful wisteria, a Japanese plant, and many varieties of camellia, a native to China, which when in full bloom are a revelation of colour.[46]

It seems fitting, historically speaking, that Dozey noted both a bifurcation between "indigenous" and "exotic" plants at the gardens, and that the tea plant adorned the footpaths that traversed these two sections. Tea, as both *Camellia sinensis* and *Camellia assamensis,* was, well before the time of Dozey's writing, an "exotic" that was civilized and trained to occupy the Darjeeling landscape *as if* it were a native.

The act of gardening domesticated tea's exoticness. Gardening was, after all, central to British ideals of domesticity. Public gardens like the Lloyd Botanical Gardens were places where English residents in India could feel English: places of relaxation and redemption. British residents could stroll through the winding paths of the garden and rest in its gazebos.[47] From the late nineteenth century until independence, the cultivation of British domestic space exacerbated tensions and literally created divisions between the British and non-British populations.[48] At the botanical gardens, colonial botanical taxonomies met colonial cultural taxonomies. Gardens physically and discursively separated wild plants from civilized ones. Gardens also cordoned off British space from that of the Nepalis, Marwaris, and Bengalis who lived among them.

Gardens are ways of disciplining bodies and environments through methodical manual labor and careful taxonomies, both of plants and of people. Through the introduction of new plants and animals, as well as other forms of landscape modification such as the construction of artificial lakes, the British remade the imperial landscape in accordance with their views of "nature."[49] The physical environment was not the only part of Darjeeling that British settlers remade in their views of nature. They also constructed representations of the people who lived there as pure and worthy of a place in these Himalayan Gardens of Eden. Popular representations of the Himalayan region often include descriptions of spiritual purity, driven by a rhetoric of a retreat from the ills of civilization.[50] Local people had to fit within the image of the recuperative garden.[51] British officials characterized hill people, like the Lepcha of Darjeeling, the Pahari of Shimla, and the Toda of Ooty, as possessing the simplicity and purity of Rousseau's "noble savage." They constructed Lepcha as the moral antithesis to the people living in the plains, in what Edward Said calls an "imaginative geography."[52] The romanticized vision of the hill stations' natives allowed colonists to view their own effect on local people as a part of an "improvement" scheme accompanying their alterations to the landscape.[53]

Gardening also shifted the function of the hill station from convalescence to capital accumulation. Lloyd Botanical Gardens was a space of experimentation and a site for the propagation of commercial plant varieties.[54] During the colonial era, officials at the gardens not only distributed plants, seed, and bulbs for home gardens and personal consumption, but also tested tea, cinchona, rubber, and other potential commercial crops to see if they would flourish in the climates of newly annexed territories. Colonial botanists and agricultural specialists, along with teams of Nepali laborers, grew out saplings of these plants for interested settlers.[55]

In his discussion of governance in colonial India, Thomas Metcalf argues that by the mid-eighteenth century, a discourse of "improvement" was consolidated into an ideology of imperial governance, inspired by the ideals of British liberalism.[56] As part of "improvement," colonial governments needed to understand the florae, faunae, and geologies of these new colonies so that they could be integrated into commercial use. Imperial botanical gardens aided colonial powers in their resource extraction and disseminated information on plants that would be "useful to the mother country."[57] Kew Gardens in London was the center of a network of British imperial botanical gardens and regulated the flow of botanical information from periphery to core and back again.[58] Decisions made at Kew had far-reaching implications for colonial expansion. As the botanical gardens succeeded in aiding resource extraction, botanical scientists working in the gardens or with trading companies became important colonial officials.[59] These scientists had a major role in turning the colonies into profitable agricultural enclaves.[60] They answered important questions, like where to find plants that would fill current demand; how to improve plants through species selection and hybridization; how to implement new methods of cultivation; where to cultivate plants with cheap labor; and how to process these plants for a global market.[61]

The imperative of "improvement" drove early tea development. The British viewed the indigenous tea variety (or *jāt*) of Assam, much like the region's native inhabitants, as "wild" and "uncivilized."[62] Colonial botanists deemed this association to be so problematic that they hypothesized that it would be wise to temper the Assam *jāt* with the nonnative, but more delicate, controllable, and civilized Chinese *jāt*.[63] Assam tea was often referred to as "*jungli* stock." *Jungli*, meaning "wild," was also used to refer to the native inhabitants of the region and later to *adivāsi* ("tribal" or "aboriginal") laborers who staffed Assam plantations. Essentializations that framed *adivāsi* laborers as exceptionally apt for jungle clearing and the more menial forms of labor (*jungli* labor) were cultural idioms that played a critical role in the staffing and organization of Indian tea plantations.[64] Botanists deemed it necessary to push for the *controlled* cultivation of Assam *and* its indigenous variety of tea. Indigenous, wild-growing Assam tea could only be useful to the empire if it was controlled, and as historian Jayeeta Sharma argues, *improved* upon through the application of both Western science, in the form of colonial botanists, and Chinese skill, in the form of imported Chinese labor.[65]

The development of tea in contemporary India's northwest in the Kangra Valley and Kumaon, and in the northeast in Assam, coincided with the appointment of Lord Bentinck as governor general of India in 1828. Bentinck saw agriculture as a key part of his mission.[66] In 1834, Bentinck formed the Tea Committee for India, led by the then-director of the Calcutta Botanical Garden, Nathaniel Wallich, and comprised of influential Calcutta merchants, opium traders (valued for their contacts in China), and various colonial officials and scientists. The first objective of the Tea Committee was to dispatch officials to evaluate colonial lands in India for agricultural potential. Committee members believed that they could cultivate a tea that would surpass Chinese tea in quality, flavor, and most importantly, efficiency of production.[67] British traders were generally contained to Canton in early years of the tea trade with China, and by the time the Tea Committee had formed, Sino-British relationships had completely eroded. To find out about tea production and acquire the material necessary for successful propagation in India, The Tea Committee also sponsored the surreptitious acquisition of tea seeds and saplings from China, most notably by Robert Fortune, a London-based bioprospector who brought them to India for cultivation in Kangra and Assam.[68]

Tea had been observed in India well before the formation of the Tea Committee. In 1823, two colonial officers, Charles and Robert Bruce, while on an expedition to the Assam-Burma border, observed that a native tea plant grew in abundance in the forests of the region. Singho and Khamti tribes used it primarily for medicinal and ritual purposes. Unlike elsewhere in Asia, where tea consumption was common, these groups were some of the only peoples observed drinking tea in India.[69] No one ever validated the Bruces' observations, and the "jungle" tea bushes of Assam remained a myth for several more years. Over a decade later, an army officer, Lt. Andrew Charlton, observed local consumption in the same area and sent leaves and seeds to the newly formed Tea Committee. Botanists from the Calcutta Botanical Garden were quickly dispatched to Assam to strategize the propagation of the indigenous Assam *jāt* of tea.

Tea cultivation quickly took off, first in Assam and then in the Northwest Provinces and the Punjab. The first shipment of Assam-grown tea was a success in London, but not because of the tea's taste; connoisseurs deemed it to be merely acceptable. The first Assam-grown lots of tea auctioned in London at twenty times the price of an average lot of Chinese tea. These high prices were credited mainly to patriotic zeal and excitement over empire-grown teas.[70] By 1839, large-scale production of tea in Assam had intensified, and within a year, the industry privatized into a single corporation, the Assam Company. The Company hired Robert Fortune as well as George Gordon, an opium trader and Tea Committee member, and Reverend Gutzlaff, a China-based missionary, to secure a continuous supply of labor and botanical matter from China.[71]

It was in 1841 at his Beechwood Cottage, near the site of the Lloyd Botanical Gardens, that the first superintendent of Darjeeling, Archibald Campbell, a self-styled naturalist, medical man, and up-and-coming British civil servant, planted tea seeds in his garden. Campbell and other officials and settlers had seen how Chinese tea bushes thrived in the Northwest Himalayas and that Assam was rapidly developing an efficient plantation industry. Campbell believed that Chinese tea bushes, or *Camellia sinensis,* could be industrially cultivated in Darjeeling. He and other early settlers in Darjeeling pointed out that Darjeeling was more climatically similar than Assam to the prized tea-growing regions of Southwest China. Shortly after his arrival in Darjeeling, Campbell arranged for Chinese tea seeds to be sent from Kangra. In Kangra, East India Company officials had recently made Chinese tea bushes profitable, with the help of experienced tea laborers recruited from China. With these seeds, Campbell began to experiment with tea in his backyard garden.[72] Like many British consumers at the time, Campbell believed that the

Chinese *jāt* of tea was superior in flavor and quality to the blacker, maltier teas produced from the Assam *jāt*.[73] While his experiments were not totally successful in his backyard garden, high up on the cold and windy ridge, Campbell and others hypothesized that the valleys below Darjeeling town could afford better sun and soil and warmer temperatures and that the fickle Chinese *jāt* would flourish there.

By the time the Darjeeling hill station was founded in 1835, tea drunk with sugar was rapidly becoming the fuel of working-class British culture.[74] Through colonial botanical garden networks, the Darjeeling municipality began to distribute tea seeds to interested settlers in the early 1850s, including Darjeeling civil surgeon Dr. Whitecombe, civil engineer Major Crommelin, and two German-speaking Moravian missionary families.[75] By 1856, individual experimentation and cultivation by Campbell and these other settlers had led to the establishment of a few commercial gardens in the warmer and sunnier valleys below Darjeeling.[76] In a January 2, 1862 correspondence in the *Friend of India*, a visitor returning from Darjeeling attests to the rapid development and sophistication of the Darjeeling industry: "Tea Planting in Darjeeling is not a mere 'experiment or amusement of gentlemen fond of a quiet life.' It is true one or two military officers conducted the first experiments, but at present time but two officers continue to be engaged in the occupation, all the rest of the planters are the same class as have settled in Assam and Cachar and it is a serious enterprise, i.e. is being conducted with as much energy and determination as characterizes the operations in the eastern districts."[77] By the end of 1866, there were thirty-nine gardens covering an area of ten thousand acres and annual production of 433,000 pounds of tea.

"GO DOWN, GO DOWN!"

Below the conservatory, there is a tiny antique iron gate tucked into a chicken-wire fence strung through a grove of *duppi* trees, marking the perimeter of Lloyd Botanical Gardens. Crunching on the dry, brown needle-covered soil, you duck and curl through the creaky egress.[78] On the other side, the slippery underbrush gives way to a pitted concrete path that hugs the hillside. After traversing over a wide gully (*jhorā*), clogged with garbage from the Chowk Bazaar, and through a settlement clinging precariously to the hillside, the path arrives at Kopibari Tea Estate's *gudum*.[79] A *gudum* is a tea-processing factory and the center of a plantation. On most plantations, contemporary workers must "go down, go down" the steep slopes of the plantation, just as the colonial planter *sahib*s demanded of their ancestors, to carry green leaf to the *gudum* for processing.

The *gudum* revolutionized the tea industry in India and enabled the creation of an economy of scale. In the early nineteenth century, tea was rolled by hand and was sourced from small-scale Chinese manufacturers (via urban Chinese distributors). Today, each Darjeeling tea plantation is still organized around its *gudum*. The smell of a tea factory is wonderfully pungent. A sweet earthy particulate-ridden fog brews inside. In the monsoon season, when bushes are their most productive (and in the case of Darjeeling, when production is in its least lucrative flush), the factory bustles with energy. Male factory workers roll empty wooden tea boxes in (often constructed from Himalayan *duppi*), and later roll them out filled with tea and stamped with lot numbers and dates. The tea machinery too, churns, burns, and shakes, sometimes twenty-four hours a day. These coal-powered machines, often embossed with the trademark of Britannia, the once-prominent British manufacturer of tea equipment and other mechanical implements for resource extraction (e.g., jute manufacture and road construction), are part of Darjeeling's landscape of imperial ruins.

Elsewhere in South Asia, tea factories have switched to diesel or electric processing equipment (some even use tea bush cuttings and waste for fuel), but Darjeeling manufacturers maintain that coal-fired machines are essential to the taste—the smoky "muscatel" flavor—of Darjeeling tea. Coal too, was of course crucial to powering the building of empire across South Asia.[80] Tea workers have been "left with" piles of coal (and its relative cheapness, thanks to the colonially forged mining industry) to fuel the postcolonial tea industry. And these imperial ruins have been the focus of labor agitations in the postcolonial era. For some workers, there was no way in which to productively inhabit them, and they presented an obstacle to future advancement.

The machinery that rolled, dried, fired, and sorted empire-grown tea was not introduced until 1873.[81] In Darjeeling, by 1870, there were fifty-six gardens on eleven thousand acres, employing eight thousand Nepali laborers and producing 1,708,000 pounds of processed tea.[82] But just one year after the introduction of machinery, in 1874, there were 113 tea plantations employing almost twenty thousand laborers. By the end of the century, the plantation labor force rose to sixty-four thousand on about the same number of plantations. This labor force constituted one-third of the population of the whole district (including the market town of Siliguri). Ninety-six percent of the tea workers in Darjeeling were Nepali.[83] The explosion in plantation development between 1870 and 1874 was due partly to mechanization. But like other imperial ruins, the factory hides a deeper and more complex history. The technology to process tea at scale did not automatically lead to a growth in the industry. People and land had to be made further governable and garden-able.

Despite the fact that tea cultivation in Assam and Kangra began some twenty years prior to the founding of the first Darjeeling plantations, thanks to the mechanical innovations in tea machinery and expeditious road and railway construction linking Darjeeling to Calcutta, Darjeeling tea production quickly eclipsed that of Kangra and became competitive in scale and, for many, superior in quality, to that of Assam. Planters credited this rapid growth to three forces: climate, which I discussed above, as well as free land and available labor, which I will discuss in the remainder of this chapter.

Land tenure rules in Darjeeling and the Northwest Himalayas were quite differ-ent.[84] As one manual for planters explained: "In Darjeeling the native cultivators have no saleable rights in the soil. . . . In Kangra the natives dispose of their surplus land or sell their homesteads at simply ridiculous prices (. . . and they almost invari-ably squander the money as soon as they get it)."[85] In other words, planters who wanted to open tea plantations in Kangra had to purchase land from local people. The fact that British colonial administrators in Calcutta classified Darjeeling and the surrounding foothills as a "wasteland" presented opportunities for entrepre-neurial British men interested in extractive industries and agriculture. In Darjeel-ing, leases for farming and the improvement of "wastelands" were exceptionally favorable for settlers. The various permutations of Wasteland Rules (in 1859, 1864, 1882, 1898) made tea cultivation a financially lucrative venture. Wasteland rules granted ninety-nine-year renewable lease periods and rent-free settlement for large tracts of uncultivated land (the 1882 Darjeeling Wasteland Rules specifically granted rent-free tenancy for tea cultivators).[86] These leaseholds were granted only to indi-viduals who vowed to "improve" the land. Under the later rewritings of the Waste-land Rules, property rights to a leasehold became transferable between individuals. This enabled settlers to sell their land tracts (and the materials on top of the land) and transfer their leases to new "owners." This ability to transfer leaseholds and sell property enabled the development of the Darjeeling tea plantation landscape.[87]

In Assam, although planters founded the industry in the image of Chinese tea production, this mode of production was deemed "inefficient" not only in its lack of mechanization but also in its organization of labor.[88] First, Chinese laborers refused to perform any labor not associated with the cultivation and manufacture of tea, such as clearing forest or portering tea and supplies. British planters attempted to attract native peoples, particularly the Nagas, who would perform such manual labors, and as an added bonus for British capitalists, worked for shells, beads, rice, and occasional feasts. Nagas were nomadic and came and went freely from tea labor.[89] The British then deemed it imperative to cultivate a *settled* labor force and recruit from more sedentary groups of people. By the 1860s, the recruitment of Chinese men had stopped, and planters looked to identify an alter-native workforce that would be cheap, disciplined, and sedentary.[90]

To Assam planters, it became clear by the 1850s that the model of producing tea with an imported Chinese labor force was unsustainable. Enticing the relatively small populations of nomadic groups within Assam to work for multiple seasons in succession was not working well for British East India Company officials and planters either. To answer what they called the "Labor Question," planters in the Northeast looked to Chotanagpur, in the famine-ridden plains of Central India, to "recruit," or more accurately indenture, *adivāsis* to work on tea plantations. Coerc-ing and maintaining the cooperation of *adivāsi* "coolies" was a violent and costly process. Indeed, the Indian Tea Association (ITA), founded in 1885 arguably for the purpose of solving the Labor Question, would struggle for decades to devise labor recruitment codes, laws, and regulations for keeping the labor force in Assam in the fields and healthy from season to season.[91] Recruiters often swindled *adivāsis* by requiring them to pay excessive amounts for recruitment fees, and British officials and planters often turned a blind eye to this practice.[92] It was in the context of labor conscription and environmental perturbations that tea planters in India and across the colonial world came to refer to their burgeoning, mechanized, and labor-intensive plantations as "gardens."

Plantations in Kangra mimicked the Chinese model of family-based cultivation, featuring smaller production plots for green leaf with a centralized location for hand rolling and packaging. This mode of production was called a *zamīndārī* system by some planters, as local *zamīndārs* (elite landowners) oversaw the manufacture of small batches of green leaf and organized its transport to government-run processing rolling and drying centers.[93] By the late 1800s, the *zamīndārī* system had been deemed inefficient by the Indian planter community.[94] Still, Kangra was slow to integrate mechanized production. For decades after Assam planters began using indentured labor, Kangra plantations continued to produce tea in small batches by hand rolling, often by Chinese laborers imported for that purpose.[95] Vocal planters in Kangra and throughout the Northwest penned letters to one other and back to officials in London and Calcutta, calling for the construction of centralized factories so that the green leaf did not need to be transported long distances to processing centers, only to be transported again for shipment back to England, which was often out of the ports of Calcutta on the other side of the Indian peninsula.

To staff their tea plantations, Superintendent Campbell and British planters in Darjeeling looked toward eastern Nepal and the Gurkha soldiers who had nearly defeated them in the Anglo-Nepal Wars.[96] Unlike *adivāsis*, Nepalis were *not* considered *junglī* laborers, and their history of army service and disenfranchisement at the hands of their king spoke to their ability to be productively controlled. They were not nomadic like the Lepcha of Darjeeling or the Nagas of Upper Assam.[97] On the contrary, they were settled agriculturalists, which made them desirable recruits for tea plantations.[98] By the time Darjeeling tea production began in the late 1850s, British administrators and settlers drew upon a cultural taxonomy of labor, which categorized Nepali migrants as industrious, loyal, and easy to control. Gurkha soldiers, associated with endurance, strength, and loyalty, were seen as good soldiers and workers.[99] The fact that British managers differentiated among "coolies" through cultural taxonomies was not unique to Darjeeling.[100] Chatterjee describes the distinct price indexes paid to labor recruiters for different *jāts* of workers in Jalpaiguri and the Northeast. In the plantations of the plains, *junglī* or *adivāsi* labor fetched a higher price than did local labor, because the British saw indigenous peoples from Chotanagpur as more suited to manual labor and the tropical tea environment of Northeast India.[101]

By the mid-nineteenth century, Nepali, or Gurkha, soldiers had also become integral to British strategies for empire preservation.[102] As one turn-of-the-century travel guide to Darjeeling explains of the Gurkhas: "They are a plucky lot, and none dare insult them with impunity; it is fortunate that they are not a quarrelsome race, for they can use their 'kookries' (or curved knives) with all the skill and adroitness of a Spaniard with his stiletto. The Ghoorkhas, which is the name of the ruling race and dynasty, make splendid soldiers, and many of them are enlisted in the British Imperial Service. They are short and slim, but wonderfully active and enduring, also brave to a degree."[103] The British maintained a friendly relationship with Nepal and by extension, a favorable opinion of Nepalis themselves, to ensure the sustainable recruitment of Gurkhas into their armies and plantations.[104]

Nepali labor recruiters, or *sardārs*, were pivotal in cultivating a resident labor force in Darjeeling. While in Assam and other Northeast gardens the solution to the Labor Question came in the form of *adivāsi* indenture, in Darjeeling, there was a surplus of labor due to the steady stream of migrants from Nepal.[105] Unlike in Assam, Nepali laborers were not indentured. Tea planters frequently spoke about how to maintain workers on a Darjeeling plantation:

> It is easy to make a garden liked by coolies. Particularly if there is plenty of native cultivation on the estate or waste land they can make use of. Always pay and advance on a fixed day, never varying, and never try to make them do extra work on their holidays. It is not good if you do, as they hear other garden's [*sic*] gongs go and do nothing or else purposely do bad work. Make them always do a fair amount of work, that is, look at the ground they are to hoe and if it is in jungle or the ground very hard, reduce the ticca, if easy work, increase. Do not try to make them do an extravagant amount, as if you do, the coolies will prefer to work until 5 o'clock and do less work. Whereas, if by working until 3:30 they can finish their task, they will work their hardest to do it and get away.[106]

Even before the formation of the tea industry, a gazetteer reported that by 1852, "the system of forced labor [had] been abolished, and labour with all other valuables [was] left to find its own price in an open market."[107] During the colonial era, Nepalis steadily migrated to Darjeeling. Over ten thousand Nepalis had resettled in Darjeeling by the time the first tea plantations opened, escaping oppressive conditions in Nepal to work as wage laborers in the construction of the hill station.

LINGUISTIC RUINS: THE PLANTATION AS GARDEN AND *KAMĀN*

In this chapter, I have argued that in order to understand Darjeeling plantations as spaces of global market production, we must see them simultaneously as part of a

larger historical project of improvement and cultivation on both local and imperial scales. Stories about Darjeeling always seem to be stories that attempt to reconcile the uncomfortable, visible material proximity of leisure and colonial production. But they are not just stories about spaces of production; they are stories
about landscapes, particularly landscapes of imperial ruins.

The duality of industry and leisure is encapsulated not only in the landscape of
material ruins but also in linguistic ruins, in the words commonly used to refer to
Darjeeling's tea plantations. In my fieldwork, I noted a complex linguistic dynamic,
between the Nepali word for "plantation," *kamān,* used by workers to describe
their workplace, and the English word *garden,* used by planters, government officials, and international tourists and tea buyers to describe Darjeeling tea plantations. *Kamān* is of disputable linguistic origin, derived from the English words
command or *common,* or perhaps even colonial British planters' use of "Come on,
Come on!" to communicate with tea plantation workers. For women workers,
kamān evoked the oppressive aspects of plantation life: the repetitive plucking,
pruning, and maintenance of a commodity crop. The use of *kamān* reminded my
interlocutors of the plantation land tenure system: that rich men "own" plantations
(though plantations are actually leased by these "owners" from the state government, in the case of Darjeeling, from West Bengal), while they are staffed by thousands of low-paid wage laborers of Nepali origin, who live in cramped villages
(*busti*) amid the sweeping fields of tea (fig. 10).

The word "garden," on the other hand, used most frequently by people from
outside of the plantations, framed tea bushes as extensions of domestic space, with
aging plants in need of familial "care" by women in order to remain productive.
The garden also framed an externalized "nature" as the product of human improvement. The use of "garden" reminded consumers and producers of Darjeeling's origin as a British hill station, a refuge from the heat and disease of the plains and a
site of social and environmental reproduction. The garden was an Anglophilic
vision of the landscape, which framed tea plantations with simulacra of English
domestic and public space—Victorian finishing schools, parks, and house-lot gardens (complete with celery, broccoli, and other plants brought from England).

At the beginning of this chapter, I identified two anthropological connotations
of "landscape," as both looked-upon and lived-in. The image of the plantation as
"garden," seen from Chowrasta, fits the first connotation. The understanding of the
plantation as *kamān,* which emanates from down the hillside, amid the fields of
tea, fits the second. In the next two chapters, I discuss the plantation in both its
kamān aspects, which I will elaborate in chapter 2, and its garden imaginary, which
I will describe in chapter 3.

The view from the ridge of Darjeeling town—the green swaths of tea plantations in every direction speckled with laboring Nepali women, or of the *duppi*
groves protecting Victorian bungalows with gingerbread ornamentation—is a

FIGURE 10. "Tea garden coolies" with planter. Photo courtesy of James Sinclair.

result of a distinct cultural, environmental, economic, and geopolitical process. Darjeeling's imperial ruins capture the contradictory history of the place itself—its history as both site of extraction and site of refuge. On the plantation, these ruins embody the binary of *kamān* and garden.

By the time planters organized the Darjeeling Planters Association in 1908, the scale of tea production would increase, tea would become more industrialized, the labor pool would grow, and the tea industry in Darjeeling, according to workers and planters, began a slow decline from its productive golden age. The construction of Darjeeling was so successful that Darjeeling ceased to be a "wasteland" by 1910, when it was incorporated into the Province of Bengal, when a partition solidified district borders in the Northeast and integrated marginal districts into the governmental and bureaucratic structures of British India. The turn of the twentieth century saw the development of tea industries in the Dooars, Terai, and South India, as well as the extension of tea cultivation into Sri Lanka and Kenya. By 1940, there were 142 Darjeeling tea gardens under 63,059 acres of land, producing 23,721,500 pounds of tea.[108] The market for empire-grown tea expanded, so much in fact that in the 1920s, British tea promoters looked to extend the tea market into the Indian middle and working classes.[109] Darjeeling, however, remained not just a predominately exported crop, but also an Anglicized one that was readily associated with exclusivity and luxury.

2

Plantation

A sheet of rain came down with a dramatic crash. We scattered into the darkness of the Himalayan forest. Despite being chastised for carrying my large rainbow-colored *gentsko chātā* (man's umbrella), I relished having it on dark dreary monsoon days like this, when I could recede into it like a turtle and feel at least a little bit dry. I had promised Neeta, an old woman in the village I was staying in on Saagbari Tea Estate, that I would keep her company while she planted baby tea bushes in a distant section of the tea plantation. All morning, it had spit rain while Neeta convinced me that planting new tea bushes was made more bearable by dancing around the recently interred sprig. "Like this," she motioned to me, packing down the dirt with rhythmic steps of her plantation-issue plastic boots. To an internal beat, she two-stepped around the plant, twisting her hands in the air and making subtle snakelike movements with her head and upper body as she turned around the bush. She commanded me to rehearse all the Nepali songs I knew, paying no mind to the monotone crackle of my voice: "*Resham phiriri. Resham phiriri. Udyera jauki dandaima bhanjyang resham phiriri . . .* "[1] Female laborers would let me pluck tea with them, but when they had to perform higher-level tea tasks, my role was entertainer.

After the rains subsided, a line of workers streamed in, each bearing a *tāukori* (a large head basket usually used for collecting tea leaves) filled with scraggly baby tea bushes (fig. 11). These workers, mostly younger women, dropped the plants with Neeta and headed back up to the tea *nurseri*. Aruni, Neeta's coworker, was hunched over, straddling the slope and clearing the ridge with a stick and her bare hands to prepare the ground for the elderly Neeta to inter the tea shoots. Looking back along the ridge, we could see the results of weeks of work: evenly placed baby tea bushes poking up from the desiccated soil (fig. 12).

FIGURE 11. Women carrying baby tea bushes in *tāukori*s. Photo by author.

FIGURE 12. Female laborers planting baby tea bushes in a new section of a plantation. Photo by author.

"Ehh, *bahini* [younger sister]," Neeta called out, motioning for me to squat with her to take a break. "They want us to retire, you know. But we won't!" she said, pulling out a small hand-rolled cigarette (*bidi*) from a cloth bag attached to the drawstring of her *chaubandi*. "We are ooold!" She curled her index finger dramatically, indicating that they had become hunched. "That is why we get this work [planting new bushes]. This is *bojyuko kām* [grandmother's work] . . . But, see these plants?" She waved toward the new sprigs. "These are our *pukka nāni* ["real (nongendered) children"]. Our daughters get married and go away, and our sons? *Aaahh!*" She flipped her hand in a dismissive backward swat. "But these bushes? They are always here. Every day, they need plucking, and pruning, and cleaning [around the roots], just like little children . . . and every day that is what we do. . . . *Darjeelingko jindagī estai chha* [Darjeeling life is like that]."

While clearing rocks and underbrush to make room for more baby tea bushes, these women, like many other female tea laborers I interviewed across Darjeeling, described what they saw as a decline in the tea industry. Neeta explained that the tea bush has about the productive life of a human being (sixty to seventy years) but that most of the bushes in Darjeeling were over a hundred years old, planted in the heyday of what she and other plantation laborers called the British tea *industri*. Older tea pluckers told me that the plantations did not produce as much leaf as once before; the bushes, too, had become "old." They often called them *thākiyo* ("tired") or *budho* (pronounced *buro*, meaning "old," or "old man"), affectionate terms of light reprimand that they also directed toward their husbands. Being *budho* was not desirable for a tea bush; women already had one *budho* to look after at home.[2]

For tea workers, it was the job of tea plantation managers, or "planters," to regularly allocate resources to replant sections of the tea plantation, replacing *budho* bushes with vibrant green sprigs. Female laborers saw it as their job to take it from there, to care for and maintain these bushes, but workers across the district agreed that in the past couple of decades, planters were not committing resources to replanting old bushes, or for any other development on the plantation. If planters did plant new bushes, as they had done on Neeta and Aruni's plantation, they did so not to replace *budho* bushes (as workers would have liked) but rather to expand tea fields into the forests and their mountain gullies (*jhorās*) in hopes of capitalizing on the growing international taste for fair-trade or organic Darjeeling tea. The choice to expand into these marginal areas, rather than to replant in existing fields, had visible, and increasingly detrimental, material effects on the landscape.

According to workers, the rapid agricultural intensification of tea plantations from the 1990s to the first years of the new century had reduced forest cover not only in *jhorās*, but also across plantation lands (according to one planter I interviewed, to prevent landslides, it was crucial to keep forest cover on the ridges and valleys of plantation foothills, in addition to the *jhorās* that separated them). *Jhorās* were dominant features of the Darjeeling landscape, but tea plantation residents knew that they had to be carefully managed. To prevent landslides, landholders either kept them forested or "trained" them by using stones or concrete to build terraces and reinforce their sides. The choice to plant tea in these areas dramatically increased the risk of erosion and, eventually, landslides.

In interviews, laborers used the planting of tea in such areas as an example of how the Darjeeling tea "industry" had become a "business." In workers' words, an *industriko mānchhe* ("person of industry"; alternatively, *rāmro sahib*, or "good planter") reinvested profits, planting trees (or refraining from cutting them in the first place), "training" *jhorās* to prevent landslides, securing water sources for laborers' use, and, crucially, replacing withered "old" tea bushes with healthy new ones on a regular basis. For female laborers, this reinvestment in the landscape signaled not just a care for the environment but also for labor. *Industriko mānchhe* who cared for *jhorās* also ensured that workers had access to housing as well as to what workers called *faciliti-haru* (using the English word *facility* with the Nepali plural postposition -*haru*), including schools, garden space, community houses for weddings, and recreational spaces for games and gatherings. *Faciliti-haru* were integral to a productive tea landscape. *Industriko mānchhe-haru* cared for laborers, who in turn cared for the land. The *bisnisko mānchhe-haru*, or *bisnis-men*, by contrast, only extracted. Instead of entrusting the care of the bushes to skilled laborers, *bisnis-men* adopted newer production practices such as organic farming and fair-trade certification. Indian planters discovered that by marketing their products as "organic" or "fair trade," they could sell at higher prices and find new markets. This revelation prompted a revival of the tea industry in the 1990s and an intensification of planting, but it did not lead to reinvestment in *faciliti-haru*. These shifts in managerial practices, or as Nepali laborers referred to it, a transition from *industri* to *bisnis,* signaled changing and degrading relationships between labor, management, and the landscape they both inhabited. *Bisnis* practices for both laborers and plantation residents were readable on the plantation landscape.[3]

Whereas planters saw in *bisnis*-based production (e.g., fair trade, organic, and other certification schemes) a revitalization of the tea industry, workers identified *bisnis* practices as severing reciprocal ties between labor, land, and management. In this chapter, I describe workers' understandings of the Darjeeling plantation landscape as undergirded by a "tripartite moral economy" that included not just humans (planters and laborers), but also nonhumans (tea bushes and the wider landscape). I trace the tripartite moral economy's historical roots to colonial and independence-era plantation life and politics, arguing that the relationship between women and tea bushes was the outcome of the labor recruitment process that brought Nepalis to Darjeeling, and the colonial and postcolonial reorganization of labor that turned tea plucking from nongendered Nepali work to Nepali *women's* work. The relationships between women, *faciliti-haru,* and tea bushes were inherited; these relationships were not on the terms of any one party's choosing. In their critiques of *bisnis,* tea pluckers were expressing an active, engaged role in the landscape they coinhabited. They were, in Donna Haraway's words, "inheriting the past thickly in the present so as to age the future."[4]

INHERITING THE PLANTATION: KINSHIP AND THE TRIPARTITE MORAL ECONOMY

Expressions of relationships to plants like those articulated by Neeta were not uncommon. Workers tended to speak about the similarities between people and tea bushes during acts of cultivation. As they planted and plucked, female tea plantation workers articulated a mutual ethic of care between people and people, and between people and plants, in kinship terms. Neeta and Aruni's talk of tea-bush "children" and caring plucker "grandmothers" reveals how in Darjeeling, discourses about the reproduction of families and landscapes blended with ideas about economic production.[5] Women's use of kinship metaphors for tea bushes provides a window into the material and ideological production, both of Darjeeling's plantation system and of workers' "consent" to remain in the labor process from generation to generation.[6] In *industri* (as workers nostalgically described it), planters were entitled to their profits, but they had to make meaningful reinvestments in the plantation. Such reinvestments rarely came in the form of increased *monetary* compensation (i.e., wages), which have become the sine qua non of "empowerment" in fair trade and other development discourses. Instead, workers valued expressions of care, for land as well as for workers, in *nonmonetary* terms: the provision of *faciliti-haru* and maintenance of the delicate plantation landscape. Planters' care for labor, manifested in the provision of *faciliti-haru,* was reciprocated through laborers' care for the land.

Tea labor, then, was not only *material,* in that it produced tea, a globally circulating commodity, but it was also *immaterial,* or affective, in that it produced feelings—in this case, of care and concern.[7] Women's discussion of a fictive kinship between themselves and tea bushes, and as I describe in this chapter, between themselves and tea plantation managers, reinforced the importance of ideas about care to the value of Darjeeling. For tea workers, care had a clear gendered dimension. Women acted as mothers and grandmothers to tea bushes and the rest of the landscape, while male supervisors played the paternalistic role of "uncles" (*kākās*) to plantation women. Plantation labor was simultaneously affective and oppressive. Women articulated their labors as care for an industrial agricultural landscape, but they also complained about the rainy monsoon days, tedious repetition of plucking, and unsympathetic management. They lived and performed caring labor on a plantation landscape that was owned and controlled by increasingly austere *bisnis-men* planters.

Discussions of *industri* provided a powerful contrast to the structural oppression workers faced in their daily lives. Importantly, women tea pluckers tended to describe *industri* in historical terms. When they recalled the past, they spoke nostalgically of colonial plantation management in order to contrast it in stark terms with the postcolonial rule of West Bengal. This postcolonial power was wielded from both down in the state offices in Kolkata, and up on Darjeeling plantations by non-Nepali management. Women identified the colonial era as a time when fictive kinship relationships and actual economic relationships ensured a productive but stable landscape.

Descriptions of a positive plantation past—a time of *industri*—framed workers' understandings of moral economic breakdown in the present. Women's nostalgic visions of mutual relationships of care formed the basis of a gendered vision of a plantation moral economy—a system of mutual obligation—on the plantation. While a discussion of the moral economy of the plantation might look at the binary relations between workers and management, in this chapter, I describe a three-way relationship that includes workers, managers, *and* the plantation landscape. For workers, descriptions of decline of the Darjeeling tea *industri* referenced not only the material plantation infrastructure, but also the deterioration of nonmonetary reciprocity between labor, management, and the plantation agro-environment, a tripartite moral economy that undergirded colonial tea production. In the tripartite moral economy, women creatively positioned themselves in the hierarchy of the plantation structure. Planters—as paternal or avuncular figures—could be both oppressive *and* caring. Likewise, female tea laborers, who had to ensure the productivity of tea, could view bushes as either partners *or* enemies.

Anna Tsing has described the social and emotional relationships people have to the plants they cultivate, drawing a comparison between her own research in Kalimantan with swidden agriculturalists and the work of Sidney Mintz.[8] In *Worker in the Cane,* Mintz describes an antagonistic—even violent—relationship between laborers and the sugar cane they harvested on Puerto Rican sugar plantations. Mintz's descriptions of taking down the cane are dramatic. The plant is a sharp, dry, and adversarial. Mintz writes:

> Just as Saturday and Sunday differ from weekdays, so the harvest time differs from *el tiempo muerto*—dead time. From Christmas until early summer, the cane is cut, and much cane is planted. The fields are alive with activity. Long lines of men stand before the cane like soldiers before an enemy. The machetes sweep down and across the stalks, cutting them close to the ground. The leaves are lopped off, the stalk cut in halves or thirds and dropped behind. . . .
>
> From a distance, the scene is toy-like and wholesome. Up close it is neither. The men sweat freely; the cane chokes off the breeze, and the pace of cutting is awesome. The men's shirts hang loose and drop sweat continuously. The hair of the cane pierces the skin and works its way down the neck. The ground is furrowed and makes foot-

ing difficult, and the soil gives off heat like an oven. The mayordomo sits astride a roan mare and supervises the field operations. He wears khakis and cordovan riding accessories. To see him ride past a line of men bent over and dripping sweat, to hear the sounds of the oxen in the fields behind, the human and animal grunting, and to feel the waves of heat billowing out of the ground and cane evokes images of other times.[9]

Tsing describes a different relationship between people in the Indonesian rainforest and the sugar they would find in a swidden. Unlike in Puerto Rico, cane in Kalimantan is a treat. Sugar cane is not the same plant in these two sites.[10] The cane in which Mintz's informants worked was a specific, standardized, industrial variety; the one that Tsing's informants discovered in swiddens was certainly domesticated, but not standardized and industrialized. That "no one loves plantation cane sugar" is certainly evident in Mintz's descriptions of male labor in Puerto Rico.[11] But if we are to take women's metaphorical motherhood of tea plants seriously, we must situate the plantation in what Tsing and others have called a "multispecies" perspective.[12] A multispecies perspective brings attention to human-nonhuman, or interspecies sociality (though we must understand a "species" as coming out of a distinct ontological frame). This focus on relationality, or what Deleuze and Guattari call "mutual becoming," highlights how human life is produced together with nonhuman life.[13] To tell the story of tea cultivation from a multispecies perspective means to emphasize how tea pluckers, as persons with particular gendered perspectives, experience the world not just alongside tea bushes, but along *with* them. The material conditions of tea, whether delicate, *budho*, or vibrant, do not just reflect the material conditions of workers' lives. Rather, these conditions co-constitute one another.

An industrial agricultural landscape might not seem like a fruitful anthropological location to employ a multispecies perspective, but a plantation is more than just low-wage labor, disinterested management, and standardized plants. Bridging theories of nonhuman sociality with an exploration of moral economies, the tripartite moral economy elucidates the relational nature of the plantation. It also adds a distinctly gendered dimension to both of these discussions. Nongendered baby tea bushes, old, impotent bushes, female laborers, husbands, *faciliti-haru,* non-Nepali male managers, and landslides (which result in both human and nonhuman death) are all "entangled," to use Laura Ogden's term, in the Darjeeling plantation landscape.[14]

The lives of pluckers, planters, and plants were entangled in more than just symbolic ways. Tea, unlike other industrial crops such as cotton, cane, and coffee, is *cultivated*—pruned and plucked—periodically, ten months a year. And tea bushes, as Neeta reminded me, can live productive lives of sixty to seventy years. Tea *cultivation,* like child rearing, cannot be artificially rushed. Thus, tea bushes and tea pluckers are both long-term residents of plantations. Conversely, cotton, cane, and coffee are *harvested,* in short, intense cycles, often by migrant laborers who do not call the plantation home. The ecological constraints on agriculture, including growing cycles, can certainly be loosened through technological innovation, but there are still constraints. Temporality in plant lives, in growing cycles, and in working days, can be manipulated through industrialization, but only to an extent. The life cycle of a plant, even an industrialized one, shapes the social and moral economic conditions in its landscape. Tea, like cotton, coffee, and cane, helps set the terms of its own industrialization.

Exchange entangles humans and nonhumans in relations of cohabitation and subsistence. Building upon a foundation laid by Marcel Mauss, anthropologists have long studied exchange relationships as *moral* relations.[15] Contextualizing plants and the agro-environment within a larger moral economic system highlights how historical processes of trade, cultivation, and capital accumulation inform local frameworks for social and environmental sustainability. If tea pluckers felt they were unable to take proper care of their tea-bush children, this had direct implications for their ability to care for their human offspring. Importantly, workers were not able to choose the conditions under which they cared for their plant *or* human children. By insisting on planting tea in *jhorās* and skimping on *faciliti-haru,* planters broke a reciprocal relationship. The results of these actions were landslides and fractured families. Workers saw such changes as rippling detrimentally through this entangled landscape.

As I argued in the introduction, drawing on the work of E. P. Thompson and James Scott, moral economies are historical constructions.[16] In the remainder of this chapter, I first describe women's tea plucking work in more detail, explaining how affective kin terminology articulated labor-management and labor-plant relations. Next, I trace the historical origins of the tripartite moral economy and Gorkha workers' rights movements to a complex history of relations between plantation owners, managers, Gorkha laborers, and tea bushes. Finally, I return to the question of *faciliti-haru,* to both historicize the concept and to show how women's understandings of the physical degradation of the plantation landscape, of which *faciliti-haru* were important cohabitants, framed their visions of plantation reform.

LABOR AND FAMILY ON CONTEMPORARY TEA PLANTATIONS

The day starts in a Darjeeling tea plantation village well before dawn, with a cup of tea and an array of domestic chores. Most plantations employ between five hundred and a thousand permanent workers, the majority of them women pluckers. Permanent workers live in small settlements of 50 to 150 people, spread across the plantation land. A typical plantation contains five to seven villages. A village comprises a cluster of small houses, lined up along a wide footpath spurred off of a rocky dirt plantation road. Houses are small. Some are made of concrete or brick, others of bamboo, and others of wood. They are packed densely together, with tea bushes often growing right up to their back walls. The spacing in most villages is so tight that it is difficult for the casual observer to tell where one household ends and another begins. This makes life in a plantation village an intensely social affair. News of large and small events, from deaths to domestic disputes to the acquisition of new cookers or televisions to the arrival of the occasional tourist (or anthropologist) spreads quickly. Although some plantation villages have water spigots, many do not. Some households collect rainwater in storage tanks during the rainy season, but during the dry season, upon waking in the cold darkness, male and female plantation residents alike load empty water and whiskey bottles into their *taukoris* and trek into the forest to the nearest spring. This spring can be as much as an hour away by foot. Early in the morning, too, women make tea. Most often, plantation women cannot afford to buy the tea they pluck. Instead, they brew a malty black tea, produced in other tea-growing areas and purchased in the local bazaar. Workers usually brew their tea with milk and sugar to make *chiyā*.

After cleaning, washing, and portering water, women workers prepare the morning meal, which usually consists of *roti ālu,* dry flatbread made from the biweekly ration of *atta* (processed white flour), accompanied by potatoes, or *boteko bhāt* ("carried rice"), rice heated up from the night before with oil and a bit of spice, and perhaps a bit of vegetables. Women workers have to make enough for their children to take a small tiffin with a rolled up *roti* or two to school. Then, at seven in the morning, working women suit up in men's button down shirts and *lungi*s or old *kurtā*s, don rubber boots and knee-high socks, and tie plastic sheeting around their waists to protect their lower bodies from sharp brambles and branches. This is the ritual from Monday to Saturday. Each day, these women work with their labor crew, composed of the same dozen or so women of various ages from close-by villages, from seven until four o'clock, with a brief respite in the middle of the day. If the section they are plucking that day is close enough to their villages, they can go home to eat lunch; but more likely, before seven, in addition to prepacking their children's lunches and sending them off to school, they have to pack themselves a tiffin lunch to eat while crouched between tea bushes, shading themselves from the midday sun or monsoon rains.

Few of the members of the household who do not go to school or work on the plantation have steady livelihoods. Some workers' husbands are lucky enough to have jobs in plantation factories, but most (if they do work at all) have to search for work in Darjeeling town or nearby villages. There was a time when the British and independent Indian armies recruited heavily among "Gurkha" plantation men, but today, men are just as likely to earn money by working as drivers, raising chickens for sale in town, working in part-time wage jobs in the Darjeeling bazaar, or brewing and selling homemade rice beer (*jāār*). If a man's plantation village is closer to Darjeeling town, he stands a much better chance of landing such a position. Farther from town, a significant number of plantation men are chronically unemployed. During plucking hours, life in a plantation village is lonely and, frankly, boring. Alcoholism and depression are rife, and women often define "good" planters as those who find occasional work for men, even if it is only cutting grass or maintaining plantation buildings. Women who are not pluckers have similarly limited options for work. Some run small stores in their villages; others spend their time seeing to the upkeep of their village homes.

On a normal day of fieldwork, I too got up before dawn and had tea and breakfast (I also found *boteko bhāt* to be expeditious and satisfying in the morning) and hiked down the ridge to a plantation. The hike to the plantation typically took one to three hours, depending on whether the crew I would join was working on an "upper" section, near town, or a "lower" one, closer to the valley floors that spread out to the east and west of the ridge. Walking (and stopping for a cup of tea here and there along the way) was key to my method.[17]

At seven o'clock, with the gong of the work bell, the plantation comes to life. Labor crews collect and unfurl across the sweeping green landscape, while snakes of uniformed children trudge up the steep washed-out dirt roads to the schools in town. I would pass them on most mornings, and they would ask me, perplexed, why I wanted to go down to the *kamān*. I tried to convince these children, who lived betwixt and between the worlds of town and plantation, that our pursuits were not that different.

At some point during the morning, I would find a group of plucking women. Using two hands to comb the bushes in a rhythmic movement, women would pull off the smallest shoots of tea from the flattened tops of each and every bush. They would then toss it behind their heads into the basket—the *tāukori*—strung from their head. Plucking is certainly a skill. It is one thing to pluck off the young shoot of tea while not slipping on the moist decomposing underbrush of tea trimmings and loose soil beneath your feet, but to do it with both hands simultaneously is quite another, all the while collecting the shoots in your hand before tossing the fistfuls over your shoulders (fig. 13).

Each day, I too would pick tea. It took months for me to be able to pluck a handful of tea at a time—but only in my right hand. My left hand never really caught up. Even days before my departure, I was jokingly criticized for being slow and clumsy as I threw my measly handfuls into the *tāukori*s of the workers around me.

Plucking dominates the yearly calendar, but during the cold dormant winter months, these same women prune each of the thousands of tea bushes on the plantation. During pruning, women's work shifts from gentle culling to flogging the bushes with a small sickle, sending tea trimmings flying in every direction. The tough gnarled bushes makes this excruciatingly hard work. Although the pruning

FIGURE 13. Female laborers plucking tea in the field. Photo by author.

season only requires a half-day's work each day, women find plucking to be much easier. One winter morning as I was crouched between bushes taking notes and shielding myself from flying tea cuttings (after a brief test administered to me by an older member of this labor group, I was not allowed to wield a pruning sickle), a worker called over to me: "Oooh, *Serā!* I have a question for you" (fig. 14).

"What?" I looked up from my notebook.

"Do women in America work this hard?"

"No, no!" Another laborer interjected. "In America, there are machines for this sort of work, no?"

I explained that, yes, in *thulo kheti-patti* (big agriculture) like the *chiyā kamān,* American farm *māliks* (owners) bought machinery to plow and cut the fields, and they often hired *begāri* (temporary laborers) to staff these *amerikī kamān.* "In America, we grow corn and soy, not tea or coffee. Corn and soy can be taken down with a big machine, but you cannot cut tea down to harvest it."

"If they grew tea in America," one laborer said, "they would figure out an easier way to do it." She turned back and took a backhanded swipe at the bush.

Throughout my fieldwork, I tried to make sense of how the plantation worked—who did what and when and how the division of labor laid over gender,

FIGURE 14. A female laborer pruning a tea bush on a winter day during the dormant period of tea production. Photo by author.

class, and kin relationships. As in other South Asian contexts, laborers referred to each other in familial terms– *didi* (older sister), *bahini* (younger sister), *kāki* (father's younger brother's wife), and *phupu* (father's sister)—regardless of biological relationships. The women referred to male field supervisors as "uncles" (*kākās*).[18] In communities across South Asia, the use of elder-male-kinship terms denotes respect, and closeness and it is not uncommon to use these terms to describe non-kin.[19] "Uncles" helped negotiate the relationships between workers and management.

HUMANS

didi/bahini (elder/younger sister): women within the same plucking group (including female anthropologists)

kāki/phupu (aunt): alternatively, women within the same plucking group

bojyu (grandmother): referring to the work of planting new bushes and to the relationship between workers and tea

āmā (mother): as in the fictive kin relationship between female workers and *nāni* tea bushes *bāje* (grandfather, or term of respect for any older man): plantation owner/ planter of *industri* (alt. "father"; often used to describe the nostalgic figure of the "gentleman planter")

bāu (father): "garden *bāu*," higher-level Nepali field managers

kākā (uncle): "father's younger brother," field supervisors, or *duffdars*

PLANTS

nurseri (nursery): where tea seedlings are grown before being planted

nāni (children): as in tea-bush children; what workers called young bushes

mudder patti ("mother leaf"): the third leaf beneath the "two leaves and a bud" (in Nepali: *ek patti dui suero*)—the young supple shoots that pluckers wanted to find

budho (old, also used to describe human men): a dry and unproductive bush that did not readily produce "two leaves and bud"

At midday, before lunch, pluckers bring the green leaf that they plucked that morning to one of the collection sheds spread across the plantation so that a *kākā* can weigh it. He records the amount plucked by each worker, and in doing this also takes attendance. To weigh the tea, *kākā* hangs a scale from one of the rafters of the collection shed. Each woman knots up her collected leaf in the scarf or scrap of fabric she uses to cushion her head from the weight of the *tāukori*, and *kākā* hooks the sack up to weigh it. *Kākā* then arranges for its transport uphill to the plantation factory, either by foot or by tractor. Morning plucking lasts from seven to noon. At noon, after a worker's leaves are measured, she can take until one o'clock for lunch. Afternoon picking, which begins at one, is generally hotter and more arduous. At four o'clock, women again have their tea weighed, before returning home. On some plantations, *kākās* inspect for darker, coarser leaves, known as "mother leaves"—the stiff older leaf that gives birth to the desired *ek patti dui suero* ("two leaves and a bud"). *Kākās* and workers use the term *mudder patti* (mother leaves) to describe these leaves, which they consider too old and tough to make proper Darjeeling tea.[20] In 2010, women received a daily wage of sixty-three rupees (just above one dollar) per day, plus a small per-kilo incentive of a few rupees. This incentive was harder to come by when plucking old, less productive bushes.

Women I interviewed explained that *kākās* were expected to treat them with a certain amount of concern, ensuring an equal distribution of labor, helping pluck leaf, or training inexperienced puckers. *Kākās* who favored certain women, chatted with them excessively during the work hours, or put extra leaf into the baskets of "favorites," had hushed snickers and indignations directed toward them. Women, too, who tried to seek preferential treatment from their *kākā* superiors were ridiculed for being sycophants, though in a more direct way, but often in earshot of the supervisor as a means of reminding him of his own indiscretions.

Such criticism sounded like: "Eh, oooh *kāki* [father's younger brother's wife: "aunt"]! What's the use? You still have to work the whole day!"

A good *kākā*, workers told me, turns a blind eye toward midmorning or midafternoon breaks. Tea not only marks the start of laborers' mornings, it punctuates the workday. In fact, drinking tea (often with milk and sugar) is part of how labor is reproduced. Tea is food for Darjeeling tea workers. Throughout the day, workers sip on sugar or salt tea from liter-sized reused XXX Rum bottles (the rum or whiskey that originally occupied the bottles was often jokingly called *bishesh chiyā*— "special tea"—as black tea, rum, and whiskey shared a similar caramel hue). Most female Darjeeling tea workers have access to low-grade broken-leaf Darjeeling tea (produced on their home factory, but not deemed fit for international circulation), which they receive as part of their food rations—350 grams every month. This only supplements women's monthly tea purchases. On afternoons and weekends, I sat with female workers as they blended this ration tea into *chiyā*, a strong, dark brew mixed with milk and sugar. They knew that Darjeeling tea was "expensive" and that a cup of Darjeeling tea in the United States cost more than they made in a day.

At the end of a typical workday, women return home to supervise the preparation of dinner. With luck, they can serve lentils (*dāl*), a green vegetable, and rice. On dry evenings, boys organize small cricket matches in the narrow lanes between the houses, and if a villager owns a working television, adolescents and adults gather to watch films, soap operas, or the increasingly popular Indian versions of reality-television shows. *Indian Idol*, whose 2007 champion was a Gorkha man from Darjeeling, was a perennial favorite. These evenings are punctuated by the consumption of *jāār* (men and women alike drink alcohol) and conversations about the future. Women speak proudly of children who are progressing to class ten (roughly the equivalent of a high school diploma) or have even been accepted to study at one of Darjeeling's several colleges. For women, knowing that men's employment opportunities are scarce, hope for the future depends on a stable plantation workplace.

HISTORICAL ROOTS OF THE MORAL ECONOMY

Women, almost exclusively, do the plucking work I described above. On some plantations, male field laborers perform tasks from carrying plucked leaf up to the factory to spraying fertilizer to repairing landslides. During the monsoon, though, they might be sent out to pluck leaf. This was rare, men told me, but is necessary at certain times during the plucking cycle, particularly during the more prolific but lower-quality monsoon flush. Male field workers begrudgingly go to pluck tea— they describe it as painfully monotonous labor.

As I will explain in subsequent chapters, the naturalization of tea work as women's work has become central to local development projects, fair trade, Geographical Indication, and the Gorkhaland movement. The feminization of Darjeeling tea labor, however, is also a relatively recent outcome of historical developments in the region, specifically its entanglement in British military and economic projects and the Indian independence movement.[21] The persistent use of kinship metaphors by tea plantation workers has its roots in colonial concerns about labor and land. From its beginnings as a British imperial enterprise, the Indian tea industry and plantation owners in particular had to reckon with what they called the Labor Question, the question of how to settle and control a steady workforce on remote plantations. Unlike in neighboring China, tea cultivation did not have a long history in India. In each major tea-growing region, the question of how to attract and maintain a willing and skilled labor force in this unfamiliar industry, often located in remote and sparsely populated parts of the colony, was answered in a slightly different way.

Whereas Assam and Dooars planters relied upon strict conscription codes to legalize the indenture of coolies—a colonial term for manual, nongendered, labor—Darjeeling planters in the nineteenth century managed to recruit a willing labor force to the plantations from Nepal.[22] They used the provision of housing, food rations, and land for cultivation and grazing to incentivize the permanent migration of entire villages from the hills of eastern Nepal.[23] In his account of the British Indian tea industry, Percival Griffiths, a planter at Tukdah Tea Estate in Darjeeling during the 1940s, paternalistically described planters' moral obligations to workers: "Men, women, and children brought hundreds of miles from their own country to the notoriously unhealthy tea districts could only survive if planters accepted responsibility for their welfare."[24] In exchange for what later became known as "facilities," Nepalis worked on British-owned plantations in Darjeeling, served in the British Army, and helped build Darjeeling's roads, railroads, bungalows, and factories.

From 1850 to 1869, the Nepali population in Darjeeling more than doubled, from ten thousand to twenty-two thousand.[25] Tea laborers, planters, town residents, and politicians all credit the first superintendent of Darjeeling, Archibald Campbell, for spearheading the successful launch of the tea industry and for getting Nepali laborers to Darjeeling to build it. Campbell remains central to vernacular narratives about the development and expansion of Darjeeling and its tea industry. It was Campbell, as I explained in chapter 1, who was credited with bringing Chinese tea bushes to Darjeeling and experimenting with them in the garden of his bungalow. In 1852, an inspecting officer to Darjeeling described Campbell and Darjeeling's labor conditions:

> [Campbell] found Darjeeling an inaccessible tract of forest, with a very scanty population . . . a simple system of administration of justice has been introduced, well adapted to the character of the tribes with whom he had to deal; the system of forced labor formerly in use has been abolished, and *labour with all other valuables has been*

left to find its own price in an open market; roads have been made; experimental cultivation of tea and coffee has been introduced, and various European fruits and
grapes; and this has been effected at the same time that the various tribes of inhabitants have been conciliated, and their habits and prejudices treated with a caution and
forbearance which will render further progress in the same direction an easy task.[26]

Most accounts of labor recruitment to Darjeeling come from planters' own
records, which tend to portray men like Campbell as single-handedly bringing
Nepalis to the region. Unlike in Assam or the Northwest Himalayas, where workers
were indentured or violently forced, recruitment in Darjeeling involved different and
less violent forms of coercion. But neither tea planters nor Superintendent Campbell
attracted Nepali laborers by themselves. In Darjeeling, labor was almost exclusively
recruited through a *sardār* system.[27] *Sardār*s were Nepali men who used their knowledge of their natal regions in eastern Nepal to bring a steady supply of labor to Darjeeling.[28] Capitalizing both on a long-standing practice of religious pilgrimage
between Nepal and Darjeeling and the Gorkha monarchy's more recent oppression
of ethnic and religious minorities from eastern Nepal, *sardār*s escorted eastern
Nepalis over the Mechi River to Darjeeling tea plantations. Once in Darjeeling, these
*sardār*s oversaw the laborers on the plantation.[29] Often, *sardār*s recruited from the
same villages in eastern Nepal over and over again. As a result, on many gardens
today, single ethnic groups and extended families dominate specific plantations.[30] On
the tea plantation, the *sardār* watched over laborers, making sure that his recruits
received food rations and salaries from the planter. The *sardār* was an important
intermediary in the plantation structure and was integral to the maintenance of
workers' subsistence and in ensuring that they stayed on that plantation (as there
were other plantations in Darjeeling on which they could conceivably secure work).[31]

Even in the early days of Darjeeling tea development, each plantation set aside
land for workers' cultivation and herding and also provided medical facilities and
housing to each laborer.[32] Crucially, the planters hired whole families to work on
Darjeeling plantations. Unlike in other British colonial enterprises, such as the
mines, jungles, railroads, and factories (usually staffed by men), children on Darjeeling tea plantations could pluck and sort tea alongside their parents.[33] Women,
children, and men all labored in the fields of tea plantations; to the British, they
were nongendered "coolies."

In Darjeeling, labor could "find its own price," in the words of the inspecting
officer quoted above, because planters, through *sardār*s, cultivated and reproduced
a labor surplus (recall from chapter 1 that this was a surplus that was nonetheless
created by the exploitation of non-Hindu farmers in Nepal). *Sardār*s managed,
maintained, and fed laborers with avuncular responsibility. In Darjeeling, plantations thrived thanks to the development of relationships of care between *sardār*s,
planters, labor, and the land. "Good" planters were those who could *independently*
retain labor on behalf of their companies.

This distinguished Darjeeling from northern India's other tea growing districts, Assam and the Dooars, where the annual bulletins of the Indian Tea Association highlighted chronic labor shortages. The Indian Tea Association, the governing body for the industry, was founded in the late nineteenth century to codify and standardize labor recruitment rules. Planter associations existed primarily to ensure that each plantation could get enough labor to last season to season, and secondarily to make sure that there were standards (often low) of labor treatment. Because Darjeeling planters used individual *sardārs* to recruit Nepali laborers, they did not see the need for such standards. The Indian Tea Association formed a Darjeeling and Dooars subcommittee as early as 1892, but Darjeeling planters initially refused to participate. Darjeeling planters believed that it was both the region's special climate and their ability to "independently" recruit the Nepali laborers who, in their view, "spontaneously" migrated to the district, that allowed them to produce the first Indian tea to be considered as good as Chinese tea.[34]

It was only in 1910, after it became clear that some planters were providing better wages and facilities than others, causing Nepali workers to move from plantation to plantation in search of the most favorable living and working conditions for their families, that planters in Darjeeling founded the Darjeeling Planters Association (DPA).[35] The DPA began standardizing labor and environmental practices across the district. While the Indian Tea Association sought to *raise* labor standards to a minimum that would motivate workers to remain in Assam and the Dooars, the DPA sought to keep planters from out-recruiting one another by providing better and better garden space, housing, and schools. In this way, the DPA actually *lowered* labor standards and the quality of "facilities." The founding of the DPA began the phase-out of the *sardār* system. After 1910, management, not *sardār*s, distributed wages and benefits, which were standardized across the region.[36] The formation of the DPA and its standardization of plantation welfare took advantage of the fact that Nepali laborers had chosen to permanently settle on individual Darjeeling plantations. It effectively ended the era in which "good planters" could distinguish themselves by offering better remuneration than their neighbors. By 1910, plantation growth had stabilized, and the demand for labor leveled off. From 1910 to the present, the amount of land under tea in Darjeeling has, if anything, decreased. Since the mode of tea production has not changed, this means that the number of workers required has not changed either. What has changed, however, is the gendered makeup of the workforce.

FACILITIES AND THE GENDERED DIVISION OF LABOR

Although men, women, and children were paid differently, there is no historical evidence that work was particularly gendered during the colonial era.[37] Instead, in Indian Tea Association records from before the First World War, Darjeeling laborers were referred to as nongendered coolies. The few elderly plantation men I met during my fieldwork remembered plucking tea as children "before the war" (World War II), when most of the able bodied men on the plantation, including the planters, were drafted into the British Army. This shift happened just after the Darjeeling Planters Association formed and began curtailing workers' benefits, and right when the longevity of the British presence in India was coming into question.

The British deployed Gurkha soldiers to suppress Indian rebellions that asked just this question. Gurkhas were central in quashing many independence movements, such as Jallianwala Bagh in 1919 and the Quit India Movement of 1942. The Gurkhas, and by extension Nepalis in general, gained a reputation within India as pro-British and anti-independence.[38] While increasing numbers of men were dispatched across India and to warring theaters in Europe, female Nepali laborers remained on the plantations. Writing in the 1947 district gazetteer for Darjeeling, Arthur Dash notes that between 1939 and 1944 the number of women workers relative to male workers increased significantly.[39]

The 1941 Indian Tea Association bulletin reported that as a result of increased food costs during World War II, Darjeeling tea workers' cost of living had increased beyond workers' ability to survive.[40] Moreover, inflation and food shortages were making plantation production less lucrative. The Darjeeling Planters Association agreed that "temporary" cash compensation should be given to workers, "quite apart from the ordinary wages . . . a special allowance introduced temporarily to meet the increase in the cost of living brought about by the war, and liable to be modified or withdrawn at any time as circumstances might dictate."[41] In addition to the cash allowances, some planters began rationing rice and other grain in order to "protect laborers against inflation," but such rations were unevenly distributed.[42] World War II thus saw the return of nonmonetary remuneration, as well as land incentives for workers, but not all planters distributed these benefits.[43] Workers began to distinguish "good," caring planters from "bad" ones who withheld facilities. While most Gorkha men were abroad fighting, women and children received these benefits. Given the changes in the work structure, then, it was women who were most aware of the separation between "good" and "bad" conditions. When women workers I met expressed nostalgia for *industri,* it seems likely that it was nostalgia for this period, when at least some Darjeeling planters regularly provided good facilities.

After a day's work, I would often accompany workers back to their houses in densely settled plantation villages (*kamān busti*) for a cup of tea; or up to town while they carried tiffins filled with rice, *dāl,* and vegetables for sick relatives in the "labor ward" of the Eden Hospital; or to the chemist to buy medicines for their children. Plantation workers are all full-time residents of *kamān bustis,* small settlements that sit within the fields of tea and whose houses were built and owned by plantation owners.[44] The *kamān bustis* began as "labor lines," akin to barracks, where the British housed the first tea plantation labor force. Over the decades, as plantation families expanded, plantation owners provided space and materials for the construction of new houses, which sprouted up around the labor lines. Beginning in the nineteenth century, *sardārs* negotiated with planters to acquire more housing and garden space, as well as crèches and community houses, turning the labor lines into *busti*s. During my visits to the *kamān busti,* it became clear that for women workers, the tea bushes were not the only part of the landscape that had become old. Stories about the bygone days of *industri* were often answers to my questions about the condition of crèches, community houses, and cricket grounds.

One day on Kopibari Tea Estate, I accompanied a retired tea plucker to her daughter's *busti* on the *kamān*. As we walked past a multistoried community house, I noted that the building dwarfed the one-room meeting houses I had seen on other plantations. I asked, "What's this building for?"

She explained:

It is for weddings and Puja . . . children can play there. . . . Isn't it impressive? The company built it years ago, before [the old owner's] children took over and started fighting with each other. They didn't care about us, or about tea even. They just wanted to make money. But the old man, he was like our *bāje* [grandfather]. There were always medicines in the dispensary, and the roads were easy to walk on. If you didn't have enough money for your own child's shoes, you could go to him—he was in the factory—and say: "*Sār*" [she dropped her eyes to the ground mimicking the necessary supplication], "my daughter has no shoes and I cannot afford them; she needs them to go to school." And he would—oh, he was so gentle—give you the money for *two* pairs of shoes![45]

This woman's nostalgic recollections of *industri* couched the plantation as a space of nurture and care. Just as replacing *budho* tea bushes signaled plantation owners' investment in the reproduction of a vital landscape, the provision of *faciliti-haru* signaled owners' investment in the reproduction and nurturing of families. Women tea pluckers spoke at length about their responsibilities to care for their children, from birth to marriage, and of children's responsibilities to care for them when they became too old to work. Throughout the course of a tea plucker's life, "good" plantation owners provided the space for this care in the form of *faciliti-haru*.

The World War II years also saw the arrival of Darjeeling's first two major political parties. The Akhil Bharatiya Gorkha League (ABGL) and the Communist Party of India, Marxist (CPI[M]), both established bases in the district in 1943.[46] The ABGL aimed to represent Nepalis throughout India. The party was affiliated with the Congress Party, and it remained so until the time of my fieldwork. During the Indian independence struggle, the ABGL and the CPI(M) worked together for the rights and autonomy of Indian Nepalis in Darjeeling and across the Nepali diaspora in the Northeast. The CPI(M) leader Mailaa Baaje (literally, "middle-oldest grandfather"), who rose to power in Darjeeling in the mid-1940s amid the struggle for Indian independence, understood that for Nepali tea workers, a political program based on hardline Marxism might not be palatable. As its union became increasingly powerful across the district, the CPI(M) began advocating to the interim central government a proposal to form an independent nation of "Gorkhastan" comprising Nepal, Darjeeling, and Sikkim.[47] The appeal to state sovereignty was a shrewd one, since the earliest organization to advocate for the rights of Nepalis in Darjeeling, the Hillmen's Association, had joined with the Darjeeling Planters Association in pressing for the separation of Darjeeling and the Dooars from West Bengal in the decades before the unionization of tea plantations. The CPI(M) capitalized on popular senses of distance from the Indian nation felt by Indian Nepalis and fomented by the Hillmen's Association's autonomy calls and intergroup alliance building. Importantly, it was during this time that tea labor became dominated by women, as plantation men had been recruited to the front lines of the British Army. Independence and the end of World War II drastically reduced military service opportunities for Nepali men. The CPI(M) exploited the malaise of these returning Gorkha soldiers and unemployed men. On the now female-dominated plantations of postwar Darjeeling, these men became active union members and leaders. The Gorkhastan movement fizzled, but regional autonomy remained part of the CPI(M) and ABGL platforms.[48]

The earliest political victories in Darjeeling went to the CPI(M). In 1946, Mailaa Baaje, who formed the Darjeeling Tea Garden Workers' Union in 1945, was elected to the legislative assembly of Bengal on a platform that promised plantation reform. Workers were aware that, thanks to the reforms undertaken during World War II, a few "good planters" were providing facilities for their workers. The party sponsored an eleven-point list of demands for the improvement of working conditions. Demands included increases in daily wages, maternity expense provision, the elimination of child labor, education, the construction of hospitals on tea estates, retirement pensions, a "bonus" or "tip," and the abolishment of rent for grazing and herding.[49] Many of the provisions were part of wartime welfare reforms, but the CPI(M) worked to ensure that Darjeeling tea plantation workers in independent India continued to receive them on a permanent basis. These provisions also mirrored those negotiated by *sardārs* during the era of colonial labor recruitment.

Planters claimed that these benefits were intended to only be temporary, but in a circular dated July 28, 1947, less than three weeks before independence, similar provisions for wages, benefits, and housing were written into the official ITA bulletin,[50] setting the stage for the passage of the Plantations Labour Act (PLA) of 1951. The PLA codified these rules, born in wartime, into the constitution of independent India. What had been planters' efforts to "maintain" an efficient and relatively healthy labor force of "coolies" during a time of war and scarcity became officially classified as "compensation." The PLA came about thanks in part to the work of Mailaa Baaje and the unions, who served, not unlike *sardārs*, as intermediaries between planters and workers, now predominantly women. The labor unions provided men, now returning from wartime service, with an alternative to the army as a source of institutional connection to the state and local and national politics.

In the face of a concerted, organized labor movement, British owners and companies sold their plantations to Indian owners at increasing rates. After 1955, Darjeeling plantations were no longer growing; in fact, they were shrinking. The post-independence years saw increased planter austerity and a declining market for Darjeeling tea. The rollback of facilities, the haphazard payment of wages, and plantation closures caused labor unrest, which planters blamed on the growing power of the CPI(M) and its unions. The workers I interviewed tersely described this "dark" phase of Darjeeling history. Their relatives were pushed so far and deprived so much, that they had no other choice but to take drastic measures to fight back against management. They murdered planters, often with symbolic resonance—throwing them into the tea plantation's drying machinery or locking them in their sprawling bungalows and burning them down. Workers also burned down tea factories. The crisis that Darjeeling tea plantations faced was multifaceted, and the options to secure a future for plantation families seemed few.

Planters saw the post-independence entry of the Communist Party as a poisoning of their "natural sympathy for the hillmen."[51] According to Percival Griffiths, "For some decades before the Transfer of Power, tea garden proprietors had enjoyed a fair measure of freedom in their dealings with employees and as labour at the time was unorganized the scales had been weighted in the favour of the employers."[52] Griffiths explains that after independence and the passage of the 1951 PLA, "the tea industry moved into a new era, in which official intervention in labour relations and government control of the remuneration and conditions of service of labour would be the rule rather than the exception."[53] Independent Indian labor laws mandated that there be regular tripartite meetings to set wages and other payments on plantations. The PLA wrote *faciliti-haru* into national law. It became the mission of labor unions in post-independence Darjeeling to ensure that the planters were providing *faciliti-haru*.

By the time the Foreign Exchange Regulation Act (FERA) went into effect in 1973, mandating that all plantations must be Indian-owned, most capital had left the region. The number of acres under cultivation and the number of gardens both declined, due to closures and conglomeration. These smaller plantations needed fewer laborers, and with the cost of production going up, new Indian owners and companies had further reason to reduce the number of permanent laborers on tea gardens in favor of seasonal employment. There were more men on Darjeeling gardens, but there was no work for them in town, in the army, or on the plantation itself. This gendered dynamic became more and more striking between independence and the Gorkhaland agitation of the 1980s.

On the post-*sardār* plantation, active unions were an important component to the ideal of *industri*. Unions, much like *sardārs* of the colonial era, ensured that planters provided workers *faciliti-haru*. The CPI(M) unions (in conjunction with the ABGL, which had a weaker foothold on most Darjeeling plantations) held planters accountable to the provisions of the PLA. Workers knew that unions were key to the codification and maintenance of facilities. But *bisnis-men* planters bought off and undermined the power of plantation unions, particularly after the Gorkhaland agitation of the 1980s, which effectively ended Communist power in the Darjeeling district.

OF FACILITIES AND STABILITIES

The deterioration of the *faciliti-haru* guaranteed by the PLA was partly a result of union buy-offs and the retrenchment of capital from the plantations that began after 1973, but by the early years of the new century, plantations were reopening, and capital was returning, thanks to the promise of fair trade, organic, and Geographical Indication status. Though these schemes brought more profits to Darjeeling's tea industry, when they were first initiated in the 1990s, by the first years of the new century, workers were beginning to ask why their lives were not improving in tandem with the fortunes of the plantation on which they lived. It was in this period that they began to speak nostalgically about the bygone era of *industri* and critically of the present era of *bisnis*. As my friend and tea plucker Bishnu described it, "These new [Indian] companies take, take, take. And, what do they give us? Nothing."

While *bisnis* practices destabilized the plantation moral economy, women workers continued to sell their labor to *bisnis-men,* even when there were other options. Take the example of Kopibari Tea Estate, the *gudum* of which we visited in the previous chapter. From 2005 to 2008, Kopibari Tea Estate was "closed," meaning that management had left the garden, all work had stopped, and plantation workers were not receiving wages. Struggling for ways to feed and clothe their children, many female tea laborers walked up the mountainside to look for work in Darjeeling town. They broke rocks for the construction of new hotels and private luxury houses and portered luggage and goods around the crumbling roads. As a porter or a rock breaker, a woman could earn more than she would on the plantation, often in the same number of hours.

When Kopibari reopened under new ownership in 2008, however, most of these women came back to work on the plantation, despite making less money and knowing that the new owner had a reputation for being a *pukka* (real) *bisnis-man,* the kind who not only skimped on facilities and cut benefits, but also had all thirteen of his plantations certified fair trade and organic. After Kopibari reopened, I accompanied a group of women as they plucked tea from the "first flush," the first harvest during the spring. After several days of plucking with these women, I asked them why they chose to return to the plantation, knowing that they could earn just as much—if not more—working in town. One woman answered: "That's not good work. On the plantation, we have *faciliti-haru*. And it is close to home."

Another woman explained that the plantation was a *stable* workplace: "It's easier here. We have to make our children food in the morning and we need to be there when they get home from school. We can't do that when we work way up there." She pointed using her pursed lips to the distant Darjeeling town, perched on the hillside above where we were plucking tea. "Here we get medicines, rice, and flour. . . . And when there is plucking we can leave our children in the crèche. We can't bring them with us when we go up there."

This worker was earnest in her insistence that working conditions on the plantation were superior. But facilities remained scarce, while tea bushes and houses alike continued to slide down into the valleys of the Himalayan foothills. Still, the *idea* held sway that the plantation was a more humane workspace than town. These plantation imaginaries were buttressed by the affective kin terminologies and idealized understandings of the British era I described above. Women "inherited" these imaginaries, like the crumbling community houses, schools, and crèches that were "left behind" on Kopibari, not to mention the plantation houses and plantation jobs themselves.[54] This moral legacy came to them from ancestral kin, and the physical "imperial ruins" of the plantation—the bushes, roads, and villages I discussed in the previous chapter—served as reminders of it. In order to "inherit the past thickly," women workers creatively assumed their role as nurturers and reproducers within an entangled plantation landscape.[55]

Tea pluckers at Kopibari spoke of the ideal plantation in ways reminiscent of descriptions of married Nepali women's discourses about their natal households, or *māiti ghar*. For married women, the home of one's own parents was a safe space, opposed to the often alienating space of one's husband's household—a *sasurāli ghar*.[56] Although marriage patterns on Darjeeling plantations did not follow the classic South Asian model of the patrilineal joint family, the distinction between *māiti ghar* and *sasurāli* provides insights into the feelings of affinity women felt for the plantation and the *kamān busti*.

On my morning walks to find labor groups, I would often pass by small crèche houses. Most were little more than shelters, with wire mesh for walls. Inside, they were empty except for a swinging bamboo basket or two attached from the ceiling, in which the crèche attendant would alternately rock fussy babies. Since *kamān busti* were situated both at the tops of the foothills and down in the valleys, many plantations contained more than one crèche, allowing women to leave their children nearer to their homes. When Kopibari reopened, the new owners did not rebuild the crumbling crèches, but they did grudgingly provide the resources to staff them. Legally, each crèche was required to be supplied with milk, but more importantly for women, a staffed crèche allowed them to work without having to entrust their youngest children to the care of older siblings, who would, ideally, attend school.[57]

Although employees paid by the plantation staffed crèches, some spaces of care were maintained and operated collectively. On most plantations, Sundays (the one day of the week on which plucking did not take place) were reserved for intervillage gatherings, most of which were organized around youth soccer tournaments. These tournaments tended to be organized and "hosted" by *thulo mānchhe* (big/important people), usually male field supervisors (*kākā*), union leaders, and leaders of local branches of the GJMM. The soccer games drew large crowds comprised of older men, children, and unmarried men and women. With schools out, women tea pluckers insisted that their children attend the games. I spent most Sundays with these women, who remained at home in the *kamān busti* doing laundry, cooking, and cleaning. Early on Sunday morning, women would shoo their younger children down to the playing ground. Older children who could finish or shirk household and market chores would soon join them, eager either to participate in the games or spend time gossiping and flirting with friends. As an unmarried and childless woman, I was encouraged to attend as well, but I tended to find the gatherings, which featured not only soccer but also hours of speechifying by the *thulo mānchhe-haru*, to be wearying. Pluckers would laugh knowingly at my complaints. "Its just *hallā!*" (literally, "noise"; colloquially, "talking for the sake of talking"). Workers, too, would mock the *thulo mānchhe*-ness of the male organizers. *Thulo mānchhe*, as I was told, liked to give their speeches, but they brought everyone to the playing fields—a key *faciliti* outlined in labor law. They were happy to let them make their petty political speeches, especially if the children came home tired and happy. I gradually began to see these daylong events as more than just *hallā* and masculine posturing. They were important acts of sociality, and the space of the soccer field supported such networking. Soccer was more than just soccer.

Back in the *kamān busti*, women's work went on much as it did in the fields. Each woman worked individually to tidy her home, but this work was interrupted by breaks for *chiyā* and gossip with other women, or even a few quiet moments with their husbands. On Darjeeling plantations, marriages tended to stem from romantic affairs. Since formal, arranged matches were rare, women and men from plantation villages tended to meet in relatively informal settings, in facilities such as community houses or playing fields. The continued existence of these public spaces, which lay outside the household, was, for women, vitally important for the reproduction of it.

I worked in a plucking group at Kopibari with Pratima, who lived at the foot of the valley floor, two hours' walk from Darjeeling town. In the winter of 2010, I was invited to the wedding of Pratima's daughter, Sonam. Pratima had decided that Sonam, her youngest daughter, would be the daughter to whom she would pass her plucking job when she retired. But Pratima could not be assured that Sonam would be able to take it unless she married the right person: someone who had prospects close to Kopibari and who could support Sonam until Pratima was ready to retire.

The ceremony was held in the plantation community house. The women of the plucking group and residents of the village prepared vats of stewed vegetables, meats, and seasoned *dāl*. Someone had brought a sound system for singing and dancing. Pratima and her husband were relatively well-to-do. Her husband worked in the Kopibari *gudum,* and she had made good money as a porter and rock breaker in town during the three years in which Kopibari was "closed." Pratima was pleased with the match. Not only was Sonam genuinely in love with her new husband, but he was also a child of Kopibari. He had a class ten education, which meant that he had been able to secure part-time employment as an office worker in town. Sonam would be able to take Pratima's plucking job, and if something befell her or her husband, Sonam would be nearby to help.

Plantation jobs were passed down from generation to generation. This meant that each woman needed a child who was willing and able to stay in the *kamān busti* both to care for her in her old age and to take her job in the field. Since the mode of plantation production had not changed since the colonial era, however, this also meant that new posts in the plantation were rare. Even as families grew and villages expanded, according to the Plantations Labour Act, planters were still obligated to provide more houses and garden space in the *busti*. In an interview over a pot of tea at Glenary's, a century-old German bakery in the heart of town, a West Bengal assistant labor commissioner explained to me:

> You walk into a Nepali house and you see a sitting room, with all the furniture covered with the finest decorations they can afford. Their house, this room, is like a bank account—you can see years and years of collective family savings . . . but, they don't even own the land under it. These housekeeping skills, you know, they learned them from the British. The gardens, potted plants, little doilies . . . you don't see that anywhere else but in Darjeeling. They don't do this in the Dooars or Assam.
>
> In fact, their houses are actually detrimental . . . they are misleading of the actual economic status of Nepali laborers. Tea buyers and tourists go down there and all they can talk about is how wonderful a tea worker's life is . . . they see their houses and they think that they are well cared for. They never ask *who* built those houses. You know, every year the garden has to build 8 percent new houses. They never do, because you know what the fine is [for noncompliance]? A couple thousand rupees [one new house costs at least fifty thousand rupees] . . . the companies pay it.[58] They have all this money and they don't care. The laws exist to make workers' lives better, but it is cheaper to just pay the fine. It makes me sick. But what can I do? This is not the era of gentlemen planters.

Of course, the gentleman planter was a vehicle of critique, more of a foil to high-light present-day *bisnis* practices than an actual historical figure. He also represented the planter that workers conjured when they spoke of *industri,* a benevolent, paternal figure. Workers' careful maintenance of houses, manifested in women's activities on those soccer Sundays, masked the house status as facilities. In this way, the pleasant facades of the *kamān busti,* with gardens, plants, and freshly painted walls, were as "misleading" of the socioeconomic status of workers as the young sprigs of tea growing in the *jhorās* were of the ecological sustainability of the plantations.

Pluckers like Pratima felt lucky if their children were able to move into houses in their *bustis,* but *bustis* had become crowded. When planters built new houses (or, more likely, allowed laborers to build their own houses), they tended to put them atop garden space—canceling out one kind of *faciliti* with another. Just as often, the children of plantations moved out of the *bustis.* Those who had some education and money sometimes looked for work in Delhi or Kolkata, but many remained in Darjeeling.

Plantation populations have grown, while the demand for labor has stayed the same and perhaps even decreased since 1910. As plantation populations grew over the decades, tea plantation residents moved up to Darjeeling town in search of work and homes (this was catalyzed by the Gorkhaland agitation in the 1980s, which compelled many non-Gorkha families in Darjeeling to leave their homes in town). This influx of "Sundays" (a derogatory term for tea plantation workers used by longtime Darjeeling town residents) into marginal areas of town—on backfill, slopes, septic tanks, and *jhorās*—has strapped the town's colonial-era infrastructure. Despite building codes that prohibit buildings taller than three stories, the market for cheap housing in Darjeeling inspires developers to go skyward, often as many as eight stories. Hastily built apartment houses, like the tea bushes of the plantation, are falling into the *jhorās* and sliding down the mountainside. "Getting off of the plantation" and into a house and job in Darjeeling town was a common aspiration among younger tea plantation residents, but those who did get out faced forms of ecological and economic marginalization similar to those that beset the *kamān busti.* In the era of *bisnis,* Darjeeling life was marked by a physical instability that mirrored the instability of labor relations. Nepali plantation residents, former or current, knew that all they worked for could wash away in the next monsoon.

MORAL ECONOMIES AND LIFE IN THE LANDSCAPE

The performance and reproduction of care in homes, fields, and factories served to mitigate not only the instability of the physical landscape, but also the uneven circulation of tea, capital, and families. From generation to generation, plantation workers inherited a landscape in which past relationships among people, tea, and land had to be reorganized in light of changing political and economic conditions in the present. What was unchanged was the link between plantation families and plantation land. Donna Haraway has elaborated the relationship between kinship and the social construction of nature by expanding the concept of "inheritance." Following the philosopher Jacques Derrida, Haraway argues that inheritance is never a given; rather it is a task. Learning to labor is "learning to inherit the past thickly in the present so as to age the future."[59] In other words, when they envisioned historical moral economic stability, plantation women were also envisioning a more stable future for their children. The precariousness of the landscape mimicked the instability of home and family life on the twenty-first-century plantation.

Darjeeling residents continue to rely upon the plantation for their livelihoods. It is the overwhelmingly dominant physical and cultural feature of the place. Over time, the lives of plantation women in particular have become more entangled with the lives of tea bushes. Tea workers are stuck with tea bushes, colonialism, and paternalism. The concept of inheritance helps move discussions of agricultural work beyond the alienation of labor to think of agriculture as a way of life that is always, already "troubled." Kin, after all, are not chosen; they are inherited, and "getting on" with them is rarely a simple task. The concept of a tripartite moral economy takes workers' senses of care seriously and it puts them into a historical frame. It permits us to think with, rather than against, the colonial and postcolonial forms that make up the tea plantation landscape. Thinking with and about the plantation moral economy, then, helps us diagnose what is not only meaningful to workers but also what their work means.[60]

In chapter 1, I discussed the landscape of imperial ruins that workers have been "left with": *what* they inherit.[61] This chapter has explored *how* people inherit. In their discussions of moral economies and their deterioration, Thompson and Scott described how workers and peasants organized revolts, participated in riots, or, at a smaller scale, adopted "weak" forms of resistance such as shirking, corner-cutting, and sabotage, to undermine oppression.[62] In the tripartite moral economy, resistance was more complicated. Narratives of a better past and an era of *industri* were more of a critique from within—a means of "inheriting the past thickly in the present as to age the future"—than an opposition borne of alienation. Workers did not want to overthrow planters, but they also did not want to return to the colonial past. Rather, they wanted to change the terms on which their children would inherit the Darjeeling landscape. Workers' stories narrated a desire for a distinct and historically specific vision of what agricultural and economic development experts call "sustainability."[63] An attention to multispecies sociality and entanglement calls into question the things and processes being sustained. Workers leveled their critique of *bisnis* practices to recover a sense of physical and familial stability, so that their children would inherit a better and more stable plantation than they did.

Piya Chatterjee has interpreted colonial discourses of *mai-bāp* (mother-father) patronage on Dooars plantations as a metaphor for postcolonial plantations. She explains that in the Dooars, "The planter sits astride a pyramid whose base is field labor."[64] While it is true that the plantation is a system governed by long-standing paternal and hierarchical relationships, I interpret metaphors of the plantation family in Darjeeling as ways for female tea workers in the hills north of Chatterjee's fieldsite to place themselves *within* the plantation hierarchy as "mothers" to tea bush "children." Laborers and their labors were not divisible from this landscape. Kinship metaphors shaped the perception of this landscape and enabled women to not only situate themselves in the plantation hierarchy, but to also to transcend its oppression through creative acts of dwelling.[65] Although *faciliti-haru* were clearly deteriorating, women workers continued to imagine the plantation a space of care.

Without this perspective, we might see pluckers as working *on* the land, and *faciliti-haru* as interchangeable with monetary compensation. Plantation life and labor are far too intertwined for such an analysis to hold. Over time, as the labor line became a *kamān busti*, and as the Himalayan foothills became a landscape where tea sat in careful tension with *jhorās* and jungles, laborers became caring subjects. The plantation was lived and worked *in*, not *on*. Attention to this process of working-in forces a reevaluation of plantations as solely "industrial farms" or "factories in the field," or even as feudal vestiges.[66] The recognition that plantation work is not only environmental work but also a form of social reproduction produces more complex moral expectations between labor, management, and the landscape. Planters, of course, say that workers "care" because they—styling themselves as environmental stewards—instill that care in workers. But such statements (lapped up by fair-trade activists and buyers of GI products) ignore the historical processes by which workers—especially women—have developed affinity for the plantation and made meaning out of their labor. Just as in kinship, multispecies affinity is neither given nor coerced; it must be cultivated.

These affinities are also reciprocal. As I described at the beginning of this chapter, Anna Tsing shows that when sugar cane moved from swiddens to plantations, the relationship it demanded of its human cultivators changed.[67] Plants play a role in their own cultivation, and even in their own industrialization. A plant's ecology shapes the forms and, more importantly, the meanings of labor necessary to produce and reproduce it. The ecology of tea is qualitatively different from that of cane, or cotton, and coffee—other well-known colonial plantation crops. The temporality of production must have a bearing on the meanings it carries. Coffee, cane, and cotton are harvested in intense, short-term cycles, at the end of which fields are barren, with nothing but stumps or fruitless bushes remaining.

Tea is not harvested in this way, and arguably not harvested at all. It must be plucked and pruned by hand to produce the right consistency and taste (the two leaves and a bud) every day, ten months a year, by skilled workers. As a socioecological system, then, the tea plantation requires laborers who live in and care about the landscape and have meaningful, long-term affective relationships to land and management. This was the challenge that British planters faced from the start of the Indian tea industry and why they provided *faciliti-haru* to ensure that they could maintain and retain skilled workers from year to year. Darjeeling planters did not participate in the Indian Tea Association's labor recruitment program, which indentured laborers and transported them to the tea-growing districts northeast of Darjeeling. Instead, Darjeeling planters competed with each other for skilled laborers. Labor was not interchangeable; it had to be cultivated. In China, tea and tea consumption were thickly woven into the fabric of everyday life and family reproduction. Pioneers of the colonial Indian tea industry like Darjeeling's iconic superintendent, Archibald Campbell, wanted to bring a rational efficiency and industrial scale to tea production, but the delicacy of the plant itself—its need for constant plucking, pruning, and cleaning up around the roots—required a willing and caring labor force. Together, British and Nepali settlers in Darjeeling made tea—another settler—an integral part of everyday life on their side of the Himalayas.

3

Property

In the spring of 2009, as flourescent green buds of tea were sprouting up on the tea bushes after a winter of dormancy, in what is known as the "first flush," I was sitting outside the manager's office of a large conventional tea plantation with Manesh Rai, a retired member of a British Gurkha regiment. Manesh had eagerly arranged a meeting for me, and he even insisted on tagging along, as he was worried about what people might think if I, a single woman, was seen in this *thulo mānchhe's* (or "big man's") office, alone, for extended periods of time.

Manesh grew up on this plantation and came from a line of *sardārs*, colonial labor recruiters who escorted marginalized peoples from the eastern hills of Nepal to British-owned Darjeeling plantations. He now lived in Darjeeling town, in a big multistoried house he built after leaving the army in 1997. A *sardār* lineage certainly came with privilege, even after the British left Darjeeling. It enabled Manesh's father to become a *garden bāu* ("garden father"), a kind of unofficial Nepali manager, appointed from the plantation population by Indian or British planters. *Garden bāu*s mediated between plantation residents, supervisors, and management, much like their *sardār* predecessors. Manesh proudly used his family's connections to secure me a meeting at his natal plantation.

While Manesh milled around the floors, asking each person who passed about his or her parents or children, and reprimanding younger men for slipping wads of Neva chewing tobacco into their cheeks, I chatted with the office *didi* (literally, "older sister") over a cup of tea. During my fieldwork, I found office *didi*s to be most helpful and knowledgeable. The office *didi* was a hybrid position of secretary and servant—depending on the plantation, her role leaned to one or the other of these poles. In this case, she held a more secretarial position. We joked about the state of the desk in the foyer, where she often had to work, examining random pieces of scratch paper with cryptic notes or lists of numbers without qualifiers. Assistant managers would dump these papers and unmarked files on the desk as they passed through. A glossy piece of paper poking out from under a stack of file folders caught my eye, and I slowly pulled it toward me, trying not to disrupt the desk's stratigraphy. It was a poster, with trails of more cryptic numbers scratched on it. I asked what it was for. She said that the *sahib* gave posters like this one out to visitors to the factory. These kinds of *Tea Boardko kāgaj,* or "Tea Board papers," frequently arrived from Kolkata with instructions about display or distribution. She told me to take this one home with me. An antique-looking scroll unfurled on the poster asked:

> "What is it that makes the world's tea aficionados rush to Darjeeling during spring-time to 'book' the first flush teas?"
>
> The answer?
>
> . . . Darjeeling Tea just happens.
>
> The reports blame it on the mixed soil, the pristine air, the well orchestrated rain-fall, the lofty altitude, the optimum humidity levels—and how they have all come together uniquely to make Darjeeling Tea *Darjeeling Tea.*
>
> To science, Darjeeling Tea is a strange phenomenon. To the faithful, it is a rare blessing.
>
> Thankfully, the Darjeeling Tea Estates have always lived by their faith—by humbly accepting this unique gift of nature and doing everything to retain its natural eloquence.
>
> So, Darjeeling Tea, hand-plucked by local women with magician's fingers, withered, rolled and fermented in orthodox fashion, with the sole intention of bringing out the best in them.
>
> Then the tea is manually sorted, packaged and begins its world tour. The only problem with Darjeeling Tea is that there is never enough of it to satisfy the connoisseurs around the world.
>
> But then, the finest things on earth are like that—very very rare—or they would not be considered the finest.

This was one of the first of many encounters I had with *Tea Boardko kāgaj,* Darjeeling tea advertisements, which the Tea Board of India distributed. While the tea industry is private, it is subject to government regulation. The Tea Board of India is the national governance body that oversees tea manufacture and circulation in and out of India. Career civil servants staff the Tea Board, much like they do other national or state (i.e., West Bengal) offices. As such, this institution, along with the Darjeeling Tea Association, a private association of tea owners and managers of Darjeeling tea plantations, worked to educate wider publics about Darjeeling tea. The advertisements were part of the Tea Board's efforts to market Darjeeling's "Geographical Indication," or GI, an international legal distinction that protected Darjeeling tea as the "intellectual property" of the Indian government. *Tea Boardko kāgaj* were of course aimed at tea buyers and tourists—domestic and international—visiting the region, but laborers, too, saw them when they dropped tea off at the factory for processing or on their way to the market on Sundays. These images attempted to affirm that Darjeeling was a unique amalgam of people and nature.

In a global market that is calling for locally sourced, socially responsible, and environmentally friendly commodities, Darjeeling tea planters and the Tea Board are looking to GI to distinguish their product from other Indian, African, and blended teas. GI is a World Trade Organization (WTO)–regulated international property-rights regime that legally protects a wide range of products, from artisan cheese to fruits to handicrafts. Notable GI beverages include Champagne, Cognac, Tequila, Scotch, Bordeaux, and Kona Coffee. The producers of these products (and the governments of the states or countries in which they are produced) advocate for GI status on the grounds that they can only be made in certain locales by certain groups of people. Marketing for these products tends to emphasize the importance of the roles both ecological landscapes and skilled artisans play in creating a unique value for a product. Perhaps the best known example of such marketing is the proto-GI campaign to distinguish Colombian coffee, which featured breathtaking views of the Colombian landscape as well as a familiar coffee grower: the friendly, humble Juan Valdez, who, beginning in advertisements in the late 1950s, personally delivered cups of Colombian coffee to discerning First World consumers. The Juan Valdez campaign started long before the rollout of WTO GI protections, but it serves as something of a prototype for the *Tea Boardko kāgaj*.

Over the course of my fieldwork, the *Tea Boardko kāgaj* became prolific, as the Tea Board petitioned the European Union (an important market for fine teas) to recognize Darjeeling tea's Geographical Indication.[1] In interviews with Tea Board officials, I learned that these posters were not just aimed at international retailers and consumers. They were also distributed within India, and importantly, within Darjeeling, to educate not only tourists, but also domestic consumers, tea marketers, and tea blenders about the national and international regulations protecting Darjeeling tea. GI protection meant that sellers could not blend teas together and sell them as "Darjeeling," as retailers frequently did, particularly outside of India. Tea mongers across Darjeeling and Kolkata used these posters to decorate their shops. Papering the walls, they formed a visual collage of the "garden" imaginary of Darjeeling—beautiful smiling tea pluckers, the Toy Train, misty Himalayan foothills, Kanchenjunga, and scenes of teatime outside Raj-era bungalows. Each time I went to a meeting or interview with Tea Board bureaucrats, Kolkata tea merchants, or Darjeeling planters, I saw these posters displayed on their walls, stacked up on desks, or poking out from forgotten file folders. And each time I visited the Darjeeling Tea Association offices in either Darjeeling or Kolkata, I would leave with a stack of the latest promotional materials, with the planter or bureaucrat's instructions: "If you meet anybody who is interested, perhaps you could pass them along!"

As ethnographic data, these *Tea Boardko kāgaj*, these "papers," provide a way of entry into a discussion of GI as a form of governance, as an intellectual property-rights regime, and as a set of performances. Justice under GI law came in the form of new property rights that "protected" Darjeeling from imitation. But who was this justice for—Darjeeling plantation owners, Tea Board of India bureaucrats, or tea laborers? The institution of GI aided in a revitalization of the industry. Stability, after all, as I described in the previous chapter, was central to workers' understandings of justice. GI, as a form of juridical justice, is aimed ultimately at helping owners receive higher prices for "rare" tea. It does so by creating a market in which the consumption of tea is linked to fetishized experiences of place and of labor. Under GI, the idea of justice is rooted in property rights. As Darjeeling's brief history as a GI shows, justice as property emerges not just from legal codes, but also from cultural performances and expressions of ideas about value. By drawing on imaginative and sensory understandings of Darjeeling as a place, items like the *Tea Boardko kāgaj* enlist tea drinkers and tea sellers in actively protecting property rights. By making Darjeeling seem like a natural home for tea, GI reinforces dominant Euro-American understandings of the relationship between property, personhood, and justice. In essence, GI appeals to a desire among planters and consumers alike to keep people and products—perhaps luxury products most importantly—firmly tied to particular places.

Through GI, the distinction of Darjeeling as a unique *taste* was legally and performatively tied to the governance of Darjeeling and the activities of tea laborers, as part of a bounded *place*. In this chapter, I draw primarily on interviews with tea planters, and officials from the Indian Tea Association, the Darjeeling Tea Association, the Tea Board of India, and Kolkata-based tea brokers, tasters, and distributors. I contextualize these interviews in insights from fieldwork on Darjeeling tea plantations and my analysis of GI-related marketing materials. The analysis of GI in this chapter highlights the work of *protection* and *perception* that this legal and market distinction performs. GI's champions in India claim that it protects Darjeeling tea—both the name and the taste—from imitation; that it protects a unique agricultural landscape and the people who work in it from being engulfed by competition in an undifferentiated marketplace; and that it protects Indian national economic interests by differentiating Indian tea from other kinds.[2] At the level of perception, proponents of GI seek to reshape how consumers understood the taste of Darjeeling tea. These proponents assert that Darjeeling has a *terroir,* or "taste of place." Descriptions of the environment of Darjeeling—the rainfall, the altitude, the humidity, and the "magical" fingers of local female tea workers—define its *terroir.* But perceptive associations of place with taste are not just environmental. GI also depends on a perception of tea-producing labor as making a unique and inimitable contribution to taste. For foods and beverages, advocates claim that these products are produced by the confluence of a distinct *terroir* and a set of "traditional knowledge" practices.

In the tradition of Juan Valdez, GI promotes a perception of an agricultural landscape that highlights relationships between craftspeople and the things they make, but not every producer counts as a craftsperson. The *terroir* of French wine and Wisconsin cheese certainly does not include the seasonal or migrant labor that goes into their production. On Darjeeling plantations, as in Colombian coffee haciendas, wage laborers were too prominent to be cut out of the marketing "picture"—literal and figurative.[3] Just as Juan Valdez offers a sanitized and palatable image of coffee production, in attempting to integrate Darjeeling tea laborers into the world of GI, the Tea Board of India and Darjeeling tea planters are working to recast tea's *industrial* production as *craft* production—a process done in small batches by "magical fingered women," not disenfranchised "coolie" labor. In Darjeeling, GI is an attempt to recast the plantation as a landscape in which tea workers and tea bushes live in symbiotic unity. In the GI narrative, laborers act as stewards for the "natural" value of Darjeeling tea. Everything else, as the posters describe, "just happens."

GI AND THE LABOR QUESTION

As I described in the previous chapter, laborers understood their relationship to tea bushes as one of affective "care." For laborers, quality tea production required the maintenance of a tripartite moral economy, a set of reciprocal, active, relationships between labor, management, and the plantation landscape. GI marketing materials also implied that tea pluckers had an affective connection to land and tea bushes. Indeed, GI has been celebrated by advocates of sustainable agricultural development as a measure that protects relationships between people and land from the alienating effects of the market. As such, then, GI labels constitute one form of "ethical trade."[4] But while the tripartite moral economy reflected workers' understandings of the plantation, GI emphasizes idealized, and even imagined understandings of the mountains and Darjeeling as a space of natural beauty, of both people and landscape.

Since Darjeeling tea's designation as a GI product in 1999, the industry has witnessed a resurgence: closed plantations have reopened, and tea is fetching higher prices. Key to the resurgence of the Darjeeling tea industry in the era of GI has been not only the legal governance of Darjeeling but also the commodification of both the sensory experience of drinking Darjeeling tea and the "craft" of its production. GI enables place to stand in for product. Many of us know that Champagne is sparkling wine, that Roquefort is cheese, that Scotch is whiskey, and that

FIGURE 15. Tea Board of India promotional poster. Photo credit: Tea Board of India.

Vidalias are onions, without being told so. The Tea Board and the DTA want consumers to associate "Darjeeling" with these GIs—*luxury* products with territorial
distinction. This association is often quite overt. Another remarkably stark poster,
which the office *didi* dug out from under a stack of papers after I expressed interest
in the first one, featured a picture of three glasses labeled: "Cognac. Champagne.
Darjeeling!" (fig. 15).

The poster continues:

> Our very own Darjeeling Tea joins the unique global elites.
> The whole world now recognises the fact that this magical brew owes its unique
> eloquence to its place of origin, the misty hills of Darjeeling.
> Darjeeling Tea has now been registered as a GI (Geographical Indication) in
> India. Which officially places Darjeeling Tea in the esteemed company of a Cognac
> or Champagne—other famous GIs.
> The unique geographic conditions of Darjeeling help make its teas such a rarity.
> Just the way Cognac and Champagne are rare because they can only come from
> specific regions in France.
> To celebrate this new rise in status for India, just raise your cup!

How did an industrial plantation crop with a less than savory colonial past
become a product with an authentic *terroir,* placed uncritically next to Champagne
and Cognac? One answer to this question lies in the way the Tea Board of India and
the Darjeeling Tea Association have repackaged tea labor. As in the Juan Valdez

campaign, a productive process that is arduous and assuredly exploitative must be replaced with something else. This replacement produces a contemporary iteration of the colonial-era Labor Question. Colonial planters' Labor Question concerned how to maintain a settled and reasonably healthy labor force in burgeoning Indian tea districts. The "contemporary Labor Question" does not focus on the acquisition of labor, but instead on how planters, hoping to export to international markets for boutique tea that demand ethically sourced products, deal with the unsavory legacy of the plantation. In asserting a luxury distinction for Darjeeling tea, as well as a natural connection between laborers and tea plants, GI relies not on an appeal to a dynamic and reciprocal tripartite moral economy but to a static image of Indian plantation life and labor, a Third World agrarian imaginary.

Darjeeling plantations have always been sites of both refinement and repression. This dual nature is encapsulated in a linguistic dynamic, between the Nepali word for "plantation," *kamān,* used by workers to describe their workplace, and the English word *garden,* used both historically and by the Tea Board to describe Darjeeling tea plantations.[5] As I note in chapter 1, *kamān* and garden evoke different visions of the plantation landscape. Darjeeling's Geographical Indication and its attendant marketing materials required Tea Board executives and planters to reconcile the polarized images of *kamān* and garden. The language of *terroir* enabled them to do so. *Terroir* enabled the consumption of tea to be linked to the consumption of the plantation. Tea planters, tea tasters, and tea brokers all agree that Darjeeling has long been associated with a *terroir;* however, when Darjeeling tea producers began seeking GI status, the imaginary of Darjeeling as a place of leisure had to mesh with the reality of Darjeeling as a mono-cropped plantation landscape maintained by low-paid, predominantly female wage laborers.

Solving the contemporary Labor Question through the deployment of a Third World agrarian imaginary requires remaking Darjeeling as both place and taste through three interrelated processes. I have already introduced the first of these: extensive marketing campaigns aimed at defining the Darjeeling *terroir* and educating consumers about the "traditional knowledge" that went into its production. I will return to this below. The construction of tea as the outgrowth of the "traditional knowledge" of female tea laborers bounded timelessly to the misty Himalayan foothills recasts wage labor and the plantation as cultural forms that can sit alongside other artisanal products, but the push of media is not enough to create place, taste, and value. The second process is the application of international law to define the borders within which and the ecological conditions under which Darjeeling tea can be produced. Specifically, planters and marketers see GI regulations as "protecting" tea produced in India by establishing the traditional knowledge of tea pluckers and the plantation environment as the "intellectual property" of the Tea Board of India and the patrimony of the nation. The appeal to intellectual property rights law as a means of justice for Darjeeling and its tea reinforces a

Third World agrarian imaginary in which laborers reside happily and stably on Darjeeling gardens.[6] As a framework for social justice, GI relies on a particular imaginary of life and labor on a Darjeeling plantation that makes this system of production compatible with "craft." In doing so, it makes laborers relatable to consumers; but this relateability aligns with what consumers already think they know about agrarian life and production. The third process is the introduction of "tea tourism" and the remaking of tea plantations into sites of "heritage." As a result of the rampant expansion of tea tourism in Darjeeling, laborers now feel compelled to perform the GI imaginary to make Darjeeling's *terroir* and GI's vision of justice as the securing of intellectual property believable and consumable.

PERCEPTIONS OF LABOR AND FLAVOR

Historically, Darjeeling's distinction as a good-quality tea came from its taste (it was similar in color and flavor to the Chinese teas favored by British consumers) as well as from ideas about its place of origin. The GI-related tea-marketing materials I discovered in the *didi*'s office depicted the plantation as an Edenic garden space and highlighted the timeless, "natural" relationships between women and tea bushes. Through GI, Darjeeling's colonial garden imaginary—where cultivation of all sorts is possible—has again become part of the value of the tea itself, but the garden image has always existed in tension with an equally powerful image: that of the *kamān,* or plantation.

In my interview with a Tea Board executive responsible for the administration of Darjeeling's GI, she explained that the historical association between place and product made the Darjeeling "brand" easier to "position": "It just so happens that Darjeeling has developed a market of its own. . . . So, when we started off on the GI exercise the brand had actually already been positioned. Maybe because of certain activities that have taken place historically or because of the fact that it is a product with certain benefits and attributes which have . . . been liked by people." The job of GI marketers, she explained, was to remind people that what they liked about Darjeeling tea's flavor could—and should—be traced to a specific place. She continued:

> If somebody thinks that Champagne is just a sparkling wine, then France will find it very difficult to protect Champagne as a GI because America would say that Champagne has got nothing to do with origin and is just a sparkling wine and would taste a certain way and that's it. You need to communicate. You need to promote. You need to tell people what it's all about. You need to convey the fact that a GI has something to do with the origin, reputation, quality, characteristics. . . . So, you have the legal side, you have the administrative side, [and] you have the side that's linked with promotion.

This executive reminded me that Darjeeling's "brand positioning," though well established, needed protection. As I explain in the next section of this chapter, that protection was partly legal and political, but it was also partly a matter of perception. In this section, I discuss what the executive called "promotion," a process of steering consumers, who had already-established desires, through the Darjeeling landscape in specific, imaginative ways. In GI marketing, drinking tea is a kind of sentimental journey to Darjeeling, one in which drinkers will inevitably "see" plantations. The question is *how* they will see them, and how that vision will affect what they taste in their cups. The tea plantation landscape has to feel like a "natural" garden, even if workers descended from Nepali migrants and laboring in exploitative conditions remain prime features of that landscape.

This process of promotion underscores that *terroir*—the "taste of place" that GI protects—is a cultural, rather than a natural phenomenon. Anthropological studies of *terroir* emphasize how perceptions of taste become linked with geology, climate and geography, as well as with the labor processes by which foods are produced.[7] In GI, labor frequently appears in the guise of "traditional" knowledge or artisan skills, even if such traditions are "invented."[8] Eric Hobsbawm defines "invented tradition" as "a set of practices . . . which seek to inculcate certain values and norms of behavior . . . which attempt to establish continuity with a *suitable historic past*."[9] Contemporary Indian tea production under GI is selectively linked to colonial plantation production. Darjeeling's colonial past does not disappear, but it is revalued and made "suitable" for contemporary consumers. Such an association with quality of taste and quality of production is essential to *terroir*. As Heather Paxson notes, what makes farmstead cheeses and other *terroir* products taste *good* is related to the values embedded in explanations for why these cheeses are *good* to make.[10]

Such explanations appear in the repeated and highly structured way in which consumers and sellers learn about the foods they exchange. Anthropological studies of *terroir* emphasize that ideas about labor are bound up uncomfortably in "taste," with taste defined as practices of consumption that are tied to class politics— what Pierre Bourdieu calls "distinction."[11] As Brad Weiss showed in a study of "local" "heritage" pork in North Carolina, these tastes must be *learned*. In the Piedmont region of North Carolina, this learning takes place in farmers markets, restaurants, and exclusive tasting events and was transmitted by trained specialists in the dietary habits of pigs and in the growing genre of "meat science."[12] As Weiss explains, "[heritage pork] (and its taste) is an amalgam of animal husbandry, marketing strategies, and social networking."[13] Similarly, consumers and connoisseurs have learned to regard Darjeeling tea, with its light smoky flavor, as the "Champagne of teas." The Tea Board of India's marketing materials are educational and instructional, not only in the how-to details of brewing, steeping, and storage, but more importantly in the messages about how to enjoy Darjeeling tea as a distinguished product. The advertisements teach consumers of this high-end GI to reconcile their desire to purchase a luxury good with the knowledge that tea is grown on colonial plantations. Without the work of marketing, it would be difficult to see Darjeeling tea as "good to make."

Darjeeling's GI promotion posters instruct consumers about how to "fine-tune" their senses to the brew. As one poster tells drinkers:

> If the fine flavor of Darjeeling Tea passes you by at first go, don't lose heart. It took us over a century to perfect the delicate art of Darjeeling Tea. You might have to allow it to grow on you. To fully appreciate the heavenly aroma and taste, treat your cup of Darjeeling as the finest of wines. Take a whiff before you take a sip. Roll the mild liquor (sans milk and sugar, ideally) around your tongue. Wait for the faint hint of the celebrated bouquet, following the signature *warm-sweet-mellow* taste. Once your senses are fine-tuned enough to discern the distinctive Darjeeling flavor, it will be a lifetime obsession—as it has been with connoisseurs around the world. To begin this journey of romance, just raise your cup . . . with finesse.

Fine tuning is not only a matter of learning how to calibrate the expectations of the taste buds. It is also about how to contemplate the origins of the brew itself: to associate flavors with natural, not industrial conditions of production. As another brochure explains:

> The crafting of Darjeeling Tea begins in the field. Where women workers begin plucking early in the morning, when the leaves are still covered with dew. The spirals of walking women gradually twist, then unfold to form a line. The tea is picked fresh every day, as fresh as the crisp green leaves can make them. The tea bushes are mystical messages on the Earth's canvas. A tale of excellence, brewed cup by cup, produced by the loving care lavished by the workers. Caressed to state-of-the-art perfection by unchanging tradition. Quality that is cherished worldwide. . . .
>
> The earth sings for you in Darjeeling. The women pluckers smile and, with the radiance of their joy, the sun rises over the gardens. Behind them, set against the rosy dawn sky, loom the snows of Kanchenjunga.[14]

In the above excerpt, women "twist and unfold" in the fields just as tea leaves in consumers' cups twist and unfold in the steeping process. The "warm-sweet-mellow" taste of Darjeeling tea echoes the radiance and warmth of Darjeeling tea workers and the Himalayan foothills they inhabit. Both tea bushes and tea workers appear to the consumer as living in a state of nature. It is important to note the difference between the "loving care" to which this passage refers and the "care" to which I discussed in the previous chapter. In the marketing brochure, soils, tea bushes, and tea pluckers all appear "unchanging" and in ecological harmony. The messages thus deploy the trope of affective connection between plants and people, even as they remove those connections from colonial history.[15]

Despite the instructional pitch of the posters and brochures, the audience for these GI-related materials is generally not individual consumers of Darjeeling in the United States or Europe. Rather, the *Tea Boardko kāgaj* are aimed at brokers, buyers, and teashop owners, both in India and abroad. Their objective is to reinforce and accentuate a set of bodily practices (the physical tasting of tea) and imaginative practices (the conjuring of the pastoral "garden" landscape). Along the way, the *Tea Boardko kāgaj* obscure and downplay the repressive, hierarchical *kamān* aspects of tea production. In essence, these are meta-instruction manuals, designed to teach tea sellers how to teach tea drinkers how to properly appreciate tea. They are a virtual version of the Napa Valley wine tour, or the intimate conversation with the meat or cheese producers at farmers markets that consumers of "local," "heritage," or *terroir* products value.[16] Part of the value of *terroir* products comes in the assurance that equitable social relationships lie behind the cup or the glass or the plate; or more simply, that there is a relationship, a commensurability of producer and consumer. Practically, however, not every consumer (or even every seller) can have such a relationship to every producer. Ironically, as demonstrated in a promotional film distributed by the Tea Board of India to retailers of Darjeeling, *Tea Boardko kāgaj* provide a simulation of the affective relations between tea producers, the landscape, and management that workers I interviewed longed for when they discussed the tripartite moral economy of tea production.[17] What is missing, of course, is the workers' clear recognition of a fundamental social inequality and moral economic relationships that define the *kamān*. On the "garden," as opposed to the *kamān*, there is no reason to speak of *faciliti-haru* or the difference between a "good" and a "bad" planter. The social structure of the "garden" is a flat one: plants, pluckers, managers, and buyers do not relate socially. They simply exist alongside one another. Indeed, in most cases, the planter is completely absent in GI's rendition of the garden.

The promotional film narrates a British teashop owner's trip to Darjeeling, and it opens with her sitting in her café in London, reflecting: "I grew up thinking that Darjeeling was just a tea . . ." Then with the exaggerated movement of a cursor on a map, we follow her from London to the plains of Darjeeling, where she climbs aboard the "Toy Train," the narrow-gauge railroad that has transported tea and tourists since the 1860s, and rides up the mountainside to Darjeeling town.

The next day, while shopping for tea in the market, she meets a tea plantation manager, Mr. Kumar. Over a pot of Darjeeling tea, the scratchy and stilted, dubbed-in voice of Mr. Kumar describes Darjeeling's Geographical Indication status: *The reputation, the characteristics, of the renowned tea that has been produced over here are, essentially attributable to the geographic location, climate, and even the soil . . . That's the magic of Darjeeling.*[18] Mr. Kumar whisks her down to a tea plantation. They stop on the side of a plantation access road. Grabbing a handful of wet dirt, Mr. Kumar explains, *"This is the soil that produces the sweet brew of Darjeeling . . . see?"* The teashop owner gingerly pinches the soil. As they walk behind a large group of female laborers, Mr. Kumar continues: *"Tea leaves are hand picked by tea garden workers, 70 percent of whom are women. Perhaps it is the warmth of their touch that gives the brew such sweetness."*

The female tea laborers in the film are clad in bright red *chaubandis*. Red is the color of fertility, and *chaubandis* are the "traditional" female dress of a united Hindu Nepal. (For the record, I usually saw them wearing men's button-down shirts to work, never *chaubandis*, which the tea workers mocked as the dress of old ladies, porters, and "backwards" Nepali farmers.) As the rains start, the laborers break out into trilled folksongs, mimicking a Bollywood musical aside. The women smile from ear to ear while they toss handfuls of green leaf into the baskets strapped to the top of their heads. Rhythmic claps punctuate the song as well as their tea plucking movements.

Later in the film, the tea buyer muses: *I started . . . exploring the mountains that are home to rhododendrons, wild orchids, and a thousand other flowers. Oh! And the birds . . . some six*-hundred *kinds. When you drink a cup of* pure *Darjeeling, you drink all of this in.*

We see the tea buyer later that afternoon, writing in her journal on the verandah of a Raj-era palace-turned-hotel. Excerpts from her journal refer not to the tea, but to the people and the environment that produce it: the "breathing mountains," "musical brooks," "hardened exteriors," "smiles of genuine people with genuine pride." After a long sip of amber tea, she remarks: *Mr. Kumar made me realize the significance of the laws protecting Darjeeling tea. It is thanks to these laws that the flavor of* pure *Darjeeling has worked its magic for me.*

In the film's descriptions, the environment of Darjeeling—the rains, the mists, the loamy soils, and the beautiful Nepali women—are integral to the taste and quality of Darjeeling tea. The viewer-consumer is reassured that the environment is not only natural and pristine but also populated by state-of-nature female workers who have such an idyllic work environment that they are compelled to dance and sing throughout the day. Workers' care becomes recast at the hands of GI marketing as something consumable. Tripartite moral economic relationships are disarticulated from the plantation landscape while fetishized, feminized, and naturalized relationships are rearticulated into the Darjeeling tea commodity chain.[19]

The taste of Darjeeling tea, then, is creatively linked to ideas about its production. The depiction of the tea plantation as a "garden" in the film and other promotional materials is part of a Third World agrarian imaginary in which low-paid workers are recast as "natural" guardians of the landscape (see fig. 16).

Their status as the descendants of colonial-era tea "coolies" and as contemporary low-wage workers disappears. The Third World agrarian imaginary centers on a selective memory of the colonial plantation. The imaginary of the plantation as a "garden" is derived from histories of botanical conquest and the experiments of the East India Company. But today, the garden imaginary has new meaning. As in other *terroir* products, marketing materials claim to unmask the conditions of food production and to shorten the social distance between consumers and

FIGURE 16. Female tea laborer, clad in a *chaubandi,* in *Overwhelm Your Senses,* a brochure distributed to tea buyers and retailers.

producers. By reinforcing an image of Nepali female tea pluckers as closer to "nature" than the refined people who appreciate Darjeeling tea, however, the *Tea Boardko kāgaj* actually extend that social distance. Indeed, GI converts that distance into value. This marks a significant difference from other specialty or geographically distinct product campaigns, which attempt to erase the distance between producers and consumers through their mutual care for quality crafts.[20] This departure from conventional GI discourse highlights dissimilarities between Darjeeling tea and other GI foods and beverages. A tea merchant or marketer might be wary of the association of affluent consumers with semibonded plantation laborers. Instructional pitches such as the films, brochures, and posters accomplish part of this work, but political and legal boundary making, what the

Tea Board executive I interviewed called the "administrative side" of GI, is just as important to the actualization of Darjeeling's contemporary market distinction.

THE BOUNDARIES OF TASTE

On a winter day in 2008, I was having a cup of tea with the secretary of the Darjeeling Tea Association in his freezing-cold concrete-slab office. He usually wanted to talk about tea-tourism projects, the hegemony of tea bags, and whether or not some planters liked him or not. But on that day, we were talking about Darjeeling's GI status.

"Do you see Darjeeling becoming the next Champagne . . . or Scotch?" The secretary asked me, tapping the ash of his cigarette onto the saucer of his teacup.

I tried to answer diplomatically, but he cut me off. "Well. It will." He said emphatically. "It has to be. We are making so much progress. But we are having real trouble in the American market. . . . It's just tea bags over there! Did you hear what happened with the Republic of Tea? They are big tea-bag producers, no? Well, they were selling this blended tea as 'Darjeeling Midnight' or 'Darjeeling Sunset' or something like that. It only had a handful, a small percentage, of real Darjeeling tea in it. And I am sure that they bought the cheapest thing that they could find. Well, we . . . along with the Tea Board, stopped them from using 'Darjeeling' to sell their blended tea."

"How did you do that?" I asked.

"Well, it was through court battles and the like. . . . The Tea Board has lawyers, you know, and that [the monitoring and regulation of GI] is their job. Tea retailers need to know that they just can't use Darjeeling whenever they want. It's our intellectual property! It needs to be used properly. If you call a tea Darjeeling," he paused to take a sip of tea, "it has to be from one of the eighty-seven gardens. For too long, unscrupulous blenders have just mixed up whatever common teas they like and slap 'Darjeeling' on the label to help it sell better."

I later learned that the Tea Board of India, backed by the rights endowed by national and international GI legislation, according to DTA and Tea Board officials, "successfully" controlled the use of the word *Darjeeling* by winning fifteen legal battles in India, as well as across South Asia, Europe, and the United States. In this conversation, the DTA secretary was referring to a case brought in the United States, in which the Republic of Tea sold a brand called "Darjeeling Nouveau," which contained little tea grown in Darjeeling. Republic of Tea lost the case because the company was not able to prove that U.S. consumers viewed "Darjeeling tea" as a generic type of tea that could be sourced from any region. The cultural cachet of Darjeeling as a place was hard to separate from Darjeeling as a tea.

"It is just like Champagne," the secretary continued, "You can't call any old bubbly Champagne. Champagne can only be from Champagne; Scotch only from

Scotland. Though . . . " he laughed. "They say that there is more Scotch whiskey produced in India that in all of Scotland!"

In this section, I consider the political economy of taste. *Terroir* has been associated with movements against the globalization of the food system, and the protection of local productive practices from the cheapening, homogenizing forces of the market. In *terroir* discourse, the locally bounded craft of artisans contrasts with the regimented (and arguably placeless) labor of industrial agricultural workers. The 1999 GI Act of India defines Darjeeling as produced on one of eighty-seven plantations in the Darjeeling district of West Bengal. These plantations and their antique coal-fired factories, Nepali laborers, tea bushes, mist, loamy soils, and Himalayan foothills are, in the language of the law, "gardens," traditional spaces of production. The number of gardens is limited to eighty-seven as a result of history and topography. The lands on which the eighty-seven gardens sit have high altitude in common, and over the course of the nineteenth and twentieth centuries, the Indian Tea Association began limiting the use of the term "Darjeeling" to those plantations that were situated in the hills above the plains, or Terai, that lead down to Siliguri. The topographical restriction is quite stark. For example, Longview, the plantation closest to the Terai, is only partly covered by GI status. Tea from Longview's "upper sections" (those higher in altitude) has GI status, while tea from its "lower sections," in the flat plains, does not (see map 2 in the front matter of this book).

Protecting Darjeeling has become synonymous with protecting agricultural practices that are presumably fine-tuned to the ecological conditions of the region. The Indian GI laws that create these boundaries help form a perception of an ecosystem in delicate homeostatic equilibrium, an equilibrium that needs protection.[21] As another poster that the office *didi* pulled out for me explains: "As Champagne cannot be manufactured in any place other than the Champagne district of France (even though the grapes used are the same kind) . . . in the same manner only tea grown and produced in the defined area of the Darjeeling district of the State of West Bengal, India can be called DARJEELING tea. Any tea grown in any other region from the same sort of tea plants cannot be called Darjeeling tea, a rare coveted brew, which is desired globally, but is only grown in India." Unlike Champagne, the GI to which Darjeeling planters constantly refer, the political boundaries of the Darjeeling district of West Bengal do not match the boundaries set by the 1999 Indian GI law (see map 1). Darjeeling is the name of a district of West Bengal that encompasses far more tea plantations than are included in the Darjeeling GI. The district's political boundaries include both hills and the Terai, both of which are dominated by tea plantations. Nepalis, almost exclusively, staff the hill plantations, while in the plains, *adivāsi*s ("tribal" or "aboriginal" inhabitants) serve as the majority of the labor force, accompanied by some Nepali workers.

Nepal, which lies only a few miles from many Darjeeling tea plantations, has a similar climate, sloping mountain tea fields, and, of course, Nepali laborers. Darjeeling and Nepali tea come from the same species of bushes (*Camellia sinensis*), and are grown and processed in similar climatic and geographic regions. Nepal tea, however, is not produced on colonial-era plantations. Instead, many of Nepal's tea estates are organized in cooperative models dating back to the 1980s. Darjeeling's GI, as the Darjeeling Tea Association secretary and numerous Darjeeling planters told me, exists in large part to protect Darjeeling tea from "imitators" in Nepal. These officials, along with tea retailers steeped in the lessons of the *Tea Boardko kāgaj*, argued that Nepal tea did not have the same flavor as Darjeeling. It was a "lesser tea," they explained. Planters maintained that tea retailers continued to pass off Nepal tea, often mixed with other teas, as "Darjeeling."

Darjeeling had to be "protected" from this blending. The secretary of the DTA often claimed that there were twenty (sometimes he would go as high as thirty or forty) tons of "Darjeeling" sold each year, but only ten tons actually grown and manufactured on the eighty-seven Darjeeling gardens. Planters, tea officials, and *Tea Boardko kāgaj* repeated this mathematical mantra. They worked to create a coherent and plausible narrative of scarcity, albeit a completely unverifiable one. Good taste, as the *Tea Boardko kāgaj* reinforce, is "rare"; protecting this rarity has become a matter of justice for planters and the Tea Board. Justice for Darjeeling, according to the Tea Board and the DTA, depends upon political and legal boundary making. One Canadian tea buyer I interviewed, who buys both Nepal and Darjeeling tea and markets them separately, called this demand-creating strategy the "myth of overproduction." He and other tea buyers argued that Nepal tea tasted fantastic—grown in the same environmental conditions with younger bushes, with an added bonus: Nepal tea was cheaper because it was not "Darjeeling." The taste was cleaner and the aroma was more fragrant than some Darjeeling teas. Marketers and sellers of Nepal tea tend to compare it favorably to Darjeeling, even using terms like "estate grown" to associate its production with that of its better-known neighbor.

Talk of a limited number of "gardens" bounded by discrete Himalayan borders not only produces the impression that "true Darjeeling" is rare, but it also gives a physical location to the "traditional knowledge" on which the Tea Board's claims that Darjeeling tea is "intellectual property" are based. A 2011 report of the World Intellectual Property Organization, an agency of the United Nations that manages global patents, defines Darjeeling's GI with reference not only to the eighty-seven gardens, with their "perfect soils and environmental conditions for tea cultivation," including wind speed, clouds, fog, and amount of sunshine, but also with reference to the "traditional knowledge" of the laborers. The report states, "Because the tea bushes in the Darjeeling region are the rare *Camellia sinensis* . . . two leaves and a bud must be picked. The traditional knowledge the women possess ensures that they can . . . pick Darjeeling tea while being careful to protect . . . the bushes from any undue stress. . . . The traditional knowledge and production practices . . . differentiates Darjeeling tea from other teas . . ."[22]

This report, which is strangely ethnographic in places, hides another story. The Tea Board claims that part of the uniqueness of Darjeeling as a tea-growing region is the presence of the *Camellia sinensis* bush—the Chinese variety of tea. *Camellia assamensis,* the Assam or indigenous Indian variety of tea, on the other hand, has long grown wild in the jungles of Northeast India and was later cultivated by the British on plantations across the empire. My ethnographic work with tea laborers not only taught me how to differentiate between the smaller, coarser leaves of the *Camellia sinensis* from the glossier, verdant, and more prolific leaves of the *Camellia assamensis,* it also helped me understand how species and political borders are subverted in the making of Darjeeling tea. Despite planters' claims to the contrary, Darjeeling plantations contain both *jāt* of tea bush. *Camellia sinensis* is a Chinese import, spirited over the border from China by British civil servants for cultivation by the East India Company. Darjeeling was favored for tea because its climate was seen as similar to that of Southwest China. While the Darjeeling plantation model was imported from Assam and other parts of the British Empire, the laborers were marginalized, but voluntary, migrants from eastern Nepal. While Darjeeling's GI couches labor and plants as being "essentially attributable," even indigenous, to the region, both are in fact colonial imports. The ecosystem itself is far from "pure" or bounded. It is historical. Indeed, Darjeeling and its plantations owe their existence to the permeability of national and ecological boundaries across the Himalayas and between monarchial Nepal and British India.

Laborers know that the geographic purity of Darjeeling tea is questionable because they maintain their own kin connections to tea workers in Nepal. Among the women with whom I worked, trips to Nepal were not uncommon. The most frequent reason plantation women traveled across the border was to find marriage partners for their daughters. Given the dearth of jobs in Darjeeling, plantation women would often marry into the families of eastern Nepalis. Women from Nepal, too, would sometimes come to the plantations as newly wedded wives. Men and women from eastern Nepal would also migrate to Darjeeling in search of low-wage work, as porters or construction workers. My tea plantation respondents found the red *chaubandi*s in GI marketing materials particularly humorous because they knew them to be the dress of newly arrived migrants from Nepal. In Darjeeling, *chaubandi*s were favored by elderly grandmothers, not beautiful young tea-plucking women.

Like young women, trucks of *hariyo patti* ("green leaf") would often arrive on plantations from outside of both the political and the GI boundaries of Darjeeling. Knowing of my interests in the circulation of *hariyo patti,* female workers would whisper to me that in the middle of the night, a truck came in from Pashupati, the nearest border crossing between India and Nepal and that that tea was from the *bāri*s ("dry fields") of Nepal, or even that that truck of leaf came from a nearby tea-farming cooperative for processing and marketing by the plantation. They often, with much disgust, explained that it was cheaper for management to buy *hariyo patti* by the kilogram from either closed gardens or tea-growing cooperatives located in Darjeeling but not included in the eighty-seven Darjeeling gardens, or from Nepal tea *bāris*, where they would not need to pay what planters called the "social costs" mandated by Indian industrial labor laws.

Like *Tea Boardko kāgaj*, GI laws portray labor as "naturally" belonging to a place that has, like many borderlands, always been a crossroads of botanical, human, and technical migrants. Indeed, nearly every aspect of contemporary Darjeeling is imported. By insisting on the hardening of borders, GI thus converts plantation labor into traditional knowledge, which has become the intellectual property of the Tea Board of India.[23] By rendering wage labor into traditional knowledge, and a plantation system into a network of "gardens," GI elides the permeability of the very border on which Darjeeling's product distinction has historically depended.

The ability of people and plants to go back and forth across porous Himalayan borders is what made it possible to make Darjeeling tea in the first place. In chapter 1, I detailed how laborers, tea plants, and colonial officials were conscripted or carried to Darjeeling to mold a hill station and later a tea enclave out of Himalayan forest. And recall that Manesh, who I introduced at the start of this chapter, was the descendant of a Nepali labor recruiter, a *sardār,* who ensured the stable supply of labor on Darjeeling gardens by going back and forth across the border to coerce and collect marginalized Nepali farmers. By making all this fluid circulation of leaves and ladies into bounded *intellectual property,* GI renders the fundamentally unequal and ethnically divided plantation into traditional "garden" heritage.

"HERITAGE" AND THE PERFORMANCE OF *TERROIR*

Workers saw GI marketing schemes and tourism projects as allowing them to stay in their plantation villages. As I explained in chapter 2, before the upturn in the Darjeeling tea market over the past decade at the hands of GI, fair trade, and perhaps even a Euro-American desire for healthy, age-defying comestibles like tea, plantations like Kopibari, located just outside of Darjeeling town, had closed. The owners had become financially unable, or unwilling, to continue tea manufacture. Women who had plucked tea there were forced to find work in town, breaking rocks and portering luggage. Workers at Kopibari and other plantations whose fortunes had improved with the market upturn over the previous several years understood that international consumer demand, both on the plantation and off of it, was critical to the stability of the plantations. Since the passage of GI legislation and the coming of fair-trade certification, plantations like Kopibari have slowly opened back up, not only to tea production, but also to foreign leisure tourism. The revitalization of *kamān* rests on the cultivation and performance of what planters and marketers couch as the region's "garden heritage."

From its early days as a British hill station, Darjeeling has been both a productive landscape and a tourist destination. Throughout its development as a hill station, Darjeeling became an increasingly popular retreat for the growing British population in Calcutta and East India. In the postcolonial years, Satyajit Ray's 1962 film *Kanchenjunga* (named after Darjeeling's iconic mountain peak) reflected Darjeeling's new distinction as a romantic pastoral escape for the affluent of Calcutta.[24] Darjeeling, with its clean mountain air, is still considered a place of wilderness and escape. This image is still so powerful that the American protagonists in Wes Anderson's popular movie *The Darjeeling Limited* did not even need to reach Darjeeling.[25] The mystique of the place was palpable just through the reference. Instead, the traveling brothers in the film arrive at a mountaintop convent, where their mother has retreated to a peaceful (and sexless) existence. As the Tea Board official explained above, Darjeeling already has a "brand," or cultural cachet. The tea just needs to be "promoted."

Tourism remains a booming business in Darjeeling. Domestic Indian tourism (informed by the *Kanchenjunga* imaginary) forms the backbone of Darjeeling town's leisure industry. In Chowrasta, Bengali tourists dress up like tea laborers, complete with red *chaubandi*s, ornate gold jewelry, and *tāukori*s, posing for photographs in front of tea bushes. These tea bushes, however, are lonely, sickly plants, growing in a rocky patch of soil adjacent to the photo booth in Chowrasta. Having a cup of *chiyā* in Chowrasta and embodying mountain life as an exotic Nepali tea plucker (and having a photographic memento of this embodiment) as well as buying a packet or two of tea and winter clothing, particularly shawls and sweater vests, are all central to the domestic tourist experience. Chowrasta—that iconic imperial center of Darjeeling—delivers this consumptive experience for domestic tourists.

Tea plantations, located deep in the valleys below Chowrasta, cater almost exclusively to international tourists. In the first decade of the twenty-first century, plantation managers are rapidly converting bungalows into tourist lodging and encouraging international visitors to experience Darjeeling tea production for themselves. Tourists are invited, as a *New York Times* travel reporter writes, to "compare styles and improve their palates," and immerse themselves in "a teetotaler's version of a Napa Valley wine tour, but with no crowds."[26]

During my fieldwork, tea planters had begun ripping up tea bushes to make room for tourism projects. In order to sell tea, they had to sell more than just tea—they had to sell a place, a taste, and an experience. In order for the plantation to be itself consumable, it had to be remade further, from relic of an oppressive colonial past to proud regional tradition. Planters now routinely refer to the tea-processing factories, the bungalows, and bushes as material elements of a shared garden "heritage." GI law and *Tea Boardko kāgaj* emphasize the emergence of Darjeeling tea from a "natural" ecosystem peopled by ecologically noble female guardians. In order to make this experience material, heritage tourism has to integrate the plantation itself, where the means of tea production (the coal-fired processing factories, the eight-hour plucking days, the head baskets) have not changed. These material aspects of the *kamān* have become reappropriated as garden heritage. GI and tourism work to co-constitute each other.

Beginning in 2008, I made regular visits to laborers at Kopibari. A prominent *bisnis-man* who owned thirteen other fair-trade- and organic-certified plantations had recently bought it and pushed it through these certifications as well. He intended to turn Kopibari into a tourist destination. When I first arrived there, construction was being completed on a new tea factory. The old one had nearly fallen down during the days when Kopibari was closed. On the top floor of the new factory, the owner had built what was to become a tea-tasting room, with panoramic views of the tea-filled valley, framed by Kanchenjunga. The lower two floors of the factory were sterile and covered in new white tile. All that remained of the original factory were the colonial-era tea-processing machines. Factory tours were central to the tourist experience. Visitors could see the coal-fired processing machines in action, following tea production from harvest to rolling to drying. Outside the factory, tourists were given the opportunity to take guided tours of the fields, and to meet a select group of laborers (fig. 17).

They were able to talk with a retired tea plucker who called herself the "five-second lady." She would invite tourists into an old one-room village shack, which she had converted into a small café, and demonstrate the "proper" way to brew and drink Darjeeling tea. She spoke remarkably good English and said that she could prepare a cup in just "five seconds." (She bought broken Darjeeling leaf tea at the market to sell and brewed it for tourists. If you swish that grade of tea in hot water for five seconds, the brew will take on the light amber hue that appears in the tea cups of the *Tea Boardko kāgaj*.) As she drank a cup of the five-second tea with visitors, she would extol its health benefits and remind them that the new owner was selling to Harrod's department store in London. She would also remind tourists that the proper way to consume Darjeeling was lightly brewed, with no sugar or milk. It was, she said in English, an "acquired taste." (She also liked to say that because this tea was organic, you could brew the tea three times before throwing out the tea leaves.)

Out of the earshot of tourists, workers on Kopibari mocked the five-second lady for being pretentious and opportunistic. She charged on a sliding scale depending on how much she thought a given tourist could pay. The price *per cup* hovered around fifty rupees (recall that in 2010, the *daily* wage of plantation workers was only sixty-three rupees). The five-second lady was able to make this kind of revenue from tourists on a daily basis, and even more during the high tourist season (September to November and April to May). Workers knew that Darjeeling tea was "expensive" and that a cup of Darjeeling in the United States cost more than they made in a day.

FIGURE 17. Tea buyers in a tea factory snapping pictures of women sorting tea in proactive clothing donned for the occasion. Photo by author.

Tourists and tea buyers who visited the plantation told them this. Messages of these high prices spread through kin networks in and across plantations.

On off days, workers would go up to town to the bazaar and see the faces of tea workers—of women just like them—plastered onto billboards. They were smiling, dressed in *pukka Nepali* ("really/totally Nepali") clothes: in red *chaubandis*, arms outstretched, handing the implicit consumer a cup of light amber tea—something that, unlike the five-second lady, they would never drink (fig. 18).

Darjeeling plantations have converted old bungalows into high-class accommodations, reminders of the spatial and class divisions of the *kamān*. At Glenburn Tea Estate, for example, a double-occupancy room complete with bed tea, laundry, picnics, bird watching, and day trips to Kalimpong and Darjeeling rents for between four hundred and five hundred dollars a night. In *Vanity Fair on Travel*'s "Best of 2010" list, the "Best Cuppa" went to: "The Glenburn Tea Estate, [a] classic old colonial. . . . The Raj lives on in rosy English porcelain teacups, the bungalow so perfectly verandahed and white-rattan-chaired it could have been a set for *The Jewel in the Crown*."[27] A review of Glenburn in *Condé Nast Traveller* reports:

FIGURE 18. Billboard outside of the Darjeeling Tea Association office in Darjeeling. Photo by author.

[The bungalow] stands as an unselfconscious reminder of an era when graciousness effortlessly prevailed. . . . The guests who stay now are given the opportunity to see the day-to-day workings of the estate . . . and its labor-intensive routines (which don't appear to have changed in centuries). . . . We hiked for about three hours each morning, happy in the knowledge that a soothing massage with green-tea oil was available upon our return. Prakesh, our delightful walking guide, kept a watchful eye on us, making sure we had enough to drink as we sweated our way up and down narrow, dusty paths that took us past clusters of brightly pained houses, the odd village shop, numerous shrines and groups of immaculate school children eager to practice their few words of English. . . . Everything thrives in this fertile place: sugar cane, bamboo, and rubber. . . . Visiting Glenburn is like arriving in a little corner of heaven—and almost as remote.[28]

Another large plantation group recently introduced Raj-era bungalow tourism on Tumsong Tea Estate. Tumsong's "Tea Retreat" website explains why this plantation is special: "The tea plants here grow very slowly and flavour the entire estate with their aroma. The locals believe that the goddess Tamsa presides over this serene landscape and in fact, the locals refer to [the plantation] as 'the Garden of Happy Hearts.' Come find out why."[29] Since all plantation land is leased by individuals or companies from the West Bengal state government, planters must petition the state Land Reforms Department to use plantation acreage and infrastructure for heritage tourism. One plantation owner who successfully received this permission explained to me that tourists wanted a British Raj-inspired luxury experience. He reminded me why Darjeeling was developed in the first place: to provide a refuge for British colonial officers. In order to compete with other plantations, he needed to provide this Raj-era form of relaxation for tourists.

Tourists also work to perform *terroir*. As one visitor to Windsor Tea Estate put it when I asked her why they came to that particular garden, "We drink their tea, and we wanted to know more about it." These tourists traveled to Darjeeling to consume Darjeeling tea in Darjeeling tea *gardens*. But they also wanted to see the material elements of *kamān*—the factory, the antique machinery, the hand-plucked tea, and the bungalows. These material symbols of British colonial development and domination over the tea industry are essential to both the high market value of Darjeeling tea and the tourist experience. "Heritage," too becomes consumable in "a cup of Darjeeling." Tourism provides a confirmation that Darjeeling plantations are not imaginary: that there are aspects of both the "garden" and the *kamān* that can be experienced materially. Tea tourism in the twenty-first century makes us realize that it is not enough to just say something is geographically distinct, whether legally or through marketing. The consumers of these products need to be in agreement. Tourism forges this agreement.

Whereas on a winery or brewery tour, tourists come to view the technologies of production in action, "heritage" tourists come to witness "living history," "the simulation of life in another time."[30] Active, visible laborers are necessary to provide both of these experiences. Tea pluckers in the era of GI cannot simply work; they have to *pose as workers*. They have to present themselves both as *contemporary* tea producers and as plausible simulators of *past* tea producers. The set pieces for this performance are already in place; again, the mode of tea production in contemporary Darjeeling *is* largely the same as in the colonial era. On Darjeeling plantations with tourism projects, workers pose for pictures, let tourists their *tāukoris*; describe how "peaceful" the plantation is; and even sing a song or two. GI casts tea pluckers as possessors of traditional knowledge that is tuned to a delicate ecosystem. In tourist encounters, workers take on the role of "gardener" for visitors.

THE DARJEELING DISTINCTION: *TERROIR*, PROPERTY RIGHTS, AND THE PURSUIT OF JUSTICE

The Darjeeling plantation is both *kamān* and garden; industry and refuge. It is both of India and a place separate from India; and it is a site of both production and consumption. Planters today are using *terroir* and Geographical Indication to yoke these dualities into a coherent image of a palatable place and product. An ugly colonial past is being sterilized into a garden "heritage." At one plantation where tea tourism comprised a growing portion of business, village activists I interviewed described the potential conversion of their village into a resort as "turning the plantation into a zoo." "Our job," one man said bitterly, "is to produce tea, not to entertain visitors." Despite these activists' strong objections to the rise of GI-related tourism, most Darjeeling tea laborers usually did not discuss *Tea Boardko kāgaj*, the protective laws defining the region as a network of eighty-seven gardens, or tea tourism as part of the larger process called "Geographical Indication." Nevertheless, they were aware that these materials signified both a revitalization of Darjeeling plantations over the past decade and new forms of labor on the plantations. It was no longer enough to produce tea. They had also to produce Darjeeling itself, in the image of advertisements and other promotional materials. While some certainly resented the need to do this, many were nevertheless quick to remind me of their identity as the laborers who produced "the world's most expensive tea."

A Third World agrarian imaginary carves discursive and material spaces in which justice can be achieved for failing plantations and their owners. The inclusion of plantations in GI highlights the problematic potentials for "justice" in industrial agriculture in the twenty-first century. Increasingly, property rights—material or intellectual—are being used as a strategy for development, yet there are deep flaws in the logic of GI as applied to Indian tea plantations.[31] The Darjeeling GI assumes that the holders of such property rights are all equals, in the sense that they are all citizens of India and equal contributors to tea's *terroir*. Doing justice, then, means simply recognizing that equality under the law. Yet most of the work of GI is not legal, but performative. As a performance, GI occludes, rather than undoes, a long history of regional and social differentiation. Darjeeling has long relied upon tourism as an economic engine, yet tourism in Darjeeling depends on the construction of Darjeeling as a foil to the rest of India: a natural, recuperative landscape populated by beautiful, exotic (and non-Indian) people. And plantations, as workers' moral economic understandings show, are places where, by definition, people are not equal. Even amid these occluding performances, some workers are finding hope that this fetishization might be worth it. After all, it is keeping plantations open.

GI depends on the assertion of a "natural" convergence of environmental conditions (the loamy soils and misty slopes) with traditional knowledge. This vision is perhaps more salient with the growing popularity of territorially distinguished, fair trade, organic, and otherwise socially and environmentally conscious labeled commodities, stoked in popular media by food activists, revolutionaries, and celebrity chefs.[32] In the case of Geographically Indicated foods, however, such labels transform place names, agricultural practice, and knowledge into property rights. Despite claims by their supporters that labeling strategies protect foods from the market, Julie Guthman has argued that this protection is overstated, since labels "extend market mechanisms into realms where they did not previously exist."[33] When tourists and laborers meet, the very conditions of production become fetishized. Workers in Darjeeling are attuned to this. After all, the conversion of wage labor-time into a commodity crop, and also into marketable and visible "traditional knowledge" constitutes a double alienation. Through GI, the culturally constructed "nature" of the garden and the labor relations of the *kamān* have become the intellectual property of the Tea Board of India.

GI replaces the plantation moral economy with a Third World agrarian imaginary, a romantic vision of postcolonial worker-plant-management relations as timeless and natural, rather than historical and social. GI requires that workers *perform* a caring relationship to plants and take on the persona of the humble craftsperson and skilled artisan. Thus, instead of protecting laborer-landscape relationships from commodification, GI makes ideas about these relationships into the essence of the commodity. GI fetishizes a *binary* relationship between workers and plants, ignoring what workers see as a crucial third element: facility-providing management. Even if an owner has a reputation for being a *pukka bis-nis-man,* if the plantation remained open, workers could still avail themselves of the nonmonetary forms of compensation that made life in the unequal plantation system more bearable, more stable.

This stability came with the added work of performance. Scholars of what has been called "hyperreality" point to the rise of "simulated" experiences in consumer culture: Disneyworld's EPCOT and history museums like Colonial Williamsburg no longer represent some "real" past or geographical experience; rather, it is the experience of these "fakes" that consumers desire. Darjeeling plantations are both productive spaces and "simulations"—performances in which the reality of agricultural labor and perceptions of it stand in tension.[34] Moving beyond the fictional image of Juan Valdez, GI as a *legal* protection promises eaters and drinkers that their perception of how tea, wine, coffee, and liquor is made reflects a reality. Bridging the refinement of luxury goods with the concerns of global citizenship, GI appeals to both romantic desires to relive the colonial plantation lifestyle *and* a liberal, socially and environmentally conscientious desire to bear witness to the conditions under which products are made. By turning the productive process into something as consumable as tea itself, GI desocializes the plantation, turning it from a problematic colonial relic into a palatable imaginative destination. Increasingly, workers are asked to participate, not in a reciprocal relationship to land and management, but in a performative relationship to consumers. GI converts moral economic relationships, in which the lives of plants, pluckers, and management are linked in a dynamic system of care and concern, into static, repetitive, simulations of colonial nature, in which the connections between plants, pluckers, and management are given rather than produced.

4

Fairness

Prakriti and I were crouched down, hovering above the dirt floor of her kitchen, chatting about upcoming weddings on the plantation. She was concerned about what color *kurtā* I should wear (I wore too much green), and how I might possibly control my wiry "ghostlike" hair for the occasions. As she got up to get us more tea—milky sugary *chiyā* made from her monthly ration of dust-grade leaf—the tethered cow in the shed attached to her kitchen let out a long aggravated *moooo,* that vibrated the brittle bamboo walls.

"What do you do with that cow, anyway?" I asked her. I had had tea at Prakriti's house many times, and I had never seen that cow outside of the shed. Despite their popularity in development projects on Darjeeling tea plantations, cows were ill suited for the landscape. Not only would it be difficult for a cow to navigate through the densely planted tea bushes, plantation owners prohibited cows from grazing on plantations. Thus, cows were confined to small sheds in plantation villages and a life of alternatively sitting and standing. Prakriti's cow stayed in the shed all day, munching on bamboo leaves.

"Oh. *That* cow? Years ago, I got it through a [fair-trade] loan from the company. We thought that we could sell the milk and the calves up in town. The manager said that the company would buy back the dung for *organiks.*"[1]

"You don't sell these things?" I asked.

"When do I have time?" she said, exasperated, pouring steaming *chiyā* into our glasses from a dented aluminum pot. "So what if I have that cow?" She pointed toward the shed. "We are all poor here. I give the milk to my sister and brother and . . . " She paused, and turned in the animal's direction. "She cannot graze anywhere! The legs of that cow are like my life: absolutely weak."

The premise of the loan was that with this cow, Prakriti would be able to supplement the meager daily wage she received for plantation work—which she performed from seven in the morning to four in the afternoon, Monday to Saturday—in addition to her domestic chores. With a cow, Prakriti could sell her dung back to the plantation management as organic compost, or sell her milk to her neighbors. With that extra money, Prakriti would be "empowered" to purchase clothes, food, or school supplies for her family. In interventions such as this, fair-trade certification schemes seek to provide tea plantation workers with alternative, individual forms of income. Loans for livestock and stores are a common feature of such schemes. Fair trade's emphasis on small, low-interest loans, which have become popular in Third World development more generally, obscures the fact that on plantations, fair-trade certification has no ability to regulate plantation wages. Instead, fair-trade certification programs attempt to shift the focus away from plantation wage labor, using individual, nonplantation work—supported by the distribution of microloans—to "empower" plantation workers. Prakriti's neighbors—her potential customers—were her siblings or other distant relatives who could trace their families back to the same regions of Nepal. The Darjeeling plantation system is an elaborate kin network, with marriages linking people across villages and plantations, and even back to Nepal. Neighbors are far more than potential customers. Workers want plantation work to be stable; they do not necessarily want more work.

Prakriti's cow, then, represents the individualizing tendency of fair trade. In this chapter, I show how fair trade is challenging long-standing moral economic relationships between Darjeeling tea plantation laborers, land, management, and the postcolonial state. Fair-trade certification alleviates some of Darjeeling tea planters' moral economic burden to provide facilities for tea workers. Fair-trade "success stories" often claim to provide these very facilities on plantations—facilities that owners have been legally obligated to provide to workers for over half a century. And, as I discussed in chapter 2, in the context of fair trade, planters are further violating moral economic obligations to replace *budho* (old) tea bushes with younger ones. They are instead planting in landslide-prone areas in an attempt to extract more tea out of their antique plantations.

Fair-trade interventions on plantations presuppose an absence of institutions that might provide social support for plantation laborers. Fair trade stakes its claim to value on the idea that such institutions must be built from the ground up, thanks to the willingness of conscientious, affluent consumers in the developed world to pay higher prices for foods, beverages, and handicrafts produced in the Third World. Fair trade posits a market solution to Third World poverty and inequality, but plantation workers live in a liminal space between market and peasantry. Fair trade's vision, in other words, accounts for neither long-standing moral economic relationships within plantations nor institutions already in place to support plantation labor. Indeed, in India, fair trade undermines existing state structures that ensure the equitable treatment of plantation laborers.

International fair-trade and organic certifiers came to Darjeeling in the 1990s in hopes of expanding the growing market for sustainable and socially responsible products. The region, still reeling from the Gorkhaland agitation of the 1980s, was in the depths of industrial decline that stemmed from decades of falling prices, the collapse of markets in the former Soviet Union, overuse of pesticides, and the proliferation of cheap teas grown in other places but marketed as Darjeeling. Savvy Darjeeling plantation owners saw international certification schemes as a way to tap new markets and make more money on decreasing yields.

In this chapter, I recount the story of Prakriti's plantation, Windsor Tea Estate, and its savvy owner, Mr. Keshav Roy.[2] In the introduction to this book, I showed how Darjeeling has become something of a testing ground for the fair-trade certification of plantations. Here, I return to the paradox of the fair-trade plantation, asking first, what made Darjeeling's plantations so attractive to fair-trade certifiers, and second, what the effects of certification have been for laborers. Windsor is a particularly instructive case, as it was among the first plantations in India to be certified fair trade, as well as biodynamic and organic. Darjeeling plantation owners like Mr. Roy made themselves attractive to fair trade certifiers by adopting a language of environmental stewardship and transparency—the language of the Third World agrarian imaginary I discussed in the last chapter. But fair trade had other benefits as well. For owners like Mr. Roy, it provided a new source of revenue with which they could build housing, schools, and the other trappings of what workers called *faciliti-haru*. After Indian independence, the provision of such *faciliti-haru* had been codified into Indian labor law. Fair trade, then, brought greater attention to Darjeeling on the global market, but it created little in the way of new material obligations between workers and owners on plantations. Indeed, by positing that plantations, productive systems that had inequality built into them, could become spaces of "fairness," fair trade changed the moral valences of the relationships between workers and owners.

LINKING PLANTATION AGRICULTURE TO
CONSUMER-DRIVEN SOCIAL JUSTICE

In the late 1980s and early 1990s, Keshav Roy began reinventing Windsor Tea Estate, drawing in equal measure on New Age spirituality and the language of luxury consumption. He did this one tourist, one television appearance, and one cocktail party at a time. Windsor was certified "organic" in 1988. At first, Mr. Roy received resentment and scorn from other plantation owners and managers for subverting the status quo of Darjeeling tea production. By the middle of the first decade of the new century, however, Windsor was the Darjeeling tea plantation most associated with fair trade, and Roy was routinely praised by fair-trade executives in the United States for his progressive social and environmental projects. Roy was among the first to appoint a female labor supervisor; he promoted the construction of biogas plants in Windsor's villages; he instituted a permaculture project; and he even began a leopard-rehabilitation project in the jungles surrounding the plantation. Instead of being scorned and shunned, Roy became widely recognized for making Windsor ground zero for a flurry of international certifications in the district. Roy's promotion of ecotourism, microloans, and other similar endeavors set an example for plantations across the district. Thanks in large part to Roy's efforts, the language of environmental and social sustainability—like that of *terroir* and GI—came to permeate Darjeeling life. By the time I arrived in Darjeeling, nearly a quarter of the district's plantations had been certified fair trade, a majority were certified organic, and several were pursuing Rainforest Alliance certification.

A discourse of transparency rests at the heart of fair trade. Fair-trade consumers believe that their purchases have the power to enact change in agricultural communities on the other side of the world.[3] Tea plantations seeking certification thus face a critical challenge. To make the colonially derived production system appear redeemable by such consumers, Mr. Roy realized that he had to allow certifiers and foreign visitors to see the conditions of tea production. Windsor was among the first Darjeeling plantations where tourists could see tea processed in the factory, walk through the fields, and even stay the night. Mr. Roy's tourism projects at Windsor are certainly exemplary of the garden-tourism dynamic I discussed in the previous chapter, but with an important twist: Mr. Roy placed himself, not workers, at the center of the plantation landscape. He styled himself as a benevolent, enlightened caretaker and environmental steward. While other plantations initially prohibited tourist access due to concerns about the dangerous terrain and personal safety (if not the moral and ethical misgivings the sight of plantation labor might induce), Windsor embraced it. Windsor is one of the few plantation factories on one of Darjeeling's two main roads, and tour groups filter in and out daily. If they are lucky, they might have an audience with Mr. Roy himself, a captivating storyteller.

I followed these tours around the factory and tasting room to hear Mr. Roy wax to visitors about the "rhythms of nature," what he called "terrestrial infirma" (an alluring neologism invented by Roy to describe an intermingled spiritual and natural landscape), and how they had become "harmonious" at Windsor. He peppered narratives about tea manufacturing with memorable and provocative one-liners, such as: "They are looking for flavor in the balance sheet, not flavor in life" (a biting indictment of other tea planters). If a guest asked for sugar or milk, Mr. Roy would chastise her: "Would you put milk in your glass of Champagne?" From the large tasting room at the factory, he would spread not only the ideas about taste that came to dominate the GI narrative of Darjeeling but also the new set of messages about the social relations of plantation production that would become key to rendering the plantation "fair."

At Windsor, this rendering was accomplished through a magical semantic dance. Mr. Roy successfully sutured the imaginary of Darjeeling as an ecological refuge to the historical legacy of colonial tea production by making sounds, smells, and sights, including the sight of plantation labor, readily available for purchase. In the agrarian imaginary of fair trade, owners like Mr. Roy were not "bosses" but social and environmental stewards. Mr. Roy intuited this and cast himself as a guardian to Windsor's land and people. As Mr. Roy put it in a speech he regularly recited to visiting tourists and potential tea buyers, "I put my heart and soul into saving the vanishing woodlands and liberating the people of the plantation." To each tour group and tea buyer, he made sure to deliver his most popular and mesmerizing monologue, about becoming a tea planter.

He spoke with candor of being the restless scion of a Bengali tea-planting family, a globetrotting playboy educated in England and uncertain about the prospect of returning to the foothills. He recalled a return trip to Windsor, when his father offered him a horse and suggested he spend the holiday back in Darjeeling riding through the plantation. It was on such a ride, Mr. Roy told his audience, that his life changed forever. He was flung from his horse. As he fell, he was struck by a vision of light and the sound of the trees calling out to him: "Save us!" Revived by caring female tea pluckers, Mr. Roy returned to his parents' bungalow and told them of his newfound resolve not to travel the world in search of fortune, but to become a tea planter in the family tradition.

The monologue was the foundation of a multifaceted fetishization project, in which he turned the workers and the environment into consumables. In the process, he fetishized himself as well, dressing in the khaki fatigues and safari hat of a Raj-era planter—a planter who became enlightened to the degradation of the socio-natural landscape of the Darjeeling tea plantation; a planter that sought to make the conditions of production fairer for both humans and nonhumans.[4]

By the start of the twenty-first century, Roy's stewardship was becoming institutionalized in the tea industry. In the 1990s, Assam Agricultural University and North Bengal University began offering degree programs in tea management. The purpose of these programs was to teach new planters to efficiently manage garden inputs, of which labor was only one. These two universities ran classes, and private tea companies and management institutes offered similar courses. In these classes, aspiring managers learned that their primary obligation was to care for the bushes and the factory's processing machines. Instead of instructing planters to rely on laborers to care for tea bushes, management courses emphasized an agrarian imaginary in which planters' responsibility was to act as environmental stewards. In this new twenty-first-century plantation model, planters were explicitly recast as "farmers."

At the National Seminar on Improving Productivity and Quality of Tea through Traditional Agricultural Practices, a 2008 course at North Bengal University, speakers advised planters who worked on gardens that would be exporting to Western countries to pursue international agricultural certification to maximize profits on decreasing yields. Organic and fair-trade certification would help planters move mediocre and low-quality tea, particularly to the United States, where the market for tea bags was booming (tea bags, which contain broken, dust-grade leaves, are considered inferior by tea connoisseurs). Despite the title of the seminar, little mention was made of tea laborers or their practices. A presentation by the head of the Assam-based Tea Research Association on "traditional" and "indigenous" knowledge in tea production made no mention of the relative novelty of tea in the Indian Himalayan landscape or of the knowledge of tea laborers, referencing instead Sanskrit texts about nature and agriculture, texts that long predate tea production. He and other lecturers replaced history with timelessness, avoiding questions of capital accumulation in an oppressive colonial and postcolonial system. The Darjeeling Tea Association was one of the sponsors of the national seminar, along with various distributors of organic fertilizers and herbicides. The DTA understood that the conversion to organic and fair-trade practice would only be effective if the narrative of "traditional" agriculture in a "mountain paradise" was made replicable.

Fair-trade certifiers who came to Darjeeling realized that they could not rid tea of its roots in plantations, nor divest plantations of hierarchy. There would always be owners and managers. Mr. Roy and, later, other planters, realized this as well. By the first decade of the twenty-first century, planters had learned to style themselves as "farmers." Consider the way that Fair Trade USA describes its mission, differentiating between farmers and workers:

WHAT IS FAIR TRADE?

QUALITY PRODUCTS. IMPROVING LIVES. PROTECTING THE PLANET.

Fair Trade goods are just that. Fair. From far-away farms to your shopping cart, products that bear our logo come from farmers and workers who are justly compensated. We help farmers in developing countries build sustainable businesses that positively influence their communities. We're a nonprofit, but we don't do charity. Instead, we teach disadvantaged communities how to use the free market to their advantage. With Fair Trade USA, the money you spend on day-to-day goods can improve an entire community's day-to-day lives.[5]

If the face of the fair-trade cooperative is that of the small farmer, the face of the fair-trade plantation is that of the enlightened planter. The enlightened planter has much more in common with fair trade's imagined consumer than does the small farmer. Whereas GI casts workers as caring stewards, fair trade emphasizes the stewardship of owners. When fair-trade organizations like Fair Trade USA certify plantations like Windsor, potential consumers must be convinced that they are entering a relationship with a fellow concerned citizen. In the language of fair trade, consumers are dealing with "farmers" whose ultimate priority is the long-term viability of "workers" in "disadvantaged communities."

In fair trade, the individual consumer is the perceived prime mover in this improvement scheme. The bonds forged between producers and consumers are elaborated in several short promotional videos to put forth Fair Trade USA's market vision of "empowerment." In *The Power of the Consumer*, a short film released by Fair Trade USA, the aims of certification are translated directly into individual purchasing power. Paul Rice, the charismatic CEO of Fair Trade USA, narrates:

> American consumers, we have so much power. Every time we go to the store, we can vote with our dollars for a better world. We're facing such huge global challenges today: poverty, climate change, environmental degradation. Americans are not indifferent to those problems, they just don't know how to make a difference. We feel so powerless in our lives in the face of these huge global problems and the old approaches, where there is *government* intervention, *government* legislation, or international development aid and *charity*—they're not working fast enough, so we have to harness the power of the market and we have to get consumers involved. So it seems to me that fair trade is empowering consumers to make a difference with every cup of coffee, with every bar of chocolate, with every banana that we eat, we can actually lift people out of poverty. We can help preserve the land. We can make a difference. People in this country increasingly want better-tasting products and healthier products. Guess what? There is a very direct connection between the money that a farmer gets for his or her harvest and that farmer's ability to produce a healthier, higher quality product. And that is a win-win, right? It's a win for the farmer. It's a win for the consumer who is looking for a better tasting, healthier product.[6]

Social justice for agricultural laborers far away from the aisles of the Bay Area grocery stores in which this film was shot is possible and attainable through market mechanisms. Governments, laws, other international development agencies cannot cultivate justice quickly enough. Individual consumers and enlightened farmers, according to Fair Trade USA's logic, have that ability.[7]

CHOICE, LAW, AND THE "SOCIAL COSTS" OF TEA PRODUCTION

Rice's statements not only trumpet consumer buying power as a tool for social justice; they explicitly question the power of governments and even traditional nonmarket development schemes to improve the lives of people in agricultural communities, or to preserve agro-environments. Fair trade's emphasis on the power of the consumer over that of the state reveals another aspect of the Third World agrarian imaginary, namely, the understanding that states and NGOs have failed agricultural communities. Rice's statement reflects a philosophically liberal model of social justice.[8] In this model, justice comes about when "involved consumers" can freely and conscientiously trade with people who provide the goods and services they want, unfettered by corrupt or inefficient regulations, particularly those of governments. Governments have little interest in satisfying consumers' desires for food that is "good," either in taste or in conditions of production. Fair-trade logic assumes that by permitting more consumers to make more "free" choices to direct their dollars to the makers of "good" food, consumer and producer desires will both be met. Importantly, fair trade envisions justice as voluntary. Plantation owners like Mr. Roy are not pressured or mandated to make conditions better. Similarly, the consumers to whom Rice addresses his message make the *choice* to satisfy their needs for good food.

In the case of Darjeeling, fair traders' dismissal of the state's role in ensuring agricultural justice was profoundly misguided. Mr. Roy and his fellow planters were not motivated only by personal desires to conserve the environment and ensure worker well-being. The provision of the basic social and environmental goods fair-trade advocates see themselves as underwriting is in fact mandated by contemporary Indian labor laws and shaped by historical moral economic practices. As I explained in chapter 2, in 1951, the government of newly independent India passed the Plantations Labour Act (PLA) to protect workers from mistreatment at the hands of plantation owners.[9] This legislation was driven in part by the active presence of Communist-backed labor unions in Darjeeling, Assam, the Dooars, and Kerala, independent India's major tea-growing regions. The PLA's tenets were based upon long-standing best practices established by the Indian Tea Association. Today, the PLA continues to guarantee plantation workers' social welfare, mandating that owners provide workers housing, health care, food rations, and schooling for their children (what workers call *faciliti-haru*). The PLA makes the plantation moral economy—the tripartite, reciprocal relationships between labor, management, and the plantation landscape—into a matter of state concern.

During the period of my fieldwork, many planters sought to "update" what they saw as the "irrelevant" sections of the PLA, namely the social welfare clauses that dictate that owners provide workers' houses, medical care, firewood, and food rations. Many owners, including Mr. Roy, saw these provisions not as "facilities," but as "social costs." Members of the Darjeeling Tea Association (DTA), the plantation owners' organization, lobbied the central government to rewrite the PLA so that they would not have to bear these costs. Owners contended that workers should provide these things for themselves. As DTA members fought against paying "social costs," they also sought fair-trade certification to find new markets for their tea. In a stinging paradox, owners like Mr. Roy gained the attention of fair-trade certifiers *because* of their adherence to the PLA, even as they foresaw fair-trade programs as a method for justifying the law's rollback or repeal. Fair-trade certification was an effective and lucrative means of reaching U.S. and European markets. With its promise of higher prices, it provided, at worst, a means of subsidizing the social costs of the PLA, and, at best, a reason for doing away with the PLA altogether.

As he promoted his stewardship of Windsor's land and its "terrestrial infirma," Mr. Roy also heavily marketed his use of fair-trade premiums to provide his workers with basic necessities. Collecting and disseminating narratives about those efforts was key to maintaining Windsor's fair-trade certification. Fair-trade "success stories"—stories about workers' lives improving thanks to the premiums provided by certification—appear frequently in websites and other promotional materials. Descriptions on fair-trade tea boxes and retail websites make lofty claims about how fair trade has provided pharmacies, money to finance weddings and funerals for laborers' families, additional housing, and roads, all of which India's PLA already mandates.[10]

Fair Trade USA explains: "All tea growers receive an additional Fair Trade premium to invest in their farms and communities."[11] But Darjeeling is actually exempt from a key obligation regarding the fair-trade premium. While on non-Darjeeling tea plantations, the premium must be spent on projects for measurably *improving* the socioeconomic situation of workers, most fair-trade certifiers make an exception, in line with the rules set by Fairtrade Labelling Organizations International (FLO). The standards states, "An exception is made in the case of Darjeeling where *basic needs* for the workers (e.g., housing, water, and sanitation) may be partly financed through the fair-trade premium. This is due to the critical economic situation in the Darjeeling region."[12] Without further explanation of the "critical economic situation," FLO has now made it possible for owners to use fair-trade premiums to cover up to 50 percent of the costs of facilities mandated by the Plantations Labour Act. While there is no clear evidence that Darjeeling planters are less economically capable than those in nearby Assam or Nilgiris of meeting their PLA obligations, the Darjeeling exception persists. I could never get a clear reason from fair-trade officials as to why this exception was in place; in fact, one standards officer I talked to did not even know that Darjeeling's uniqueness was written into the standards documents. It is clear that powerful Darjeeling planters like Mr. Roy have been able to convince fair traders that Darjeeling is exceptionally troubled. In order to use the fair-trade premium to pay for PLA-mandated projects, however, Mr. Roy and other fair-trade plantation owners are supposed to seek the approval of a council made up, in part, of laborers. This council is known in fair-trade language as the Joint Body.

THE JOINT BODY

On a cold winter night in 2008, I was sitting in a village at Windsor, in a house occupied by the relatives of Gautam, a former Joint Body member. Mr. Roy insisted that I rent a room in Gautam's family's house, which was one of the few he had designated for foreign "homestay" visits, for which he charged three hundred rupees per night. That night, our dinner conversation kept returning to plantation politics and life in Darjeeling. On this, as on many other evenings, Gautam's family argued about the effectiveness of the factional leaders who fronted the Gorkha political parties, the Gorkha National Liberation Front (GNLF) and Gorkha Jan-mukti Morcha (GJMM). Cynicism about these politicians, whose power base was partly drawn from plantation workers' unions, ran high among Windsor residents. At the time, Gorkha politics revolved around the revived movement for a separate, Nepali-majority Indian state, Gorkhaland. While the Gorkhaland movement depended on the mobilization of plantation laborers in its calls for subnational independence, it had a complicated relationship to the plantation system. I describe this complex relationship in more detail in the next chapter, but it is important to note here that an overthrow of the plantation system, which was dominated by non-Nepali elites like Mr. Roy, was not a part of the Gorkhaland agitation.

Slamming his hand down on the sticky plastic table, Pranit said of the politicians, "They eat all the money and buy new clothing and cars with it."

"Wrong! We will get our separate state and they [the politicians] will help us get better wages on the plantation," said Kancha, cigarette hanging out of his mouth as he heaped white rice onto a plate.

Someone else chimed in: "All that happens are [party-mandated] cultural programs—dance, dance, dance; clothes, clothes, clothes—that is all they want to talk about." Gorkha leaders had chosen not only to keep the plantation system largely out of their political discourse, but had also enforced dress and behavior codes based on essentialized definitions of Nepali identity.

"*Darjeelingko jindagī estai chha* [Darjeeling life is like that]," said Bhoju, the oldest woman in our little group, crouched in the corner without looking up from her dented stainless steel cup of tea.

Later, the cups were filled with military-issue whiskey, and our conversation turned to the politics of the plantation itself. Bhoju told the story of a younger male relative who approached management to inquire about getting a fair-trade loan to fix his house. Although the fair-trade Joint Body had provided loans for livestock like Prakriti's cow in the early years of Windsor's certification, more recent Windsor "success stories" were larger investments in projects like biogas plants and new latrines. The fair-trade "exception" that allowed premiums to be spent on the "basic needs" of Darjeeling workers had made individual loans difficult to obtain. While the livestock loan never really made much sense on the plantation, workers who wanted new beds, furniture, appliances, or even modest additions to their homes had relied for generations on the ability to petition the *māliks* (plantation owners) for loans against their salaries. Such loans, even with their exploitative attachment to wages, were rare these days. Bhoju lamented, "The company used to give loans."

I was confused. "Isn't that what the [Joint Body] does?" I asked. I assumed Mr. Roy had boarded me with Gautam's family because they represented something of a fair-trade success story. As close kin to a Joint Body member, they were, according to my findings, in the minority of Windsor workers who even knew what fair trade was! I had raised my observations about the generalized ignorance of fair trade at Windsor, but Mr. Roy ensured me that workers were involved in the system.

"Not anymore . . . the company eats all the money and we drink this black, black tea," Bhoju replied, referring to the cheap CTC tea we had been drinking, produced in the plains south of Darjeeling.

Everyone turned to Gautam. Silence. As one of the few people privileged with knowledge of the higher-level functions of the plantation, perhaps he could explain why his own relative couldn't get a small home-improvement loan from the Joint Body. Several years earlier, Mr. Roy had appointed Gautam out of the rank-and-file male workforce and transformed him into a "ranger." Officially, Gautam's job was to manage the forests that surrounded Windsor's tea fields. This job, which took him back and forth across the area, raised suspicion among the workers that he was Mr. Roy's spy, looking for disgruntled or dissident elements in Windsor's seven villages. Gautam was also related to almost everyone in his village through marriage or blood. His relatives were as suspicious as anyone else about his work, but tea buyers and United States-based fair-trade executives thought that the appointment of a forest ranger was a truly revolutionary step toward environmental sustainability. For years, people in his village would ask him to explain the inner workings of management, or perhaps even the whereabouts of promised fair-trade benefits, but eventually they stopped asking him. After a few years, he had fallen to the margins of the Joint Body in favor of individuals with better English-language skills and homes closer to the factory.

"What is the Joint Body anyway?" I asked. Silence. He stared at his cup, shaking his head.

"*Man-pardaina* [I don't like it]," he said shaking his head and hands, still looking down into his tea.

"Why?" I asked.

"*Man. Par. Dai. Na*," he repeated deliberately. I gave him a puzzled look. After some contemplation, he explained, "You know the problem with Darjeeling politics? That is why I don't like it [the Joint Body]." He lowered his head into his tin cup, signaling that the conversation about plantation politics was over. His implication was that, like Gorkha politicians, Joint Body members were enriching themselves with fair-trade premiums. I had no way of knowing whether or not Gautam's implied accusation was true, but suspicions about his own possible sycophancy and embezzlement showed that fair trade at Windsor had amplified—rather than minimized—the social distance between Mr. Roy and his workers.

In "hired labor" situations, fair-trade certification requires the establishment of a "Joint Body," an elected group of individuals composed of representatives from both labor and management. The Joint Body must be democratically selected through "regular" elections, but neither FLO nor Fair Trade USA defines the intended regularity of meetings. On coffee cooperatives, cooperative members democratically decide how to spend the fair-trade premium,[13] but on tea plantations, the Joint Body distributes the premium in consultation with ownership. According to FLO, the Joint Body must: (1) "inform and consult all workers of the company about fair-trade standards and the fair trade premium and its use"; and (2) "manage and invest the fair trade premium transparently and responsibly."[14]

For laborers at Windsor (at least those like Gautam's relatives, who were aware of the Joint Body's existence), this supposedly democratic institution reflected one of the shortcomings of what they called the *bisnis* model of plantation operation, namely, that owners were able to manipulate favored workers through the unequal distribution of favors and resources, as I learned in a conversation with two older children of a tea plucker at Windsor, who were familiar with the workings of fair-trade certification:

> *Jigme:* You try calling for a Joint Body meeting. You will not be successful because people will not be around.
>
> *Sarah:* I stayed here for six months but they didn't come for the meeting.
>
> *Bhumika:* [They] work under the *sahib* [describing who is in the Joint Body].
>
> *Jigme:* How much money has come for the Joint Body in [Windsor]? It's more than one *crore* [ten million] rupees!
>
> *Sarah:* It's more than one crore?
>
> *Jigme:* It's more than that. It's useless, the company made all the profit, and there was no development! . . . It is all the company's, nothing has been used! What has Joint Body done till now? Have you seen?
>
> *Bhumika:* He [Roy] is the president!
>
> *Sarah:* How many years has it been since you have taken a loan?
>
> *Jigme:* Now it's been several years since they have stopped giving loans. There is no money. It's all over. . . . I don't know what the company did. . . . Before they use to give loans up to ten thousand rupees for a worker. . . . Now they don't even give that! They say they don't have the money.
>
> *Sarah:* But [people] don't speak about it?
>
> *Bhumika:* They are under the *sahib*.
>
> *Jigme:* No one can speak! No one can say these things.
>
> *Bhumika:* They are afraid.
>
> *Sarah:* What happened?

Bhumika: Because [the company] . . . restricted them from work, that's why.

Jigme: But still, follow it, give it a try, understand it. Here, the Joint Body meeting is impossible. . . . You should really follow it. What development has been done to date for Windsor with the Joint Body funds? . . . You will not be able to find it, even if you search for it. It's disappeared . . .

Bhumika: Actually, you know what is behind all this, Sarah?

Sarah: Hmm.

Bhumika: Actually, it's the culture. What we have here is that the *sahib* has kept all the clever people under his hands, while the simple and foolish people are greedy for work. They want to learn and understand the work. We are residents of this place, we have a *bodi* [body, using the English word], and we respect them, but they [the Joint Body representatives] never say that they want to do something. So, all of the members are all under his hands, because he provides them with extended facilities. And they get extremely light work, with more facilities, and whatever else.

At Windsor, workers claimed that there were never elections. Instead, Joint Body members like Gautam were "appointed" by Mr. Roy, and when Mr. Roy saw fit, they could be replaced. Similarly, at Kopibari, the organic and fair-trade certified plantation I described in the last chapter and among the most visible fair-trade certified plantations in the district, I found few workers who were aware of the Joint Body's existence, and I was never able to meet a member of the body. According to FLO, the composition of the Joint Body should reflect the composition of the workforce, meaning that on a tea plantation, where 60 percent of the workers are female tea pluckers, the Joint Body should contain a proportional number of pluckers. On Windsor's Joint Body, there were more women then men, but these women overwhelmingly came from one village: the one closest to the factory and to Mr. Roy' house. Other tea pluckers would often say that these women on the Joint Body were the recipients of special favors from management (*bakshish*). On all fair-trade plantations in Darjeeling, managers and other higher-level plantation functionaries were visible on the Joint Body, and on Windsor, the Joint Body "president" was Mr. Roy himself. Residents of Gautam's plantation said that the Joint Body included few pluckers. Some cynically said that the Joint Body had ceased to exist. All the money, they said, had been "eaten."[15]

Jigme: If the [Joint Body]'s funds are used, then there will be no problem.

Bhumika: If the tea garden workers themselves say all this, it would be better. We do not work in the tea garden. If we say it, they will say: "Where did they come from and why are they saying these things about me?"

Jigme: If we talk about these things, they will say: "He is fresh here. It's only been one week that he is staying here. He is an outsider and he does not know anything."

Bhumika. "He has come to stay with his relatives." . . . The workers who work hard and have problems do not say all this. What to do? It's difficult to bring changes. . . . The situation of the tea gardens is like this, and this is why the workers are poor. It's because they deprive themselves. They cannot demand anything and they are afraid. If they create a little fight they will send the police. The police will arrest them and file a case. Who will fight the case? Earning fifty rupees as wages, they cannot afford to fight a case. It's very difficult. . . . Maybe changes will come in the future generation.

Workers knew what nonmonetary forms of compensation planters were supposed to provide them. A 1971 amendment to the PLA mandates that each plantation have a labor welfare officer, whose job is to translate labor law, which is written in English, into Nepali. Across Darjeeling, however, owners installed labor welfare officers as assistant managers and saddled them with other duties on top of their obligations to laborers. On fair-trade plantations, the labor welfare officers were also appointed as the "fair-trade officers" of the Joint Body. After Gautam's dismissal of the Joint Body, I began asking around Windsor again about its activities. Eventually, I asked the labor welfare officer to explain the Joint Body's work, and to answer workers' concerns about the lack of loans or other visible projects. He told me that there was no more money left in the Joint Body coffers and no additional funds had come in for some time.

Darjeeling's assistant labor commissioner, who was in charge of the training of the labor welfare officers, was angered by how the officers had been coopted by management. When I interviewed her, she told me that all the work that she and Labor Department staff had done to select and train these individuals had been "for nothing." These officers had been saddled with extra tasks on most every plantation, but on what she called "showcase gardens" (those, like Windsor, that were backed by international certifications and labels like fair trade), that double-duty was particularly upsetting. "All these buyers and tourists come here and they think that it is just so lovely, but they have no idea." She told me about a promotional poster for another fair-trade plantation she had recently seen, which pictured two little Nepali children—a boy and a girl ("*kāncha* and *kānchi*")—torsos extending out from the cavernous darkness of a beautiful British Raj-era bungalow, waving. "That is the manager's bungalow!" she exclaimed. "The only way those children would ever have been in there is if they were mopping the floor!"

Workers showed little knowledge about what fair trade was and how it operated. This finding contrasts with other ethnographies of fair trade, which highlight that workers or cooperative members were dissatisfied with the operations of fair-trade certification.[16] That dissatisfaction, of course, indicates that cooperative members did have some basic knowledge of fair trade. This contrast raises the question of whether all workers on plantations need to be fully aware of the operations of fair trade in order for that plantation to be fair-trade certified. In Darjeeling, even though workers were not all aware of fair-trade certification, they did see significant changes in moral economic relationships. Workers saw the changes wrought in the name of fair trade as emblems of "*bisnis*-like" cronyism and an undermining of the state's ability to guarantee the presence of "facilities" through laws like the PLA. The PLA provides a legal counter to the inequities of the plantation system by defining the nonmonetary forms of remuneration that planters should provide. Darjeeling tea was likely deemed a good candidate for fair-trade certification because of the stability the PLA guaranteed, yet fair-trade certification schemes failed to acknowledge the importance of labor law to the maintenance of labor relations on plantations.[17]

A HUNGER STRIKE ON A FAIR-TRADE PLANTATION?

In practice, the involvement of ownership in the Joint Body undermined rather than promoted workers' ability to access knowledge about their labor rights, and the state-appointed labor officer's presence did little to make the Joint Body effective. Workers at Windsor had few ways to become involved with fair trade's central institution, even when it was funded. While Gautam disparagingly compared the Joint Body to Darjeeling's political parties, the parties, unlike the Joint Body, *did* provide a mechanism for worker action. In the summer of 2008, the leading political party in Darjeeling, the GJMM, told its affiliated union leaders to mobilize workers to enact hunger strike for higher wages. I was staying at one of Windsor's villages at the time, and I joined workers from the village on the morning of the event in a slow march up the hill to the processing factory. The march seemed incongruous. How could a fair-trade plantation play host to a hunger strike? Was this not the kind of unrest that fair-trade certification was designed to stave off (fig. 19)?

As it turned out, plantation strikes were highly orchestrated affairs. On that day, workers across the district—not just on Windsor—were following a familiar script. Whereas the inauguration of one of Windsor's fair-trade projects might draw a dozen or fewer nearby workers, attendance at the strike reached the hundreds. The walk up the hill ended at the gates of the factory, where party-backed union leaders commenced the first official phase of the strike: the "gate meeting." Before the plucking day began, and before Mr. Roy arrived to his office, workers, male and female, gathered at the locked entrance to the plantation factory. They awaited Mr. Roy's arrival, blockading the entrance to formally express their demands. In this case, they were seeking a wage rise. Mr. Roy came prepared for this, since union leaders had registered a memorandum with all owners in the district in advance. Mr. Roy had reviewed those demands, and like the other owners in the region, he refused to meet them. The workers promised not to go to the fields until he met with union representatives (fig. 20).

Perhaps the most problematic aspects of the inclusion of tea plantations in the fair-trade system are the popular misrepresentation of the wage relationship in the

FIGURE 19. Female laborers proceeding to the factory from the *kamān busti* for a gate meeting. Photo by author.

FIGURE 20. Waiting for a gate meeting. Photo by author.

Indian tea sector and misguided beliefs about fair-trade certification's ability to increase or guarantee it. Plantation workers receive a daily wage, supplemented by very small per-kilogram plucking incentives (often only a couple of rupees, and there is a remarkable amount of green leaf in one kilogram). Wages on Indian tea plantations are negotiated every three years in three-way meetings between the state (represented by the Department of Labour), the workers (represented by local labor unions), and the planters (represented by regional planters' associations).[18] These negotiations occur independently in each Indian state that contains plantations (the most notable tea-producing states are West Bengal, Kerala, Assam, and other states in the Northeast that were part of colonial Assam). The Darjeeling wage negotiations, therefore, were part of the larger wage talks for the state of West Bengal. The wage agreed upon in these meetings would apply to multiple tea-growing regions in the state, including the Dooars, Terai, Jalpaiguri, and Darjeeling. The protest at Windsor in the August 2008 was thus not just against owners, but against the state of West Bengal.

At Mr. Roy's refusal, the workers demanded to be let into the factory to begin their hunger strike. Mr. Roy resisted, but he eventually permitted the group to enter the gates and occupy the factory foyer. The reasons for this were unclear. Mr. Roy would certainly have liked to keep the workers as invisible to passersby on the road as possible, but he also did not want to appear overly threatened. He thus permitted the strikers to enter, with the proviso that they should not enter the factory floor. Once Mr. Roy relented on the demand to strike, workers initiated a rotating occupation of the factory foyer. Most of the women who had marched up the hill that morning went to the fields, as usual, but a few women and men remained on strike in the foyer. They sat against the walls, men on one side and women on the other, chanting party songs and discussing their plan of action: each group of men and women would spend twenty-four hours on hunger strike, to be replaced the next day by another.

On that day, hunger strikes were taking place on every plantation in Darjeeling, but they had particular resonance on fair-trade plantations. Thanks to fair-trade- and GI-related tourism and development projects that brought Europeans and Americans to Windsor, workers were beginning to learn more about the market for the tea they grew. During the 2008 strike, workers told one another that a cup of Windsor tea sold for *hundreds* of rupees. At the time, there were about forty-four rupees per dollar, and Windsor's tea pluckers were making fifty-three rupees a day, or just over one dollar. The rumors of high tea prices among workers were not far from the truth. Indeed, a cup of Darjeeling tea, bagged from the lowest-grade leaf, costs between three and five dollars in tea and coffee shops in the United States today.

"Do *you* pay that much for a cup of tea?" a worker asked me.

"Just the tea? Not the milk and sugar?" another woman asked.

Another man interjected: "No, only rich people can afford this tea, like the people who stay in the owner's house. . . . Our earning of twelve days, they finish in one cup of tea."

His compatriot added, "Some of the ones plucking tea, some of the ones who work the machine inside, the ones working at the machine don't even get time to wipe off their sweat."

Despite the fact that Darjeeling tea is some of the most expensive in the world, Darjeeling tea laborers are paid some of the lowest wages in India's tea sector. Other tea-producing states in India, such as Kerala and Assam, produce lesser-quality tea, which sells for less on the domestic and international markets. In 2010, wages ranged from 50 rupees in Assam to 147 rupees in Kerala. The plantation wage is kept artificially low because of the provision of *faciliti-haru*. The plantation daily wage is actually lower than the minimum state wage for agricultural workers (in 2008, from 120 rupees to 154 rupees per day depending on kind of labor and skill level). For example, to offset holiday expenses, permanent laborers are granted a "bonus" before the Pujas, the main Hindu festival season, usually in early October.[19] The bonus enables workers to participate in religious festivities and rituals, including hosting and feeding visiting family. True poverty, according to many workers I interviewed, is the absolute inability to buy a new outfit for your children, or paint your house during the Pujas.[20]

Attempting to diffuse the strike, Mr. Roy tried to use fair-trade Joint Body meetings to discuss the union's position.[21] The main complaint of the workers was that owners like Mr. Roy were failing to supplement wages with *faciliti-haru*. At the time, the statewide daily minimum wage in West Bengal was 120 rupees, but plantation workers only received 53 rupees in cash. The remaining 67 rupees was to be paid in kind, through the provisions of schools, electricity, water, and care for houses. As one union leader put it to me, "Today they do not whitewash your house, but they show the government that they have spent for whitewashing your house! You do not get the ration, but they charge the government money for that ration also. And so the things which we are not utilizing, why should we let the company deduct money for that?" The Joint Body was scheduled to consider these issues, but a meeting never materialized. Instead, the district-wide hunger strike ended with a promise to begin three-way wage negotiations between owners, the state, and unions. It is doubtful that Windsor's Joint Body could have done much at all to assuage workers' concerns because this strike, like all wage negotiations in Darjeeling, was not limited to Windsor alone. Fair-trade regulations require that labor unions be permitted in "hired labor" situations, but fair-trade standards explicitly link better wages to fair-trade premiums earned by workers on *specific plantations,* not regionally connected plantations who enter into negotiations together. Most importantly, fair trade, by treating plantation workers as "hired labor," fails to acknowledge the unique combination of cash and in-kind payments on which plantation laborers rely.

Wages were a key element of compensation for workers at Windsor and other fair-trade plantations, and wage hikes were certainly something Windsor workers wanted. But plantation residents I interviewed put little stock in the capacity of democratic representation under fair trade to improve their wages. Despite this, Fair Trade USA makes bold claims that fair-trade certification can institute "fair minimum wages."[22] The mistake in such claims lies in the characterization of plantation workers as "hired" in the sense that wage earners in other industries are hired. Fair Trade USA calls its hired labor regulations "farm-worker standards." Like other certifiers, Fair Trade USA studiously avoids using the term *plantation* to describe places like Windsor, even though the colonial plantation model, which relied on tenant laborers, who worked for low wages and in-kind benefits and lived in cramped settlements on huge mono-cropped tracts, is alive and well. Fair Trade USA tends to call plantations "large farms," as in this excerpt from its website, which describes tea certification: "Warm on a cold winter's day and or chilled to beat the summer heat, your favorite tea starts with skilled workers on farms around the world. Fair Trade Certified tea comes from both cooperatives and large farms. Fair Trade helps tea farmers and workers gain access to capital, set fair prices for their products, and make democratic decisions about how to best improve their business, their community and their tea."[23] Fair Trade USA's use of "farm worker" to describe this type of organization makes it seem as if workers freely come and go from land, when in fact the plantation system has historically tied them to the land. "Hired labor" evokes a vision of a pure wage relationship between workers and the commodity they produce. Plantation laborers do not spend fixed amounts of time "at work." Home *is* work for the Darjeeling plantation worker. Fair-trade standards for hired labor avoid engaging this compression of home and work because in the context of plantations, this duality evokes not rugged individualism but indenture, sharecropping, and permanent marginalization—unavoidable elements of plantation life and labor. The PLA has taken this tie into account, protecting not only wages but also benefits for workers' latrines, water, housing, and food rations. In other words, Indian labor law, unlike fair trade, acknowledges that laborers live where they work. The frequent deployment of the term *wages* on fair-trade advertisements makes sense as a marketing strategy. Wages are certainly more comprehensible to first world consumers than "facilities."

Fair Trade USA explains: "A minimum sales price is guaranteed to ensure a sustainable wage is paid to tea workers and a sustainable income is paid to tea farmers."[24] In practice, a minimum sales price in no way guarantees a sustainable wage. Fair-trade standards recast the minimum prices—a figure central to fair-trade certification on coffee cooperatives, where farmers might be vulnerable to selling their coffee at below production costs—as a project that could make a difference to tea plantation workers in India (and, after 2012, to the coffee plantations that are coming under fair-trade certification). In Darjeeling, workers make the same wage regardless of the price at which their plantation's tea sells and regardless of the fact their plantation is certified as fair trade. Whether a kilogram of tea sells for eighteen thousand or two hundred rupees, a Darjeeling tea worker makes exactly the same amount of money, her state-mandated daily wage.

CAN A PLANTATION BE FAIR?

The 2008 wage talks in West Bengal raised the wage from fifty-three to fifty-eight rupees a day, just over one dollar per day. The president of the Darjeeling Tea Association (DTA), who was also the owner of several other fair-trade plantations, told the press that the 2008 wage hike was "unprecedented," far too high for the economic conditions of the area. (It was in fact, not unprecedented, as the rate of inflation between the last wage talks in 2005 and 2008 was much higher than this.) This hike, he said, set an "unhealthy trend for future negotiations."[25] Throughout my fieldwork, owners of both conventional and fair-trade plantations continued fighting to keep workers' wages down.

The DTA president's assertions reflected an assumption that is written into fair trade's "exception" for the use of premiums in Darjeeling. Darjeeling tea plantations are allowed to use fair-trade income to cover "basic" needs: the in-kind benefits that accounted for just over half of workers' daily income. His assertion was that workers' hardships were somehow coeval with those of planters. This is not to say that workers were not aware that their well-being was tied to that of owners. During the hunger strike, one of the male activists spoke of the laborers' connection to Mr. Roy metaphorically: "The owner has become like an egg right now down there. We have to stay careful. He has become like an egg. If we move him a little bit and if he breaks, then he is finished, then at that time we will also be finished. But forget it! He will also not get on. We will also not get on. *I will break an egg at that time,* in the last moment." Whereas the fair-trade discourse about plantations, reflected in the DTA president's complaint about the wage negotiations, was that workers and owners in the tea industry were both vulnerable to economic hardship, this laborer's remark signaled that that vulnerability was not the same for labor and ownership. Importantly, however, workers *did* understand the plantation, represented by Mr. Roy, to be somewhat fragile. In the final sentence of the excerpt above, the striking laborer signals his intention to "break an egg": to sever the reciprocal relationship between himself and Mr. Roy.

The laborer's metaphorical remark thus speaks to a fragile, politically mediated *moral economic* connection between owners and workers. Moral economies, as I explained above, do not operate on assumptions of equal vulnerability. Quite the opposite. Moral economies are reciprocal relationships of care among *un*equal partners. In the laborer's metaphor, part of workers' jobs is to care for a fragile owner whose "wholeness" is essential for their own survival. Moral economies such as those that govern plantation politics do not eliminate exploitation; they regulate it.[26] The worker's egg metaphor stands in direct contrast to the fair-trade imaginary that tries to equalize producer-consumer-worker relations, and the persistence of moral economic ideas in Darjeeling raises questions about the role of fair trade on plantations in the first place. Why would planters like Mr. Roy (with the help of fair-trade certifiers) feel the need to alter something that—according to workers—is not yet broken? Why present an alternative system when there is still a viable system at play?

The presence of fair-trade tea on store shelves implies that a consumer can help fix conditions on plantations by buying that tea. But not all agricultural systems can be made compatible with market-based solutions based on consumer benevolence.[27] To paraphrase Fair Trade USA's promotional materials, "the money you spend on day-to-day goods can [not] improve an entire community's day-to-day lives." After years of fieldwork on Windsor and other fair-trade Darjeeling tea plantations, I am left to conclude that the extension of fair trade to tea plantations is little more than a movement for retailers and consumers to engage in "solidarity-seeking" consumption.[28] Fair trade's "fairness" is a market-driven version of justice that assumes that workers and owners share common interests, common strengths, and common weaknesses. Fair trade is a way for consumers to tell a story about themselves through their consumption practices. Fair trade is selling a moral economic fetish, a dream of equitable relations in empirically unequal productive conditions, and sales are booming. In this booming market for justice, the extension of fair trade is also beneficial to fair-trade certification organizations. Increased certification means increased certification fees.

Beyond this broad problem lie two deeper shortcomings of fair-trade logic on plantations: its equation of individual entrepreneurialism to "empowerment," and its privileging of democratic but "antipolitical" decision making.[29] Fair-trade logic hinges on the idea that individuals can better their economic and social standing by using improved wages and/or loan schemes to become entrepreneurs. Political scientist Gavin Fridell has argued that fair trade extends a "neoliberal" economic emphasis on nongovernmental economic regulation and individual empowerment—the kinds of values that undergird the logic of calls for "free trade"—even as it challenges the disenfranchisement that such policies cause.[30] In both free trade and fair trade, private-property rights and individual entrepreneurial identity confer "empowerment." Sangeeta Kamat, examining NGO-driven policies based on such a vision of empowerment, writes: "A fundamental cultural transformation involved in the transition from state-led development to a deregulated market economy is that citizens have to forego their sense of entitlement and have to acquire an entrepreneurial citizen identity that derives from liberal values of independence and autonomy. . . . The new economic institutions are engaged in this process of advancing a new citizen culture . . . in which all citizens, including the poor, are encouraged to be enterprising and seize the opportunities of the global economy."[31]

Tea laborers on Darjeeling plantations are decidedly *not* adopting ideas of individual entrepreneurship. The story of Prakriti's cow is a prime example. The cow was meant to be an income generating strategy, but Prakriti resisted using it in this way. By *giving* the milk and dung to her relatives and neighbors, rather than selling it, Prakriti was ensuring that their relationships remained healthy. Prakriti's cow failed to work as a tool for "empowerment" because plantation moral economies among workers depend upon nonmarket solidarity. As anthropologist Daniel Reichman argues in his analysis of fair-trade logic in a Honduran coffee-growing community, fair trade's emphasis on individual economic empowerment attempts to force such forms of solidarity into the narrow arena of market transactions.[32] Reichman shows that some coffee growers *were* embracing the liberal ideal, even when that embrace contributed to the fracture of their vulnerable village. In Darjeeling, by contrast, plantation workers did not seem to want to be entrepreneurs. They wanted higher wages, to be sure, but they were convinced that owners like Mr. Roy were failing in their obligations to provide basic facilities. Wages would buffer against this neglect. In the main, though, they wanted plucking and processing tea to remain a minimally stable form of work.

Workers at Windsor (not to mention Mr. Roy) knew all too well that moral economic relationships were politically mediated. Yet as I have argued in this chapter, planters like Mr. Roy saw fair-trade certification as a way of extricating themselves from obligations to labor that were underwritten by the state. For international buyers and fair-trade certifiers, fair-trade institutions and ideologies supersede existing state institutions aimed at protecting workers' rights. While the PLA and fair-trade regulations both nominally protected workers' rights to organize into politically affiliated labor unions, fair trade also created a separate institution, the Joint Body, which was supposed to enact plantation governance through an equal partnership of owners, managers, and rank-and-file workers. Again, the success of the Joint Body hinged on the illusion that owners and workers on fair-trade plantations shared a common interest in securing and distributing fair-trade premiums. The system of party-backed, union-driven negotiations shows that workers were much more prone to mobilize across plantations, fair trade and conventional, against both owners *and* state governments. After all, it is state governments, not individual plantations, that set plantation wages in India. By ignoring and even disparaging the state institutions already existent on the plantation that work to ensure the equitable treatment of workers, fair-trade schemes aggravate, rather than alleviate, the tensions of plantation life. The appointment of rangers like Gautam, temporary favorites of fickle owners, to weak Joint Bodies, and the extension of loans to reluctant plantation entrepreneurs like Prakriti, were just a few of the practices that workers identified as *bisnis*. Workers saw *bisnis* as divisive to plantation village life, social solidarity, and to a larger system of moral economic reciprocity between workers, management, and the agro-environment.

Fair-trade standards need to reflect that plantations are hierarchical, colonially derived industries in which workers depend upon owners not just for money but also for food, medical care, schools, and housing. This has been the case in Darjeeling since the 1850s. Their hierarchical structure makes it impossible for resources to be managed "jointly" (and certainly not democratically). Instead, international certifiers must privilege workers and take measures to prevent owners from manipulating the system for their own benefit. Recasting plantation work as "hired labor" will not benefit workers.

The 2008 hunger strikes, led by the GJMM, show how politics penetrated plantation life. Workers, as I show in the next chapter, believed in the power of political movements to achieve social justice, even more than they believed in the power of the market. As Gautam's family's conversation in this chapter shows, they were occasionally cynical about the potential of party politics to make life on plantations better. But where fair-trade projects consistently failed to engage workers in significant numbers, or with significant passion, Gorkha separatist politics consistently succeeded. Gorkhaland politicians' relationship to the tea industry and its moral economy, however, remained complex. The next chapter examines that complex relationship.

5

Sovereignty

I delighted in weaving back and forth across an invisible line—"Now I am in Nepal." I jumped. "Now I am in India." I jumped again. Grazing goats passed by and shot me suspicious glances as I examined the small stones that demarcated the border (see figs. 21 and 22).

I repeated the game of hopscotch several times over the week I spent on Meghma, an organic-certified tea estate near Darjeeling. Meghma straddled the Nepal-India border, high up in the Sandakphu range. As a geographically liminal plantation, it was not included as one of the eighty-seven Darjeeling plantations with GI status, nor was it certified fair trade.[1] I watched not only goats and other grazing livestock come across the border, rather unceremoniously, but also vintage Land Rovers filled with people, goods, meats, and sacksful of fermented millet, or *chang*, for sale in the markets at the base of the range in the bazaar at Sukhia Pokari. The same Land Rovers would return to Nepal filled with supplies for sale to passing trekkers and vista-seeking tourists: perforated strings of ten rupee bags of potato chips and *wai-wai* (ramen noodles) fluttering off the roof.

The Nepal-India border, often marked only by stones like these or three-foot-high posts on which market goers tether livestock or hang laundry to dry, is a fluid one.[2] In my time at Meghma, I saw people and materials of all kinds ply up and down the long bumpy road to Manebhanjang, the small bazaar town at the head of the Sandakphu trekking route.[3] There was a small Indian army post adjacent to the house in which I was staying. Other than daily walks and evening serenades of Bollywood hits (accompanied by the melodic sounds of smashing glass), I was not really sure what the twenty-five or so Indian soldiers were doing there. When I asked (here, high up in the mountains of the Nepal border was, ironically, one of

FIGURE 21. India side of a border marker. Photo by author.

the few times while living in Darjeeling that my Hindi language training proved to be useful), they explained that they were "looking for Maoists" amid the normal flow of livestock and Land Rovers coming over the border from Nepal. For most of the previous ten years, a Maoist-led insurgency had raged in Nepal, and the Indian military had packed the border with extra security in order to prevent Nepali Maoist rebels from moving into Darjeeling and other border regions.[4]

Following Indian independence and the end of the Kingdom of Nepal's century-long isolation, the two governments signed the 1950 Peace and Friendship Treaty. The Treaty grants citizens of Nepal and India the same rights in the opposite country. Citizens of India can own property, hold a job, and live without any restrictions in Nepal. The same holds true for Nepali citizens in India.[5] The treaty gives residents of both India and Nepal what Aihwa Ong calls "flexible citizenship."[6] As a document, the Peace and Friendship Treaty serves a purpose similar to that of the dual passports that Ong describes for Hong Kong businessmen, enabling Indians and Nepalis to travel freely across the border.[7] According to the Peace and

FIGURE 22. Nepal side of a border marker. Photo by author.

Friendship Treaty, if a person of Nepali descent settled in India before the adoption of the 1950 Indian Constitution, that person was declared a "natural citizen" of India.[8] Gorkhas were thus "natural citizens" of India by the terms of the treaty, but since 1950, their sense of belonging within India has remained precarious.[9]

The fluidity of the boundary between India and Nepal has historically provided opportunities for both capital and labor, as I have described in previous chapters. But the "open border" has paradoxically erected a barrier between Indian Nepalis, or Gorkhas, and the Indian state. Gorkhas I met during my fieldwork described how the treaty left them in an uncomfortable liminal space.[10] Although their jobs were located in India, the farther Indian Nepalis from Darjeeling got from the plantations, the less they felt like Indian nationals. As jobs in Darjeeling dwindled, they migrated to Delhi and Kolkata in search of work. When traveling, even my most urbane Nepali friends told me that they would routinely have their identification questioned. "You're not Indian. You don't look Indian . . . " guards outside airport terminals would often say, "You look Chinese." There are over 2.5 million Nepalis living in India today, but as anthropologist Michael Hutt argues, the more secure Nepalis have become in their linguistic and cultural identity outside Nepal, the more *in*secure the "dominant political orders" within which they live and work have become about their presence.[11]

Since the early twentieth century, Darjeeling has been a bastion of Indian Nepali activism and the stage for a series of Gorkhaled agitations for Indian citizenship.[12] Gorkhas were plagued by what they often called an "identity crisis," and the accusations of "being Chinese" were just one manifestation of this. As Hutt describes in his account of the Nepali diaspora across India, Burma, and Bhutan, beginning in the 1960s, after a series of Indo-Chinese border disputes, thousands of Nepalis and other "foreigners" were expelled from states in Northeast India, where they had been living for generations, and by the end of the 1980s, tens of thousands of Bhutanese Nepalis had been evicted from the country they had called home all their lives.[13] When Gorkhas moved back over the border to Nepal, their behavior, especially the way they spoke Nepali, marked them as outsiders as well. According to Gorkhas in Darjeeling, the flexibility and reciprocal rights granted by the Peace and Friendship Treaty actually undermined their sense of *Indian* citizenship. For Gorkhas, belonging was predicated on geographical *inflexibility.* It was against the backdrop of evictions, migrations, and fluid boundaries that the Gorkhaland agitation, the movement for a separate Indian state comprised of a majority of Nepali-speaking people, took hold.

This chapter explores the connections between tea labor and the Gorkhaland movement. I argue that material and symbolic ties to land, which emerged in part from the history of plantation tea production, lay at the heart of Gorkhas' claims to Indian citizenship. The Gorkhaland movement's vision of "justice" was one of territorial sovereignty. As permanent residents of Darjeeling, Gorkhas spoke of justice as a set of rights rooted in innate ties to place, buttressed by a common language. These claims were complicated by the fact that Gorkhas owed their sense of distinct identity to a history of displacement from Nepal and servitude in the colonial tea industry. Gorkhas alternately articulated their belonging in historical, relational terms (in which the history of plantation labor and service to the British and later Bengali planter class was central), and in primordial terms (in which timeless ideas about natural behavior and natural connections to land were at the forefront, divorced from the history of tea production).

One possible interpretation of the Gorkhaland movement might highlight its similarities to other subnationalist struggles in India. Movements by marginalized populations for statehood have been common over the past few decades. For example, the Uttarakhand, Nagaland, and Jharkhand movements all succeeded in creating separate states (seceding, respectively, from Uttar Pradesh, Assam, and Bihar) by convincing the Indian government that residents of these places constituted indigenous populations, united—like Gorkhas—by the use of a common language. In each of these struggles, primordial arguments about belonging appeared to hold more sway than historical ones. I call attention to the coexistence of primordial and historical understandings of belonging in the Gorkhaland agitation, then, for two reasons. First, most Indian Nepalis—especially tea workers—are well aware of their ancestral ties to Nepal. Second, as I found in my analysis of the second major Gorkhaland agitation, which I witnessed and documented between 2008 and 2010, while primordial ideas were important for positioning the Gorkhaland struggle on the national stage, among rank-and-file political activists, historical connections between people—notably tea workers and other descendants of British colonial servants—and the Darjeeling landscape were at least as salient.

In what follows, I pay particular attention to the ways in which Gorkhaland activists deployed images of and ideas about soil, plants, and other aspects of the landscape as they framed the Gorkha "identity crisis." I suggest that this version of the movement failed to achieve "justice," which tea workers understood as the sovereignty of Nepali speakers over Darjeeling and its territory, because of the contradictions between primordial and historical understandings of the relationship between Gorkhas and land. The prominence of tea labor, which emerged from histories of migration rather than timeless connections to land, may have undermined Gorkha claims to indigenous belonging. Both the first and second Gorkhaland agitations used violence, attacks on property, and death threats to achieve their goals, but neither manifestation of the movement ever attempted to stop the tea business. Neither questioned Darjeeling's main economic engine. While the prevalence of violence in the Gorkhaland movement was not unique (the subnationalist struggles for Uttarakhand, Nagaland, and Jharkhand also included considerable death and destruction), in Darjeeling, these contending discourses led to a mix of actions and ideas that linked gender, work, and social class in uniquely volatile ways. The story of Madan Tamang, Meghma Tea Estate's owner, provides a tragic but instructive example of this.

THE ASSASSINATION OF MADAN TAMANG

Madan was not thought to be Gorkha, despite the fact that he grew up in Darjeeling. It was true that Madan was not like most other Nepalis in the district. He was not born on a tea plantation. Nor were his parents. He grew up in a large farmhouse on the land that became Meghma Tea Estate. Although the Peace and Friendship Treaty between India and Nepal meant that all Nepalis had reciprocal rights in both countries, Madan, as the owner of land that straddled the border, was a "dual citizen" in a much more palpable sense.[14] His claims to Indian and Nepali belonging were strong in that he owned land in both countries, but his claims to Gorkha identity were tenuous for the same reason. Well educated and traveled, he neither served in a Gurkha army regiment nor worked on a tea plantation. Instead, he became a successful real-estate developer in the area and a prominent politician. Yet Madan was an avowed Gorkha activist. He served as President of the Akhil (All) Bharatiya (India) Gorkha League (ABGL), the oldest political entity representing Gorkhas in India. When I knew him, Madan relished the role of dissenter.

Indeed, Madan's embrace of life-in-opposition, along with his failure to meet either historical or primordial definitions of Gorkha-ness, might have cost him his life.

As I was told time and again, Madan did not carry himself in a way becoming of a typical Gorkha male. These statements took awhile for me to comprehend, but after going to dozens of GJMM rallies over the course of my fieldwork, it started to make sense. During my fieldwork, Gorkha maleness was tied to military service and stereotypes of heroism and aggression. Male politicians banged on the podium while screaming their message. In fact, they screamed and banged a lot, peppering their discourse with threats of violence to the movement's enemies. The more politicians yelled and fist-pounded, the more the crowds cheered. Madan, by contrast, talked calmly in a refined oratory cadence that betrayed his British-style college and university education. He told stories and talked about contingencies. He never threatened to hold a *khukuri* to the throats of those opposing him (though this was a threat commonly voiced toward him by GJMM politicians). For many GJMM politicians, being a Gorkha was about being brave, loyal, and industrious, not refined and critical. "Don't listen to *Madan dāju,*" GJMM leader Bimal Gurung would often roar across the loudspeakers at rallies. "He is only going to confuse you."

Referencing his privileged upbringing, GJMM politicians routinely denigrated Madan. As a child of wealth and privilege and not of the plantations or army, Madan did not have the background to be a "proper" Gorkha. During a March 2010 Gorkhaland rally, the chief secretary of the GJMM Youth Committee put his party's feelings about Madan in stark terms:

Madan Tamang is a teacher who cuts the paper of Bengal ... we will erase you [Tamang] if tomorrow the public are betrayed. What will be done to Madan Tamang is in the hands of the public. You remember that, you understand this. We have said, we have loved our *jāti* [race, group, kind—also used in plant taxonomies (see chapter 1)], we have come for the poor public, we are not the sons who have come from a rich family ... we are also the sons of families who eat the rice which we get from rations. We are also the sons who carry a tumbler and stand in line. Mr. Bimal Gurung [the GJMM leader] is the son of a mother who worked in the tea garden. We have suffered ... so ... today we are doing it for *our sad mother* ... we know what is hunger. We know what it is to study and not get a job. We know what it is when we have tension in our minds. . . . We have come to wipe the tears of the public . . . for the ones who understand, please don't listen to the things said by others. *The people from the tea gardens and the village area, please go and sit up front!*

Veiled threats to Madan were common among male leaders like this one, as were gendered and classed appeals to the suffering "mothers" who worked in tea fields while their sons struggled to find work.

Female Gorkhaland activists, however, were more ambivalent about Madan. "Madan-*dāju* is pretentious," some women would tell me at rallies. "When you *namaste* [put your hands together as a form of respect], he will not *namaste* in return." Others thought that Madan's elite education, political connections, and ability to "talk to the center" could be an asset to the movement. At one GJMM rally, a female supporter said to me with a hushed voice: "Well you know, we need someone like him. These men [pointing to the stage], they are good at what *they* do. They get attention, but they can't talk in Delhi, or even Kolkata [meaning that they did not speak Hindi or Bengali] . . . maybe he could just be an advisor."

Just four days after I returned to the United States from Darjeeling, in May 2010, the threats to "erase" Madan came to fruition. He was assassinated in Darjeeling town, less than two hundred yards from Chowrasta, the central plaza where the GJMM held its rallies. He was killed by a group of men wielding *khukuris*, the curved knives that are the "traditional" weapons of Gurkha soldiers. He bled to death beneath a gleaming billboard (reproduced in chapter 3, figure 15) advertising Darjeeling tea's GI status. "Darjeeling joins the global elites," the billboard's lettering read, beneath a giant row of pictures: a teacup, a Champagne flute, and a glass of Cognac.

In the days that followed Madan's murder, my Darjeeling friends talked about how they felt betrayed. Certainly, they had heard the threats to Madan, but they had also heard constant pledges to nonviolence from GJMM politicians. This permutation of the Gorkhaland movement was intended to break with the previous one (1986–88), in which violent clashes between separatists and the Indian police were commonplace. Such pledges rang hollow, since property destruction and death threats remained among the GJMM's tactics, though the violence never reached the level of all-out insurgency that marked the 1980s. Senses of fear and loss were still palpable. Everyone knew someone who died in that first agitation, and they did not want to experience that kind of loss again. As I read the news reports and Internet message boards, however, others celebrated the murder. Elite centrists like Madan, anonymous posters said, were the only obstacles to obtaining a separate Indian Nepali state of Gorkhaland.

Madan's murder provides a starting point for exploring the contradictory connections between the Gorkhaland movement and the twenty-first-century tea plantation complex. A laboring identity born in the colonial plantation context, I argue, was key to Gorkha activists' notions of "justice" and regional sovereignty. Being at once a brave and loyal soldier and an industrious laborer was a part of Gorkhas' ideas of who they were. The ancestors of present-day Gorkhas came from several ethnic groups in Nepal and beyond, but in Darjeeling, as I explained in chapter 1, these identities melded into an identity that corresponded to British cultural taxonomies. In short, Nepali speakers would not constitute Darjeeling's majority population without tea. The colonially rooted tea plantation system depended on gendered cultural stereotypes that couched Nepali men as aggressive, *khukuri*-wielding fighters, and Nepali women as submissive, comely figures. Scholars in other South Asian colonial contexts, notably Jayeeta Sharma and Piya Chatterjee in their studies of Indian tea in Assam and the Dooars, have documented this condensation of labor-based and ethnic identities.[15] In rhetoric and in practice, Gorkhaland politicians and their supporters wrestled with the paradoxical legacy of the plantation. They wanted to overcome the continued economic oppression that the plantations represented, yet they routinely appealed to essentialisms about Gorkhas, as men and women and as laborers, that were rooted in the plantations themselves.

Gorkhas articulated their visions of justice around their care for Darjeeling and its landscape, even as they recognized the role that their own subjugation played in making that landscape. In the Gorkhaland agitation, historical, relational senses of care for place sat in tension with primordialist ideas about the connection of Gorkhas to place. Primordialist discourses hinged on the kind of simplified, ahistorical relationships presented in the "Third World agrarian imaginaries" manifested in GI and fair-trade discourses. Such imaginaries, which posited a timeless, ecologically harmonious Gorkha, proved as politically potent for politicians and activists as they were economically lucrative for GI and fair-trade advocates. But as with other essentialist ideas about persons and places, these imaginaries were impossible to sustain, and, as Madan's murder shows, they were internally destructive to the Gorkhaland movement. The tea plantation and ideas about plantation labor were both the making of Gorkha identity and its undoing.

Below, I will explore the relationship between gendered labor and Gorkha ethnic identity. Hegemonic colonial discourses about Nepalis, embraced today in tea marketing and in Gorkhas' own reflexive descriptions of themselves, rely on associations between Nepali people and service work.[16] References to colonial service were central to Gorkha discourses of belonging. In the iteration of the Gorkhaland movement I witnessed, women and men collectively recalled histories of affective labor to make claims to political sovereignty over the region. Affective labor produces not just material things but also emotions. As tea pluckers, soldiers, and servants, Gorkhas took pride in making tea as well as building and defending infrastructure, but they also took pride in immaterial productions: taste, loyalty, and nationality. As I will argue, however, these ideas about service and other forms of immaterial production limited the effectiveness of the Gorkhaland movement and converted sensibilities about care for land and kin into narrow and morally conservative ideas about gender and work, reinscribing rather than unmaking colonial taxonomies of labor.

THE GORKHALAND MOVEMENT

The 1980s saw a rise in Nepali political action in Darjeeling. In 1980, Subhash Ghisingh, the child of a tea garden, and his Gorkha National Liberation Front (GNLF) joined forces with the Pranta Parishad, a group founded by Madan Tamang, in a movement to push for the autonomy of the Darjeeling district from the state of West Bengal and the formation of a separate state within India.[17] The Gorkhaland movement gathered steam in the early 1980s, and Ghisingh quickly became its most commanding voice.[18] The GNLF broke with the Pranta Parishad in 1984, and in 1986, the first Gorkhaland agitation began in earnest. In that year, Ghisingh dispatched a group of supporters to the town of Kalimpong. There, they publicly burned a copy of the 1950 Peace and Friendship Treaty. A police detachment forcibly put down this rally by firing into the crowd, killing several GNLF activists. The state's violent reaction to this and other protests sparked a two-year revolt that changed the contours of Darjeeling politics. As long as the Peace and Friendship Treaty existed, Ghisingh argued, Gorkhas would always be treated like migrants, not Indians. Gorkhaland supporters claimed that all the other Indian states were drawn along linguistic lines, but that Nepalis were literally left off the map of independent India. Gorkhas were plagued by what politicians then and later have called an "identity crisis." The first Gorkhaland agitation also had a material basis.[19] By the mid- to late 1980s, there were many men living on tea gardens, as opportunities subsided for males to work off of the gardens. In particular, the Gurkha regiments, in both the British and Indian armed services, curtailed recruitment of Nepalis.

In 1986, the Communist Party controlled the West Bengal government, and for a time, it seemed as if the Congress Party government of Rajiv Gandhi might support Gorkhaland as a hedge against the Communists.[20] A standoff between Gandhi's national government and the West Bengal government over how to deal with the GNLF opened space for the outbreak of violence. Late that spring, strikes and violence reached a boiling point. There were not clear sides in the agitation. Some violence and counterviolence was between the GNLF and West Bengal's Communist government. Throughout 1987, GNLF activists burned West Bengal institutions in Darjeeling, such as police stations, libraries, and schools. At other times, the struggle was between the GNLF and India's Central Reserve Police Force (CRPF). The GNLF attacked and sometimes even decapitated its opponents, while the Bengal and national governments officially invoked the Terrorism and Disruptive Activities Act, which justified the CRPF's arresting, shooting, and beating of GNLF members, often leaving burned villages in their wake.[21] Everything in the hills—education, transportation, commerce—ground to a halt. Even tea production slowed. Many plantations "closed," meaning that all work stopped and workers did not receive wages or in kind benefits, and the rest experienced drastically decreased production. Strikes and destroyed or otherwise militarized roads prevented wages, food rations, wood, and other materials from getting to tea plantation workers. They were stranded, but in the midst of over two years of violence, tea pluckers on open plantations had to continue plucking.[22]

Because of the hold the Communist politicians and labor unions had on plantations, a great deal of the Gorkhaland violence took place in and around them.[23] The GNLF and the CRPF carried out nighttime assaults on plantation villages, looking for Communist union sympathizers. Women at home with their children were raped and forced outside of their homes to watch them burn to the ground, and men who could not escape into the jungle were dragged off, sometimes to be disappeared. Other times, dead bodies or heads would later appear on display in the bazaar.

Even though tea planters were the objects of previous Gorkha agitations in Darjeeling in the 1950s and 1960s, planters actually backed the 1986–88 movement, in hopes of breaking the hold the Communist Party and its powerful labor unions had on the region. Partly as a result of this support, Ghisingh made linguistic and national recognition, rather than workers' rights or plantation reform, a central pillar of his eventual reconciliation deal with the West Bengal and Central Indian governments. In place of a separate state, a tripartite peace agreement between the state of West Bengal, the central government, and GNLF led in 1988 to the formation of the Darjeeling Gorkha Hill Council (DGHC), a semi-autonomous regional administrative arm of the West Bengal state government. The formation of the Hill Council effectively ended multiparty politics in the hills. The DGHC, headed by Ghisingh, would become the dominant local political force in Darjeeling for the next twenty years. It had the power to levy taxes and regulate transportation and infrastructure, but no power whatsoever over the plantation system.[24] Ghisingh promised at the time of the 1988 reconciliation—and continually throughout the 1980s and 1990s and the early years of the new century—that statehood remained the ultimate goal of the GNLF, but faith in his leadership had waned by the time my fieldwork began.

In the early years of the twenty-first century, ethnic and caste organizations became increasingly powerful on the Darjeeling political stage. These ethnic organizations (*samāj*) began mobilizing to gain "Scheduled Tribe" status. At this time, Ghisingh was an ardent supporter of Sixth Schedule, a form of affirmative action for all ethnic groups in Darjeeling, including various Nepali *jāti*s, or groups (Tamang, Gurung, Lepcha, Rai, Limbu, Sherpa).[25] Under the Sixth Schedule of the

Indian constitution, groups can be approved for government-sponsored community development. With Scheduled status (either Scheduled Tribe [ST], Scheduled Caste [SC], or Other Backward Classes [OBC]), marginalized "tribes" and "castes" are "scheduled" for advancement through the provision of quotas for seats in government jobs or schools. Many Darjeeling town residents, but only a small fraction of tea plantation workers, were active in their ethnic *samāj*.[26] For Sixth Schedule supporters in Darjeeling, according to anthropologist Townsend Middleton, ST and SC status were about more than quotas—they were about forging a sense of belonging in India.[27] Middleton explains that in the middle of the first decade of the new century, there was popular sentiment that the Gorkhaland movement of the 1980s had failed.

But in October 2007, calls for Gorkhaland were renewed. Bimal Gurung, well known as Ghisingh's deputy and chief *gunda* (thug), parleyed the success of Prashant Tamang, a constable in the Kolkata Police who was born in Darjeeling, in the *Indian Idol* singing competition. To marshal Gorkha patriotism and revive the Gorkhaland movement, Gurung called on all Gorkhas, those in Darjeeling and those working and living further away, to phone and text their support for Prashant Tamang, whose mother worked in a luxury hotel in Darjeeling. If a Gorkha won *Indian Idol*, Gurung maintained, the belonging of Gorkhas in India would be affirmed.[28] Ghisingh offered nominal support for the *Indian Idol* campaign, but Gurung made it his personal crusade. When Prashant Tamang won the competition, Gurung used the success of the campaign to argue that Ghisingh's long tenure at the head of the DGHC had diluted his enthusiasm for the advancement of the separatist cause and the development of Darjeeling. And, as Gurung and GJMM activists claimed in rallies, the Sixth Schedule, by dividing people in the region into many distinct "tribal" or ethnic groups, precluded the possibility of a united, panregional Gorkhaland. Ghisingh, they argued from the stage of Chowrasta, had "sold the dreams of the Gorkhas and Gorkhaland lovers."

In January 2008, when I arrived in Darjeeling to begin my second fieldwork stay, the only mention I heard of the Sixth Schedule came in rallies on the Chowrasta stage, where processions of chanting women would cry: "Sixth Schedule, go back! Go back! Go back!" coupled with shouts of "Death to Subhash Ghisingh!" and "Long live Bimal Gurung!" I tried to engage tea workers and town residents in discussions of the Sixth Schedule, but the topic was taboo outside of outright denouncement. Furthermore, it seemed that for plantation workers, Sixth Schedule concessions were not as politically salient as the promise of Gorkhaland. Workers with whom I spoke had vague understandings of the concessions of the Sixth Schedule and what it would do for them. The legally and bureaucratically fraught affirmative action process seemed less comprehensible than the promises of a free, separate, and prosperous Gorkha state. This disconnect was partly because the work of Sixth Schedule recognition was done largely in town *samāj* offices, spaces to which rank-and-file tea workers had little access given their work responsibilities (and their gender). More affluent town men dominated the ethnic *samājs*. When workers *were* engaged in ethnic *samāj* politics, they were called upon to dress up and dance traditional dances. They described these events as great fun, but they did not view them as a form of political action.

In February 2008, less than a month after I arrived in the field, Gurung had managed to oust Ghisingh from the Hill Council and drive him out of Darjeeling with threats to his life and property. Gurung and his party, the Gorkha Janmukti Morcha (GJMM), began holding regular rallies in Chowrasta. At the rallies, Gurung and his deputies denounced Ghisingh and the Sixth Schedule, instead calling for separate statehood. The transition from GNLF to GJMM rule in Darjeeling was less of a rupture than one might expect, however. Gurung did not change the unitary authority of Gorkha leadership or the Hill Council. Like Ghisingh before him, Gurung and his party also enforced their authority with threats and acts of violence, attacking or vandalizing the property of those who did not acknowledge the supremacy of the GJMM in Darjeeling politics. As one cynical Darjeeling resident told me over a cup of tea on a sunny afternoon in Chowrasta: "It's just old wine in new bottles."

SERVICE AND LAND

Starting in 2007, in public rallies and strikes in Chowrasta, Gurung and his supporters began articulating a new vision of Gorkhaland. Gurung argued that the quest for "tribal" recognition was dividing the region's Nepali majority, whose common experiences—particularly of work in tea plantations and of service in the British and Indian armies—gave them a unified justification for regional sovereignty. In the early days of the second Gorkhaland agitation, Gurung and his supporters reframed Gorkha identity in terms of a shared history of service and care. Opportunities for work among Nepalis in Darjeeling had long been limited to military, domestic, and agricultural labor, overseen by the British and later by Bengali elites. Yet a history of service, while predicated on subjugation, also implied a history of care. The rallies in Chowrasta in those early months of the second Gorkhaland agitation were filled with metaphorical and historical appeals to a population united not only in its marginalization, but also in a cultivated affect toward the place it called home.

Images of plants and soil dominated those 2008 rallies. Mindful of the association of the first Gorkhaland agitation with violence, politicians sought to strike a softer tone. As one politician put it, railing against the "divisive" tribal rhetoric of the Sixth Schedule movement: "We are flowers of different colors born on the same hill. . . . I say, we are the garlands made from different flowers and different colors *growing in the same soil*. . . . We are flowers ourselves, and we have been strung together on the same thread. So, in the same way, in the entire area of our Gorkhaland, we are like a garland of flowers with different colors, living together, with unity as our prime aim." The floral imagery conveyed two distinct messages. At one level, the references to "soil" are primordial, tracing Gorkha identity to the land itself. At another level, the references to people "having been strung together" indicates an indirect acknowledgment of the historical and involuntary proximity of Rais, Limbus, Gurungs, Tamangs, and other Nepali groups (not to mention Lepchas, Tibetans, and other residents) in the Darjeeling hills. Gorkhas were attempting to claim rights to the region based upon a cultivated belonging.

On a rainy monsoon afternoon in the center of Darjeeling town, a GJMM politician screamed through a crackly PA system to a sea of men and women huddled under bright umbrellas: "*Dāju, bhāi, didi, bahiniharu-lāi* [Older and younger brothers and sisters]! . . . We were the servants of the British, their gardeners and maids. . . . And we made their famous tea—Darjeeling tea—the most expensive tea in the world. Even today, despite corruption by Indian businessmen who took the tea industry and the whole town of Darjeeling. . . . Darjeeling does not belong to Bengal. It belongs to us! We built it! Our grandfathers built the railroads and planted the tea. . . . We Gorkhas are the *sons of the soil* [in English]."

Banging on the podium with his closed fist for emphasis, the next speaker echoed his fellow politician: "We should not remain in Bengal. Kolkata takes, takes, takes. They take our tea and they auction it in Kolkata, but that money never comes up here. . . . The British replanted bushes and invested in medical facilities, but these Indian owners do not reinvest." This speaker, voicing the concerns of many other politicians and residents, went on to talk about the important role that Gurkha regiments played in the making of both the British Empire and of Darjeeling: "We served in the British Army. We are the famous and brave Gurkhas. Bengal cannot take that from us, but they did take our land. We were the servants of the British; we built this land and this tea industry. Darjeeling tea is our tea; Gorkhaland is our dream, our destiny."

Gorkha leaders, many of whom had grown up on tea plantations, drew deftly on colonial history and the British cultural taxonomy of labor (fig. 23).[29] In my field recordings, the Gorkhaland activists' claims to being "sons of the soil" were commonplace. This particular phrase had several connotations. First, it linked the political rhetoric of the second Gorkhaland agitation to that of the first, when notions of deep connections to place were the justification for the GNLF's rejection of the 1950 Peace and Friendship Treaty as an exclusionary statute. Second, the phrase referenced relationships between Nepali workers, British planters and the Darjeeling landscape. Primordialist language and references to rootedness in "soil" or land have been documented in other Indian subnational movements, but in the second Gorkhaland movement, such cries oscillated between referenc-

FIGURE 23. The Gorkha Janmukti Morcha (GJMM) flag on the Chowrasta stage at a rally. Photo by author.

ing the timeless, ancestral belonging of Nepalis in Darjeeling and the historical construction of the Darjeeling landscape by Gorkha laborers.[30] "Sons of the soil," an evocative English phrase, positioned Gorkhas as both the indigenous inhabitants *and* the rightful inheritors of Darjeeling. In the early twenty-first century, the history of the tea industry entered Gorkhaland political discourse in a more overt way than it had in the 1980s, when Ghisingh reached a tacit detente with the tea planters who, like Ghisingh, saw the Marxist unions backed by the West Bengal government as enemies.

In a 2008 rally, a representative of the GJMM student wing put it this way: "I am ... a Gorkha son. I have few words to share with you. In 1835, Lord Campbell planted tea in Aloobari. But our mothers and fathers were the ones to sweat in the plantation. Today, Gorkhas are there in every regiment of the Indian Army. Many soldiers die every year. But what an irony today, the same Gorkhas ask for protection they are trampled. They are kicked and spurned. This is the oppressive regime of the Bengal government. Today we have been deprived of our fundamental rights."

Another student, also speaking of military service, joined in this line of argument, associating West Bengal with the British, and then accusing Bengal of being *more* exploitative than the colonial oppressor: "The state government uses us. As a result, we can see no development here. Our uncles had been involved in the world wars. *The British knew their value.* But today, the Bengal government accuses us by saying that we are not Indians!"

These overtly historical calls for Gorkha sovereignty appear tinged with a sense of unrequited reciprocity. In this narrative, West Bengal has failed to reciprocate Gorkha care for land and nation. Gorkhas traced their belonging in India to men's military labor and women's tea labor. The servile but patriotic military man and the toiling, motherly woman were the key human anchors of the movement. For them, justice, through Gorkhaland, could right the moral economic relationships between tea plantation land, labor, and management, and between nation, soldier, and citizen.

At Kopibari Tea Estate, I interviewed Kamala, a retired tea worker, and her son, Rupesh. While we were drinking tea one afternoon, I asked them to describe what they meant by "justice." Kamala defined justice through control over land. As she told me, "The plantation—the factory and other things—will be the owner's, but the *whole land* becomes ours. . . . That means the *soil* is ours too . . . at that time Darjeeling tea will become *Gorkha* Darjeeling tea."

Reminded of the "sons of the soil" rhetoric I had seen on the Chowrasta stage, I asked Kamala and Rupesh to elaborate. She continued:

> *Kamala:* When we get our land, we can say that we are Indians. Land is important for us. . . . Without it, we are not regarded as Indians. We say that we are Gorkhas—Gorkha Nepali from the British time—who came a long time ago, but stayed here. Everyone got their separate state. Why don't we have our state? . . . When the Britishers left they had given the state only to us Nepali. At that time, our leader could not rule by himself, he had taken the help from Bengal and suddenly the leader died and then Bengal said: "Darjeeling is ours."
>
> *Rupesh:* We died for India. We died on every border of this country. That is why we want our own land—this land—the land we built.
>
> *Kamala:* That is why we want justice! . . . Those who protected the country should have rights. . . . It's very important, but sometimes I feel sad. We are in India. Yes, we are Indians. India is our country. But we Gorkhas live on the borders of India. Whenever India is being attacked by its enemies, at that time the Gorkhas come forward. So why don't we get Gorkhaland?

A GJMM central committee member, also mounting a critique of the West Bengal government, spoke of a common history of migration:

> We [Gorkhas] have lived here for over a hundred years now. When the people from Bengal come here, they just have one suitcase but when they leave they have loads of things that they accumulate while they are here. What I see here is that the officers of the government of Bengal take advantage. They are fooling us and ripping us off. . . . The ministers of Bengal are calling the Gorkhas separatists. Who were the people who separated Bangladesh and who created East Pakistan? Was it us? You people

were the ones who created East Pakistan. You all must leave. We were born in India and we will bring our Gorkhaland home!

For tea workers and their families, rights to Gorkhaland—indeed, justice itself—stemmed from the same set of moral economic obligations that connected workers, management, and the tea plantation landscape.

For plantation laborers, separating the history of Gorkha labor and migration from belonging made little sense, yet these historical associations were consistently refuted by primordial appeals from powerful Gorkhaland activists. In fact, when I interviewed A. J. Lama, the president of the GJMM tea plantation labor union, he avoided admitting that Nepalis *ever* migrated to work on Darjeeling plantations. Instead, he centered his appeal to Gorkhaland on the story, which I recounted in chapter 1, of Darjeeling's brief time as a part of the kingdom of Nepal (even if Rais, Limbus, Tamangs, Sherpas, and Gurungs didn't reside there).[31]

> *Sarah:* It is said that Darjeeling tea is different because in the British opinion, people from Nepal were good at plucking; they were good at work.
>
> *Lama:* People from Nepal?
>
> *Sarah:* Yes, the ones the *sardārs* brought here.
>
> *Lama:* No! *This very thing* [tea, land] *came with us!*
>
> *Sarah:* Yes, and . . .
>
> *Lama:* This [tea] came with the land, and *we* came with the land, too.
>
> *Sarah:* Ah.
>
> *Lama:* People alone didn't come.
>
> *Sarah:* They didn't?
>
> *Lama:* This was all already in Nepal. The whole land was Nepal. If it was all in Nepal, then it should be returned.

Lama actively disputed the history of labor migration, but he was correct that at one time Darjeeling was a part of the Kingdom of Nepal. That the region passed to the control of Sikkim before becoming a British colony was not important in this retelling. When I spoke to workers about GJMM leaders' denial that tea workers were recruited to Darjeeling by the British through *sardārs* (in the system I described in chapter 2), they chuckled and explained that he had to say this "to be legitimate."[32] Establishing a primordial connection between Gorkhas, land, and tea, they insisted, was crucial in the larger field of Indian subnational politics. The denial of the history of Nepali labor migration to Darjeeling was a deliberate political strategy to naturalize Indian Nepalis' claims of belonging in India. Like GI marketers, Gorkha politicians publicly traded on the perceived "naturalness" of Gorkhas in the tea landscape. Similarly, while Gorkha politicians used primordialist language in political theatrics, the local success of these performances relied upon a consent from Darjeeling residents that was based as much on a sense of historical time as on timeless belonging.

EMBODYING TRADITION

If one were to visit Chowrasta on a day in October between 2007 and 2009, one might mistake the scene for something out of a Darjeeling GI film: throngs of Nepalis, most of them tea plantation workers, most of them women, all dressed in "traditional" Nepali clothing (fig. 24). The float pictured in figure 24 appeared at a rally held on Phulpati in October 2009, the seventh day of the Dashain, the yearly month-long celebration of the Hindu pantheon, marked by feasts, family visitation, and parades. Dashain was part of the Pujas, a time of year when people across India trekked to the homes of their maternal kin.[33] To mark the occasion, Gurung and the GJMM mandated that all Darjeeling residents dress in "traditional clothing." For Darjeeling Gorkhas, this meant *chaubandi cholo* for women and *daurā sural* for men. A *chaubandi cholo* is a wrapped and tied top with a *sārī*-like wrapped skirt bottom, usually made out of cotton in a red and white geometric print. A *daurā sural* is a solid colored long shirt and fitted pants combination, resembling a *kurtā*. In tea plantation villages, enthusiasm for this mandate varied. Ardent supporters of the movement insisted that every household send at least one member to the celebrations. Younger female tea workers were often the most enthusiastic about doing so. For unmarried women, the appeals to "tradition" were less of a motivating factor than the chance to dress in formal clothing, dance, and gossip with friends. Like the soccer matches organized by the village "big men" (*thulo mānchhe*), Gurung's exponentially larger Puja celebrations had a strong social attraction for tea workers.

At the launch of the traditional dress mandate at the GJMM "cultural program" in October 2008, one of the central committee members explained:

> We really have to show the West Bengal and central government our cultural dress for our identity. This is the guidance of our president of the GJMM. We are wearing *chaubandi cholo* and *daurā sural* and *topī* under his guidance for our identity. And for this, Kanchenjunga must be proud of us. We are wearing our cultural dress not to show to our own people but to show to the Bengal government because we want to be free from the domination of Bengal. . . . In the area of Gorkhaland, we are not Rai, not Chettri, not Bahun, not Magar, and we are not Tamang, but we are all Gorkhas. We don't need to wear our own *jāti*'s dress. Therefore, we request to all Gorkhaland lovers not to confuse themselves. . . . We should not confuse ourselves in wearing our own cultural dress, because in our country's history, Gorkhas never thought about profit and loss. . . . Gorkhas had always sacrificed their blood and sweat.

FIGURE 24. "Let Us Protect Our Heritage," a float at a 2009 GJMM rally. It depicts the Toy Train, a whitewater raft, mountaineering, two leaves, and a bud of tea, the Clock Tower (hidden behind the woman dressed in a *chaubandi cholo*), and a red panda. Photo by author.

These garments were symbolic of the united Hindu Nepal, but when they were first mandated during the 2008 Pujas, one was hard pressed to find a *chaubandi* in Darjeeling. To supply demand for the 2008 traditional dress mandates, seamstresses and tailors were brought to town from Nepal.

Bimal Gurung himself, drawing again on floral and agricultural (even gardening) imagery, made the case for traditional dress:

> Nowadays people are using chemicals and destroying food. *Saipatri* [marigold] and *makhamali* [a red or purple flower] grow in both the hills and in the plains. But now, we are not able to hear the rhythm of *saipatri* and *makhamali* because they are disappearing. We are not thinking about *why* these things are happening. We are now wearing traditional clothes, but people's dignity is being degraded because women are not able to put flowers like *saipatri* and *makhamali* in their hair. Why are these things disappearing from the hills? Why are they getting destroyed? We have to think about this matter. We are not noticing these things and because of this, the Bengal government is dominating us. Nowadays we are compelled to buy *saipatri phul* from Siliguri because it is disappearing from the hills. We planted *saipatri* and *makhamali* in Darjeeling, but it is disappearing. So we have to know what is the mystery behind

this. Our intellectual people should know this. Why these flowers are not willing to blossom or flourish in the hills. . . . Now, Bengal is trying to encourage people against each other [through Sixth Schedule], and they are trying to destroy us like they are doing to the *makhamali* and *saipatri*. We are all enjoying our festival by wearing traditional clothes, but the history has awakened our past. So we have to keep it in a proper manner. And we should be able to utilize them. . . . Flowers like *saipatri* and *makhamali* are disappearing but we Janmukti Morcha will carry on with the program to wear *duarā sural* and *chaubandi cholo* from the 7th of October to the 7th of November. Those people who are not willing to wear traditional clothes should understand that it is like selling their own dignity and respect . . . selling them to Bengal and the central government.[34]

Paradoxically, while the GI advertisements overtly sold the images of "traditional Nepali" bodies to tea buyers, the GJMM saw its celebration of the traditional body as an anti-exploitation measure. In this, the traditional dress campaign betrays a fluidity, rather than a rupture, between calls for Sixth Schedule recognition and Gorkhaland. In rallies, the Sixth Schedule was flatly rejected as a "divisive" measure that would preclude the achievement of Gorkhaland. But ethnically specific clothing, *khukuris*, and dance became central to being a Gorkha and a "Gorkhaland lover." The calls for "traditional" clothing reminded many tea workers of the diverting invitations to dress and dance during Sixth Schedule activities organized by the *samāj* (fig. 25).

As I explained in chapter 3, such garments were not symbols with which older tea workers readily identified. Longtime residents, forced to don "traditional" garb, would joke to one another, "Go get me a gas cylinder!" Before 2008, *daurā surals* were associated with male transmigrant laborers while *chaubandis* were the quintessential dress of elderly women back in Nepal. These laborers often found work carrying liquid propane tanks in and out of villages, where jeep access was limited or nonexistent. During the 2008 Pujas, a new joke arose. It was said that the owners of pay toilets were making extra money, because the garments took so long to take on and off. One-rupee "short" visits to the toilet were fast becoming two-rupee "long" visits. Arguments between needy toilet visitors and toilet attendants became commonplace in town.

GJMM politicians consistently cited two reasons for the wardrobe: first, to show to the rest of India that Gorkhas were a united people, distinct from others in West Bengal; and second, to regulate the behavior of wayward younger Gorkhas. The Pujas were a high tourist season in Darjeeling, when an influx of Bengalis from the plains and international tourists would visit the hotels, parks, and tea plantations. The GJMM used the occasion to display Gorkha unity and discipline. "If you wear a *daurā sural*," Bimal Gurung said in a rally, "You will not drink and smoke. . . . You will read and study . . . and be reminded that there is work to be done for your land."

FIGURE 25. *Daurā sural* and *topī* (with *khukuri* pin). Photo by author.

Tea workers knew that such dress was part of a larger language of Indian sub-nationalism: a set of cultural performances needed to "gain legitimacy," in female tea workers' words, in Indian politics. Just as traditional clothing helped substantiate the Tea Board's claims about Darjeeling tea's natural place in the region, clothing became part of the work of national legitimation, but workers maintained that a history of service work was also important. While traditional dress emphasized imagined unity and moral discipline, the float in figure 24 highlighted key symbolic aspects of the Darjeeling *built* environment.[35] The Darjeeling Himalayan Railway, or "Toy Train," constructed by migrant Nepalis, carried tea down to the plains for transport on to England. River rafting and mountain climbing, pictured at the center of the float, were popular tourist activities that capitalized on the rugged mountain landscape. The image of the raft complements that of the red panda, the iconic endangered species of the Eastern Himalayas. Nepali men, whose ancestors worked with the British as hunting and expedition guides, now served as trekking guides, hiking up the mountains of the Himalayan interior with international outdoor adventure tourists.[36] Darjeeling native Tenzin Norgay, along with Edmund Hillary, was the first to summit Mount Everest. Locals celebrated Norgay's birthday and marked the rock where he trained. Norgay grew up in a Sherpa *busti* adjacent to Aloobari, the oldest tea plantation in Darjeeling. Behind the *chau-bandi*-clad woman is the "Clock Tower," the home of the Darjeeling municipal offices and icon of British architecture. Finally, the tea leaf—the iconic two leaves and a bud—sat as a reminder of the area's real economic engine.

"BRINGING GORKHALAND HOME": CARE, MASCULINITY, AND THE TEA PLANTATION SYSTEM

We have the tea gardens here, but why is the tea auction and the Tea Board in Kolkata? All the companies are in Kolkata. . . . You know why this is? This is because the political elites in Bengal believe that Darjeeling should always be kept by them alone, like a God, right? . . . And they have kept Darjeeling, Dooars and Siliguri as a colony. Otherwise why would we have the tea plantations here? We have our laborers here, and we shed the blood and sweat. But the companies are in Kolkata, the auctions are in Kolkata, and the Tea Board is there. If we have our own state, then automatically the auction, the Tea Board, and the companies will come up here. So we must think about this as broadly as we can.

DR. M. P. LAMA, SPEAKING AT THE DARJEELING DISTRICT AND DOOARS INTELLECTUAL FORUM, JULY 2008

Be conscious, save Darjeeling tea!

MOTTO, DARJEELING TEA MANAGEMENT TRAINING CENTRE

Alongside claims to linguistic and cultural heritage, the second Gorkhaland agitation—at least in its early days—grappled with its complex material heritage. The party's 2009 manifesto, "Why Gorkhaland?" identified the deterioration of tea plantations, the "major source of sustenance" for Gorkhas, as an intentional act of discrimination. "The Government," reads the manifesto, "has made no concerted effort to reopen the large number of sick and closed tea gardens." For at least some Gorkha activists, reform and revitalization of the tea plantation system was one of the main potential benefits of separate statehood. Between late 2008 and early 2009, the GJMM attempted to use tea plantation reform to harness and redirect long-standing ideas about Gorkha (particularly male Gorkha) aptitudes for service. As I argued in chapter 2, tea plantation labor had long been gendered female, but this meant that male residents were constantly in need of work outside plantations. The image of the wayward Gorkha male, with a possible propensity to violence, was of concern to Gorkha politicians and tea planters alike.

In 2009, I sat on the verandah of the Darjeeling Planters Club with two senior planters and discussed problems on "the gardens." One planter explained what he saw as "the real problem" of the plantations: "It's the men. They have nothing to do. They sit around all day and drink and then they come into town and get up on that stage [at Chowrasta] and talk about how they demand their own state. . . . It does not make any sense; they think that they deserve this and this and this. That is the problem with Darjeeling—it is these Gorkha men. At the drop of a hat, they will hold up a *khukuri* to your throat and demand more."

"That's a little brash," the second planter interjected. He explained that the difference between the modern period and the colonial past was that there were no communists in Darjeeling during the "days of the Britishers." This second planter started in tea before 1973 and the enactment of the Foreign Exchange Regulation Act (FERA), which ended the control British companies held over the region. He joined a British company after college and came up to Darjeeling after a couple of years in Assam. He explained, "When the British were here, they ran their gardens like fiefdoms, but they kept the men under control. . . . They brought in army recruiters to take the smarter ones and they sent others to town as porters or to the forests as wood cutters. . . . They were productive and there was much more respect." Then he turned to me and said: "They called it paternalism for a reason, dear."

The second planter's comments about respect provide a window into the perspective of the planter class on the plantation moral economy, but his companion disagreed that "respect" came only from control over men.

The first planter placed his teacup down on its saucer, which rattled as he spoke: "But supplies were so inexpensive back then. . . . Planters cannot provide all these things anymore; the workers have to do it themselves. The plantations are no longer that remote."

Planters I interviewed in Darjeeling felt that the mid-twentieth century "crisis" in the tea industry came from their own inability to properly "manage" the male population on the gardens. Some suggested that "too many males" on the garden created unrest, both on the plantation and in regional politics. At the same time, Indian planters exalted British colonial-era planters for finding work for Nepali men and women on and off the gardens. By providing supplies and jobs, British planters created a stable system. Some acknowledged that the plantation system was akin to a "fiefdom"—the feudal land tenure system readily associated with peasant agriculture—but most planters I interviewed contended that in the colonial era, stability on the plantation came from a symbiosis between the tea industry and the government, military, and other economic enterprises ancillary to it. Planters could provide "facilities" (food, land, medical care, schooling) to those who worked for them, but their relatives depended upon employment in town, in the military, in forestry, or in construction. A racist taxonomy of labor couched "Gurkha" men and women as suited in different ways to on-plantation and off-plantation labor, but in the second Gorkhaland agitation, the complaints of students and scholar-activists like M. P. Lama, quoted above, blamed not British racism but *Bengali* mismanagement for the "sickness" of tea plantations.

In conversation and even in public political rallies, Gorkha men assented to the characterization of them as industrious but sometimes violent and dangerous.

Gorkhaland leaders, like the planters I interviewed, were well aware that there were few jobs for Nepali men in Darjeeling, and that male unemployment was a key motivation for their rank-and-file supporters. The (sometimes educated) unemployed male was a central figure not only of Bengali elites' racial anxieties but also of the Gorkhaland agitation. To support male Gorkhas, the GJMM launched several campaigns aimed at what the party called "development." For the party, development meant, in large part, finding work and controlling wayward Gorkha boys through job training, particularly in the tea industry. These strategies hinged upon a desire to harness the sometimes "unruly," but nonetheless "power- ful," fierce, and loyal Gorkha male subject that British colonial racial taxonomy constructed, and that Indian-born Darjeeling residents both feared and respected. Job-training strategies underwritten by the GJMM became the party's way of inte- grating colonially derived male labor roles into its subnationalist vision. The par- ty's vision of the new Gorkha man, then, relied on colonial ideals. In the discourse of "inheritance" outlined in public political rhetoric, Gorkhas saw themselves— men in particular—as taking on *new* roles, as managers and leaders. Rather than questioning the tea plantation structure or the racial association of Gorkha men with a penchant for violence, Gorkha activists tried to insert themselves in new ways within that structure and to redirect those racial associations.

From the colonial period to the present, the ability of Gorkha men to advance in the tea plantation economy has been severely limited. In a British taxonomy of labor, Nepali men were suited to both manual labor (clearcutting, road build- ing, and factory work) and army service, but the British almost never allowed Nepalis to work in management positions on plantations. If there were non-Brit- ish managers on plantations in colonial days, these were usually Bengali, Pun- jabi, or of other non-Nepali ethnic extraction. This exclusion continued after the takeover of plantations by Indian companies in the postcolonial period. Gorkha activists saw the forced out-migration of Gorkha males as one of the principal crimes of postcolonial plantation management. In the absence of any investment in infrastructure males had little choice but to leave the district in search of work.

In the summer of 2008, former Nepali assistant plantation managers, with sup- port from the GJMM, founded the Darjeeling Tea Management Training Centre. Modeled on the tea schools at North Bengal University and at the Assam Agricul- tural University, which I described in chapter 4, the Training Centre's goal was to prepare young Gorkha men to work as tea plantation managers. As the President of the center declared in July 2008, echoing the words of the "Why Gorkhaland?" manifesto, "The tea gardens in Darjeeling are in a deplorable condition. They need love. To get back our lost glory is . . . one of our objectives."

The Training Centre's goal was to prepare Gorkha boys to work as managers on tea plantations. Gurung, in a classic display of unilateral political power, permitted

the center to be housed in a stately old "holiday home" on the main road to Lebong, where British colonial officials and tea barons had once lived. The home was
technically the property of the state of West Bengal, and though Gurung had no
official authority to seize it, no one contested the move.

Gurung was named "school patron" to the Training Centre, while another party
cadre was named "legal advisor." The GJMM was now in control of all the municipal funds for the maintenance of Darjeeling, as well as millions of rupees allocated
for disaster relief (during my fieldwork there was a major cyclone as well as massive landslides, for which the central and state governments dispatched funds). As
a patron, the GJMM president was a nominal supporter of the school, though the
extent to which the party was a financial supporter of the school was never dis-
closed. The center's president rightly assumed that if potential managers were
deemed to be directly affiliated with the GJMM, they would never gain employment on the plantations of Darjeeling, all of which were owned and operated by
non-Gorkhas.

At the inauguration of the Management Training Centre in July 2008, the center's president drew on plantation history as he outlined its purposes:

> The reason why we are starting such a tea management institute in Darjeeling is out
> of necessity, because since 1820 . . . planting and cultivating was done by our ances-
> tors only. But our people are still laborers, and they [non-Nepalis] are still occupying
> the executive posts. But today most of our [Nepali] young brothers and sisters are
> educated. They are all competent. Our brothers and sisters can outshine the outsid-
> ers. We need such people. So if we open such an institute here, then such youths will
> get an opportunity. The [non-Nepali] outsiders just come and make money. They do
> their jobs and quit. Then they go to another garden. But if we have someone from
> here, he will love his place. And if he loves this place, the tea garden will be well.

The president invoked not only Darjeeling's colonial history but also what I have
called a plantation "moral economy," whereby Nepalis "cared" and "loved" the land
on which they worked, in exchange for facilities and—in the Gorkha rendering—
an inherited right to increased responsibility and control over that land.

The president was one of the few Gorkhas who had succeeded in becoming a
tea manager, working on a small, remote garden on the Nepal border. In his classes,
he told his forty-five students to be more than economic stewards: "You should not
only think about the people in the tea garden but . . . the future of the tea garden."
The tea school mimicked the university courses I also attended at North Bengal
University and the Birla Institute in Kolkata. Courses of study included Field Management; Nursery (the propagation of new tea bushes); Maintaining the Old Tea
Bushes; Cultivation (including weeding, hoeing, forking, and irrigation); Manufacturing and Tasting; Office (budgeting and record keeping); and Driving. Labor
Relations comprised another key course category. The president explained, "Labor

always sees the management as its enemy. That ruins the relationship for everyone. So we have to work toward repairing their relationship and to bring them together. Their relationship affects the working of the garden. So, I think only our local boys can mend this relationship, in my opinion. They can manage their own household matters better. . . . We are looking for someone who understands our pain." Gorkha managers-in-training thus had a practical goal, to get work that kept them in Darjeeling, and also a moral goal, to right what they and their teachers saw as a deteriorated relationship between labor and management. Neither the party nor the Training Centre desired to overturn the plantation system. In fact, they envisioned improvement via a return to the "lost glory" of mutual care between labor, management, and the agro-environment.

Tea Management Centre students came largely from tea garden villages. Their mothers, aunts, and sisters worked as tea pluckers—the āmā (mothers) to Darjeeling's tea bush nāni (children). Even Darjeeling Gorkha men who were able to get work with tea companies found it impossible to stay close to home. For example, my friend Sanjay, who grew up on a tea plantation in Kurseong and managed to finish university, was one of the only Nepalis in his class to find employment with a tea company. When he requested a posting in Darjeeling, he was denied and dispatched to Assam. His superiors explained to him: "Nepali women would never take orders from one of their own." After a few years in Assam, Sanjay took his saved earnings and returned to Darjeeling, where he opened up a cyber café. The ranks of Training Centre students were filled with such stories: young Nepali men who managed to find educational and work opportunities, but whose skills actually pushed them away from their homes. The discourse of the Gorkhaland movement, which emphasized the connection between Nepalis and the "soil" of Darjeeling, was especially resonant with these aspiring tea managers: they belonged in Darjeeling.

The center wanted not only to improve labor-management relations but also relations between people and plants. The president liked to tell stories about these relationships:

> I sometimes feel that even the bushes here recognize [their] own people. They may say—"Ah! Look. My own relative is here. He knows me and will look after me." When outsiders come, they may say—"Look! Here he comes to suck the life out of me," and they may get startled. If they had life they would have said something like this.
>
> Let's take an example. One man had some problem in his eye. So he was very worried. He did many things to treat the eye. He went to South India and to Delhi. He spent thousands of rupees, yet he did not get well. . . . And at last a doctor from a tea garden cured him. He found a small splinter in his eye. So he took it out. The big doctors had thought that he has some big problem. We too do not have a big problem. They think of all these big schemes to take care of the garden, when all they need is something simple and basic. Our local people have been taking care of the garden for ages. They can do it, but they have not been given any opportunity so far.

There was a boy who worked in a sweatshop—he got an appointment as the assistant manager [of a tea plantation]. Then there were few boys who were working at the hardware store—they too have become assistant mangers [of plantations]. These people have never seen tea bushes. But our people who have been raised in the plantation since birth still have no chance. But we believe that if we have local people, the lost glory will come back. This is our prime motive.

Gorkha managers asserted the connections to the land that they had forged over generations of tea labor. In the opening ceremony, the president said: "All of us here believe that one day we will have our Gorkhaland. Then we will be the caretakers."

Since the decline of the tea industry began in the 1970s, waves of improvement projects had come and gone in Darjeeling, from biodynamic certification, to International Federation of Organic Agricultural Movements (IFOAM) "model farms," to fair trade, to Geographical Indication. As I explained in previous chapters, none has solved the problems of land degradation and continued unemployment. Aspiring Gorkha managers asserted the connections to the land they had forged over generations of tea labor as potential sources of plantation revitalization. The goal, as the president said, was a "return to lost glory." This nostalgic objective, mirrored in the Gorkha discourse of "heritage" and "sons of the soil," gave a political slant to the center's curriculum.

Beneath it all, however, was a sense that Gorkha men thrived when they cared as much for themselves and their neighbors as for the bushes. The Training Centre had a moral and disciplinary code. Smoking, drinking, and gambling among students were prohibited, and although most students were adult men, their parents were invited to discuss their courses with center staff. A nostalgic idea of the Gorkha man's need for moral discipline was woven into the GJMM's rhetoric, and enforced among men at the Tea Management Centre as well as the Gorkhaland Police, a quasi-governmental force founded in 2009. Both institutions combined self-consciously "traditional" ideas about Gorkha masculinity with a developmentalist rhetoric of community improvement. Ideas about Gorkha manhood rooted in colonial taxonomies combined with newer ideas about national autonomy and cosmopolitanism.[37]

In chapter 3, I introduced Manesh, the descendant of Nepali labor recruiters, or *sardār*s, who was something of a self-appointed wise man on his plantation. He was also an elder statesman in his neighborhood GJMM ward. When the new party formed, he eagerly took this position, he explained to me, because he had a penchant for telling moral stories. He considered himself fairly uninfluential before the formation of the new party, but he felt now that his voice (which was usually quite judgmental) could be heard. His cause in 2008 was youth alcohol consumption. Party leadership dispatched him to spread messages of social control: that the only way Gorkhaland was to be achieved was through the disciplining of young men.

Manesh proudly sent his nephew (who grew up on the same plantation that Manesh did) to the Tea Management Centre, but after the first year of courses, the center's momentum began to slow. It became clear to students that despite the zeal of their teachers (and the party that backed them), the plantations—the one element of Darjeeling that was not quite under the GJMM's control—would still not hire them.

The Darjeeling Tea Management Training Centre graduated its first class (about half of the original forty-five students) in May 2009. I did not hear much from them over the monsoon season. In September of that year, I made my way out to Lebong to check in on the progress of the second class. To my surprise, the gate was locked. I climbed over it and was greeted by a shirtless teenager brushing his teeth. He was clearly as surprised to see me as I was to see him. Knowing that some Tea Management Centre students lived in the house during the school year, I asked him, "Are you in tea management school?" (Perhaps their discipline had slipped a bit.) He responded with incredulity: "This is a barracks." He had never heard of the Tea Management Centre. He was instead a member of the Gorkhaland Police (GLP), which, sometime during the monsoon, had taken over the mansion and remained there until I left Darjeeling in May 2010. The GLP began as a group of "social workers" who were supposed to roam the town helping the elderly, cleaning parks, and watching out for inappropriate behavior, particularly public drunkenness. Response to the early recruitment advertisements was overwhelming. By mid-2009, the GLP, with the help of ex-Gurkha soldiers, had begun training young men and women not only to how to help their neighbors but also how to fight in hand-to-hand combat, to perform military-style calisthenics, and to march in formation.

FEMALE TEA LABORERS' ENGAGEMENT WITH GORKHALAND

After each rally at Chowrasta, the Nari Morcha (the GJMM's women's wing) would march out of the square, chanting in call and response (fig. 26):

> *Hāmro bas bhūmī pharkai diye . . . pharkai diye . . . pharkai diye.*[38]
> *Hāmro bas bhūmī pharkai diye . . . pharkai diye . . . pharkai diye.*
> [Our subjugated land, give it back . . . give it back . . . give it back.]
> *Hāmro māto pharkai diye . . . pharkai diye . . . pharkai diye.*
> *Hāmro māto pharkai diye . . . pharkai diye . . . pharkai diye.*
> [Our soil, give it back . . . give it back . . . give it back.]
> [In English:] *We want justice . . . justice . . . justice.*
> *We want justice . . . justice . . . justice.*

The unceremonious end of the Tea Management Centre suggested some important limitations to the Gorkhas' ability to channel affective labor into an

FIGURE 26. The Nari Morcha. Photo by author.

inclusive and caring resistance movement. While the image of the brave, loyal, and morally grounded male Gorkha represented the imaginary future envisioned by the movement, it was the suffering female tea laborer who represented Darjeeling's harsh present. The Nari Morcha were generally mothers (mostly over twenty-five years of age). According to Bimal Gurung's order, every household had to have a "Nari Morcha member" (any able-bodied older woman) present at the rallies. Though most of the female tea plantation workers with whom I worked supported the movement, few had the time or inclination to trek uphill to town for political rallies. Plantation workers were often excused from rallies that took place on weekdays, and plantations were almost never subject to general district-wide strikes (with the notable exception of a select few tea plantation strikes, like the one I described in chapter 4). Most rallies took place on Sundays, when plantation women would often send their younger daughters to attend.

I asked Manesh, the moralizing son of *sardār*s, why, in a movement that was so clearly dominated by men, the Nari Morcha played such a prominent role in the Sunday rallies (see fig. 26). "You know my wife," he told me. "What would I do without her? She keeps me organized! Nepali women are strong—much stronger

FIGURE 27. The Nari Morcha marching into Chowrasta. Photo by author.

than we are!" I suppose I agreed, as I worked with so many plucking women whose husbands were absent (many men worked away from the plantation in army regiments or in cities, remitting money home), drunk, or otherwise *budho* (old, unproductive). As I began studying the connections between Gorkhaland and women, I noted not only that the women activists of the Nari Morcha served as important political operatives but also that nonactivist women were drawn into the movement, not because of its moral and military rhetoric (and neither because they considered themselves, as Manesh intimated, moral guardians), but because they saw the promises of more jobs and plantation revitalization as a direct benefit to themselves, their children, and the future of Darjeeling (fig. 27).

At most rallies, the Nari Morcha were the first to arrive and the last to leave. They would march around town, up the hill via a circuitous route from the bazaar to Chowrasta, the town square. But their work began days before the rally began. In fact, if I wanted to know the date and time of the next rally, I asked my female friends. Nari Morcha activists were each responsible for "wards," relatively small subdivisions of Darjeeling town. Plantations were divided into "branches" (*shākhās*), usually one to two per plantation, each with its own Nari Morcha organizers. These organizers would go from house to house, or simply SMS their contacts via cell phone, reminding them that each household must have at least one family member present at the rally.

Those who did not attend would be assured of a visit from Nari Morcha organizers and their cohorts. These visits were couched as caring and concerned. My friend Omu, a storekeeper in Darjeeling town, regularly skipped the rallies. Her brother had been active in the first agitation and was held prisoner by the Indian Central Reserve Police Force, which was sent by the central government to suppress the Gorkhaland movement. Omu's brother was arrested and chained to a building just south of Chowrasta. For weeks, Omu brought him food, until the Central Reserve Police finally freed him. Shortly thereafter, Omu's brother committed suicide. Omu still believed in the idea of a separate state, but when the second agitation started, she became disillusioned. She wanted no part of the zealotry that had swept up her brother. She told me that people didn't remember the turmoil that took over the district just twenty years earlier. But when she failed to attend a rally, Nari Morcha organizers would visit. They would start by inquiring about her health and that of her mother. But conversation quickly turned to the subject of loyalty. Was Omu *not* a supporter of Gorkhaland? Did she *not* want Darjeeling's children to have a better future? This last question stung Omu particularly, because her ward organizer would quickly follow it by saying, "Oh, right. You don't have children."

The Nari Morcha promoted political discipline through a conservative, maternal ethic of caretaking—a version of the caring ethic that many women tea workers actively asserted in their descriptions of their relationships with tea bushes. For these women leaders, on plantations in particular, participation in Gorkhaland was about children and the reproduction of Darjeeling families. Plantations were sites of production and reproduction. In order to keep their houses, food rations, and other *faciliti-haru* (all the welfare structures that made the plantation livable), women felt compelled to continue plucking. Plantation jobs were passed down from generation to generation. This meant that each woman needed a child who was willing and able to stay in the plantation village both to care for her in her old age and to take her job in the field.

Women workers talked about a future of opportunities—for education and employment for their children. The desire to be "like Sikkim," the Indian state and former kingdom directly to the north of Darjeeling where Nepali was also the lingua franca, was powerful. Darjeeling residents told me that in Sikkim, the roads were free of potholes, jobs paid exponentially higher than in Darjeeling and they were plentiful, and there was access to quality primary and higher education. Early in the movement, workers were adamant that the formation of Gorkhaland would cause plantation *māliks* to be more accountable. Jethi, a worker at Kopibari, described life on the plantation under new ownership and the potentials for Gorkhaland to change owner negligence:

Sarah: What has changed since the new owner took over?

Jethi: Nothing! They just eat lots and fill up their stomach. The poor people are still poor.... There are no improvements, there is nothing.

Sarah: Do you think that anything will change in Gorkhaland, or not?

Jethi: Yeah, if we get Gorkhaland then there will be lots of improvements.

Sarah: On the tea garden?

Jethi: Yes, on the tea garden there will be lots of improvements. Because at that time our tea from here will be named as Darjeeling Gorkha tea, Darjeeling Gorkha tea.... In Gorkhaland, our children will be educated here—in Darjeeling! It'll be like Sikkim here, if we pass class ten we'll get thirty thousand rupees here.... In Gorkhaland, we will process all of the oranges, cardamom plants and many other kinds of fruits and vegetables. They are Gorkhas, but we do not benefit. And on the plantation, we'll get good money ... we will get facilities, we will get houses, we will have our own area. We will obtain lots, but the most important is Gorkhaland.

But as the movement progressed, women's visions of increased stability also waned. The references they heard in GJMM rallies to women as the suffering center of the statehood movement became hollow.

While we squatted down over a postplucking cup of tea in the late-winter sunshine near the end of 2009, close to a year after that conversation with Jethi, I asked an older female plucker at Windsor about what might change with Gorkhaland. She told me: "When we get Gorkhaland I don't think there will be any improvements in the tea garden. I think it'll be like this only in the tea garden, this is the area of the company. This is his own place, why will he give us the facilities? These days the money is more all over, but the things are expensive, so what is the use, even though there is more money?" This worker suggested that the vitality of the plantation might conflict with the vitality of the movement. Around this time, the GJMM began to abandon its support for plantation reform, and party leaders started to criticize people like the president of the Darjeeling Tea Management Training Centre and intellectuals like Madan Tamang for "confusing" the public with complex economic and social development schemes. But female tea workers were not confused. From their perspective, plantation reform and statehood had to come together. When they did not, tea workers began to question the efficacy of the movement.

This was remarkably clear on a Sunday in July 2009 when the GJMM called a special rally for tea workers—a "Rally to Give Thanks"—that coincided with the beginning of a strike, from which tea plantations were exempted. The GJMM labor unions organized processions of mostly female laborers from all of Darjeeling's plantations. These women streamed into town in shared jeeps adorned with GJMM flags to give thanks to GJMM leaders, who with the help of the right-wing

Hindu nationalist Bharatiya Janata Party (BJP), had brought the issue of Gorkhaland before parliament in Delhi. While rallies just one year earlier had routinely appealed to tea workers by reminding them of the fact that all the profits from the tea industry flowed "down the mountain" to Kolkata but never came back up, GJMM representatives in this rally only made vague statements about their vision for plantations under Gorkhaland.

The majority of the speakers, in a change from the norm, were women. A Nari Morcha leader's speech was typical of the day:

> Let's talk about the main cause of today's meeting. The movement for Gorkhaland is going in the right direction. . . . We should not think that people are not hearing our voice! We are shouting here and our voice is being heard [in the central government]. . . . We should not talk bad things about ourselves. We should be thankful today because today, even the president of India is a woman. So, we should be able to respect women. . . . Today I feel that Gorkhaland will be for real. I feel the love of Gorkhaland in my heart and soul and I think that you all are feeling the same way too. We will get Gorkhaland soon . . . We should pray for that. . . . Let us all move forward together.

The rally made no reference to tea or tea plantations. For hours, the loudspeakers blasted hopeful statements like this.

As the movement retreated into this abstract language, women tea workers became disenchanted. The gap between the plantation and the movement—a gap that, early on at least, seemed to be closing—was widening once again. Rallies began to focus, almost exclusively, on expressions of identity in dance and dress, and not the ideas about righting economic wrongs, which had garnered tea-worker support in the first place. By the end of 2009, the movement fell back onto the divisive identity politics that it initially repudiated in the Sixth Schedule. And this was for good reason. Indian subnationalist movements, which were raging across the country during the first decade of the twenty-first century, were nearly all tied to linguistic and cultural identity, not to natural resources or economic inequality. Gorkhaland followed this script. Workers wearily acknowledged that creation of difference through primordialist imaginaries was the best way to "gain legitimacy" on the national political stage.

CONCESSIONS: JUSTICE IN RUINS?

Madan Tamang was particularly critical of the GJMM's rhetoric. He would often ask supporters, "If Gorkhaland is achieved, then what?" He would ask this publically (or attempt to, though ABGL rallies were usually quashed by the GJMM), provoking people to consider how the attainment of Gorkhaland would make the substantive changes they desired. As a result, he was denounced by GJMM political leaders, who reminded their supporters that Madan had not suffered, not served, and thereby not really lived as a true Gorkha. Madan just could not understand them. Nevertheless, Madan's murder in May 2010 dealt a decisive blow to popular support for the movement.

By the next summer, the GJMM had agreed to the formation of a replacement for the Darjeeling Gorkha Hill Council (DGHC), what Gurung claimed would be a more autonomous Gorkha Territorial Administration (GTA). The GTA, headed by Gurung and resembling the Hill Council in almost every respect, was designed to act as a semi-autonomous overseeing body for the Darjeeling district within West Bengal. Few of my friends in Darjeeling, on or off plantations, were satisfied with this outcome. Despite the fact that almost everyone agreed that Madan's murder was a tragic and unjust act, the dream of Gorkhaland remained strong.

Notwithstanding the charisma of leaders like Madan Tamang, Bimal Gurung, or Subhash Ghisingh, Gorkhaland remains a salient idea for tea workers because it evokes nostalgia about the material relationships between Nepalis, the British, and the landscape that enable a distinct vision for the future. It evokes a desire for belonging in India, a place to which workers forged a connection through generations of labor. The case of Gorkhaland and the short life of its second incarnation reinforces the way in which identity in the region emerged due to the inheritance of colonially formulated ethnic taxonomies and the inherited experience of tea plantation labor. Though other anthropologists have identified such a connection,[39] including in the Indian tea industry,[40] the interface between colonial ethnic discourse and colonial labor organization in postcolonial Indian life has seemed to fade away in discussions of Indian subnationalism. The plantation was essential to everyday articulations of Gorkhaness—after all, it brought people in droves to Darjeeling in the first place—but remained the movement's biggest obstacle.

A tight connection between Gorkhas and the Darjeeling landscape was central to Gorkhaland politics. In the years since independence, Gorkha activists constantly reminded one another, their ancestors worked to make a colonial landscape a national landscape by defending India against China and Pakistan. But those border wars made the place of Nepalis in India precarious. During the same period, they worked to convert what I referred to earlier as Darjeeling's "imperial ruins" and colonially rooted enterprises (tea, timber, rubber, and cinchona) into productive *Indian* industries.[41] These ruins and resources were part of what Gorkhas referred to as their rightful "heritage," much as the plantation owners sold the "garden" as a site of "heritage." Ironically, for Gorkha activists, a *separatist* movement that took land rights as its core offered a more just means of *connection* to India, as well as a more equitable form of political and economic citizenship. Being Gorkha meant sharing a common history of work, of servitude, and of dispossession. Historically speaking, the ancestors of most people who claimed Gorkha identity were recruited to the region. How, then, could they make believable claims to Darjeeling as a "homeland"?

When it was at its most powerful and persuasive in the lives of tea workers, the Gorkhaland movement worked to convert these historical ties to land into a meaningful pretext for territorial sovereignty. Tea workers felt attracted to the movement because they wanted to keep the plantations viable. Indeed, they saw "justice" and the revitalization of the tea industry as potentially commensurate with one another. Beneath the ruins of the British experiment in tea, after all, lay the "soil" of Darjeeling. In my conversation at Kopibari with Rupesh and Kamala, they elaborated their thoughts on justice:

> *Rupesh:* Justice means that we're asking for our own land. If we get our state, our land, then we will be free.
>
> *Sarah:* So, will life be different on the tea plantation in Gorkhaland?
>
> *Kamala:* It becomes our own land.
>
> *Sarah:* But it will still be owned by the companies, no?
>
> *Kamala:* Sure, but that it is not important. The plantation—the factory and other things—will be the owner's, but the *whole land* becomes ours. . . . That means the *soil* is ours too. The owner will need to pay us. Today we get sixty rupees. At that time we will get . . . two hundred, and facilities! . . . It's like this, at that time Darjeeling tea will become *Gorkha* Darjeeling tea, because we Gorkhas are working. But the land is not the owner's; it's the government's. Right now they pay taxes to themselves on the land. In Gorkhaland, they would pay taxes to us. And they would have to provide facilities. . . . They will do it; otherwise they cannot have their big *bisnis* here. Darjeeling has its name for tea.

"Darjeeling" had its name for tea, but Gorkhaland had its name for people like Kamala and Rupesh, for whom "justice" entailed a recognition of the particular conditions—historical *and* natural—that kept them there. The ultimate failing of the Gorkhaland political elite was its reliance on a discourse in which the connection between Nepalis and land—indeed, between landscape and identity—existed outside of or prior to historical conditions. For tea workers, and indeed for many rank-and-file Gorkhaland activists between 2007 and 2011, to strive for justice was to acknowledge histories of service and care, the repressive and hopeful pillars of Gorkha identity.

Conclusion

Is Something Better Than Nothing?

One sunny spring afternoon, I sat in a village at Windsor with Som, an older garden supervisor and former union activist. Jamuna, a tea plantation worker, and
Maya, Jamuna's unmarried oldest daughter, joined us. In the early spring, during
the first flush, tourists and tea buyers flock to Windsor. In fact, in the weeks leading up to our conversation, tourists had stayed in the homes of the village where
Jamuna, Maya, and Som lived. Windsor's management and Mr. Roy himself had
chastised them about the poor quality of the food they prepared, the state of their
houses, and the overall quality of their hospitality. In part because of this, and in
part because of tensions about wages, described in chapter 4, relations between
Mr. Roy and the workers at Windsor were strained. As Som explained, "It's not like
we don't support him, but he says things to us like: 'Take an interest in the tea—go
inside the factory and look!' or 'It's your property. Take care of it!'"

Maya added, "He says that, but we will be scolded and chased out of the factory
if we try to go in." Mr. Roy was criticizing workers' lack of care for the state of the
plantation. A lack of the right kind of care might be construed by tourists as imply-
ing something negative about the quality of Windsor's tea. Thanks to both GI and
fair-trade marketing as well as the Gorkhaland movement, Nepali tea workers had
become used to being put on display, essentialized by dress, language, and vague
implications of primitive ecological nobility.

Som continued, "Mad! He is mad! Without brains! He cannot recognize the
good in people. They care! Of course they care! The ones that are bad, they will do
only for themselves."

The accusation that tea workers were not concerned about the state of Windsor
was offensive, given workers' sense of moral economic responsibility to the

plantation. As Maya explained, "He will always get love from all the tea garden workers, won't he? Tell me? He definitely will, because he gave us education, saw us grow. He gave publicity to the tea. Yes, he did. People like us would not have been able to bring publicity to the tea. We still love him and respect him. But he also has to trust us. But he never does."

Maya's discussion of trust indicated a sense that moral economic ties between workers and Mr. Roy remained, even if in a weakened state. Her moral economic discussion bled into a discussion of Gorkha citizenship in India, inflected with the rhetoric of Gorkhaland. She continued, "We have the right to question. Our country is a free country. In a democratic country there is right to speech. You can go to the parliament and can lecture. You can say: 'The Prime Minister of India is a cheater, he is bad, he deprives the poor.' Remember the people. We are the people and we can say it!"

Surprised at the analogy between plantation labor relations and citizen-state relations, I asked incredulously, "Can people actually do that?"

"It's very difficult," Jamuna explained, "It is *his* land, *his* plantation, and *his* seeds. And so he has to pay the taxes, right? . . . And I also work . . . but the one who makes the honey, will taste his hands [the one who works, deserves the spoils]. . . . It's hard to work and live. That is why we need our land. We need our land. That's it!"

Ad hoc evaluations of the functioning of fair trade, the increasing presence of tourists coming to taste Darjeeling tea as part of GI- or fair-trade-related tourism projects, and the potentials and shortcomings of the Gorkhaland movement drifted in and out of tea laborers' conversations about the state of what I have called the "tripartite moral economy," which undergirded their understandings of how plantations should work. When Mr. Roy accused workers at Windsor of "not caring" about the plantation, he was not only playing the role of the paternalistic, benevolent "farmer" imagined by fair trade's "hired labor" discourse, he was refusing to acknowledge the deep social investment that workers themselves made in the landscape. GI, fair trade, and Gorkhaland were undermined by the difficulty of dealing with this long-term, multigenerational relationship between workers, plants, and planters. Proponents of these revitalization strategies misread the breakdown of that relationship—and it was most assuredly breaking down by the early years of the twenty-first century—as a sign that what plantation workers needed was a rescue, in the form of economic or juridical justice, or the attainment of territorial sovereignty. From the outside, it seemed plausible that more income, property protections, or a separate state would solve plantation inequality, but each of these frameworks for justice largely ignored the ways in which plantation workers explained what was unjust about plantation life.

In the introduction to this book, I noted Anna Tsing's observation that justice is an effective mobilizing idea for both powerful and powerless people alike around the world.[1] My main critique of fair trade, GI, and Gorkhaland is that none of these movements asked how workers themselves understood their own powerlessness. They either presumed that their powerlessness was inevitable (fair trade's ignorance of the Plantations Labour Act); replaced it with ahistorical ecological nobility (GI's depictions of plantation women as "magic-fingered"); or attempted to fetishize it as a symbol of national suffering (Gorkhaland's treatment of those same women as the movement's "suffering mothers"). I have tried to understand how workers theorized their own exploitation in response to these strategies for reinventing the plantation. Workers described powerlessness not as an inevitable condition of plantation work but as an outcome of the shift in the organization of plantations from a model of *industri* to one of *bisnis,* from a complex hierarchical corporate plantation structure run by companies, to what fair traders might call a "farmer-run" model, in which charismatic owners like Mr. Roy took a direct interest in plantation operations. Workers described their relationship to tea bushes not as timeless and "completely natural" but as the inherited outcome of generations of work, homemaking, and moral economic relations. Workers described their suffering on the tea plantations as the result of a political order that had failed to deliver the benefits of tea's global market value back to the people of the plantations. For workers, British, Bengali, *and* Gorkha politicians each bore part of the blame for this.

It was the shift from *industri* to *bisnis* that my friends at Windsor were describing on that spring day. Mr. Roy's mistrust was a sure sign that he was not an *industriko mānchhe,* but in truth, no twenty-first-century planter was. Workers judged planter quality based on their deviation from that ideal. He was failing to reinvest in land and in people, despite the fact that Windsor's workers felt as if they were invested in the fate of the plantation. In terms of anthropological exchange theory, Mr. Roy, as a *bisnis-man,* was failing to play his part in a reciprocal relationship that went beyond money. He and other plantation owners promised more facilities through GI and fair trade, but they failed to deliver. Som explained,

What does he say in the meeting? He says: "I will not be able to run the *kamān,* I don't have money." "I don't have the money. No money!" He cries! He acts serious! Even the supervisor is serious, the garden is going down, and the garden is going down because we are not working. It's sinking! The garden is going down; it will not be able to run. There is no money. The quality of tea has gone down, the wages have gone down. *But* there *is* money. Simple and innocent, [workers] agree to what ever [management] says. They just say: "Ok, ok!" The cost per kilogram of our tea leaves is so expensive, it's so many rupees more than the other *kamān,* if the other *kamāns* are operating, why not ours? No one questions!

Moreover, owners, like Gorkhaland politicians, were promising that change on the plantation would come in a dramatic shift of fortunes, rather than in an extended, recursive process of mutual support. Change was necessary, but that change, according to workers, should be in the structure of the plantation. Som continued:

> There should be a change. The whole company should change. If a different company comes they will get a lot of support, but it should not be a personal king type. [It] should have a manager system. It should be through the manger, it should be through the company, it should not have a "self-owner." What we have here is a "self-owner" company. Every thing is under him, in his hands. . . . It is sad, Sarah. A bonded laborer will always stay bonded . . . *because of poverty and politeness, one's self is being cheated.*

Som was critical of his fellow workers for continuing to be "polite" and deferential to Mr. Roy, when he was shirking his obligation to reciprocate workers' care. Loyalty to a single patron was risky, whereas loyalty to a *company,* represented by managers and responsible to the state and its regulations, was more secure.

To older tea workers, what was perhaps more worrisome was that the practice of *bisnis* was corrupting the younger generations. At Kopibari, my friend Ganga singled out political and union activists in particular:

> Darjeeling is the best in the world . . . the most expensive, but the laborers are invisible. They are the least. . . . And *what is* the union *doing?* They are sleeping! They eat a lot. They fill up their stomachs and then sleep. Isn't that it? And when there is a union, where are they really? Even if they look like humans speaking, they are dead bodies—living dead bodies. Do you know the meaning of living dead bodies? Dead body—there is nothing. It's over. They should speak for the workers, but this new generation will not do it, because it's hard.

Young political activists' search for immediate gratification, often in the form of payoffs from owners, undermined the moral economy their parents worked to maintain through hard work. Ganga continued, "Daily, every day, it goes on deteriorating. . . . It's almost finished. Day by day. They do not pay much; they don't even maintain the houses. . . . We are working here, but if I am a worker and I get sick, they [the owner] does not want to pay for the medicine."

"Where is the dispensary?" I asked.

Ganga answered my question with a wave of her hand through the empty air, "Where *is* it?"

"Where is the ambulance?" I prodded.

"It's not there. They let the poor people die while they eat a lot and sleep. . . . I feel like cutting them like this," Ganga made a diagonal cutting motion at her neck. "Do you know? I feel like killing them." I left the encounter unsure whether she meant harm to the owner that had failed to provide adequate *faciliti-haru* at Kopibari or the complacent local GJMM representatives and union bosses who failed to represent workers' interests.

IS SOMETHING BETTER THAN NOTHING?

As I explained in chapters 4 and 5, union action surged in the early days of the second Gorkhaland agitation, but this surge was short-lived. The ethic of *bisnis* undermined that progress. By the time I was able to interview Gorkhaland leader Bimal Gurung, in late 2009, I asked him the question that Madan Tamang and countless plantation workers had also asked: "How will plantations change if Gorkhaland is achieved?"

He repeated my question. "How will plantations change?"

"Yes," I repeated back, "How will life on the plantations be different?"

"It will be like that [it will be like it was before]," Gurung replied. "The owners will still be the same."

I looked at him, puzzled.

"But it will be *in Gorkhaland*," he added with dramatic emphasis. He had no specific plans, beyond sovereignty, for addressing the plantations, but he and his supporters believed that with sovereignty, it was at least plausible to think that some of the financial benefits of the tea industry would remain in the new state.

During my fieldwork, I heard a common refrain from fair traders, plantation managers, and Gorkhaland political activists, including Gurung. "Something is better than nothing." By this logic, fair trade made incremental positive changes in (at least some) workers' incomes; GI's legal protections allowed Darjeeling tea to enjoy a higher market value and more global prestige, possibly benefiting plantation laborers; and Gorkhaland promised "development" to the district's residents, including plantation workers. The notion that some intervention is better than no intervention is something of a development imperative, but in Darjeeling, it was profoundly misleading.[2] The "something" that each program promised did not replace "nothing." It replaced another something.

I do not deny that fair trade, GI, and Gorkhaland are meaningful forces. They are all powerful visions of justice with real impacts. Saying that something is better than nothing, however, presumes that a "nothing" exists: that a program for justice will fill some kind of void. As I have tried to show in the preceding chapters, doing justice requires not just a powerful vision of justice but a powerful framework for imagining injustice. Envisioning "something" requires symbolic, linguistic, economic, and political framings of actual conditions. This entails imagining a suitable "nothing." While the proponents of fair-trade certification, Geographical Indication, and even Gorkhaland (all of whom claim to *speak for* plantation workers) have declared each of these programs successful, none of these strategies for reinventing the plantation has engaged with plantation workers' understandings of the current conditions of plantation life and their visions of its future.

While it seems clear that there *is* a market for justice, this market is not just. To make agricultural justice a market value, to make it something that is consumable, requires the conversion of wage labor time not only into a saleable product, but also into a marketable *image*. For workers, this constitutes a double alienation. Workers only obliquely participate in this market for justice; it is a market that transforms them into different kinds of imaginary agricultural subjects, none of which correspond to plantation reality. Fair trade, GI, and Gorkhaland all involve a disciplined forgetting of the colonial histories, unequal power relations, and structural inequality that remain fundamental to the functioning of plantations. The message of this book is that these histories cannot simply be willed away. For workers, the plantation is a living set of moral economic relationships that transcend wages and monetary value. Justice requires regulating juridical, kin, ecological, *and* economic relations among workers; between workers and management; and between workers and the agro-environment.

If they hope to have a lasting impact on workers' lives, fair trade, *terroir*-based initiatives like GI, market-based strategies for social justice, and even local politics must be more reflexive about what a plantation is: a colonially rooted system of exploitation. Because workers' understandings of social justice are rooted in the tripartite moral economy, short of strengthening labor unions, expanding employment opportunities, and providing health care on plantations—short of the reconstruction of *faciliti-haru*—there may be no chance for workers' visions of justice to ever be realized today's world of *bisnis*.

Workers understand what living on a plantation means. Over generations, plantation labor has bonded them to Darjeeling's land, and, for better or worse, the stability of the land matters to the stability of their families, houses, and futures. These bonds to land link them to a broader political order. The land under Darjeeling has never belonged to single owners or companies; it has always belonged to a colonial or state government. It is collective property. Workers know this, and their ideas about justice are thus rooted in histories of landscape and politics. This does not mean that workers' ties to the landscape are not natural. It just means that those ties are also historical.

Fair trade, despite its lofty claims, fails to provide meaningful change in the majority of workers' lives in line with workers' understandings of the plantation and of the concept of justice. If, as I outlined in the introduction to this book, Fair Trade USA, the largest third-party certifier of fair-trade goods in the United States, is to include plantations, it must acknowledge a plantation for what it is and do justice to workers' senses of justice. A one-size-fits-all model of "improvement," in which the conditions of the global commodity trade are made "fairer" through the choices of conscientious consumers, has not seemed to work in Darjeeling. Different crops have different social contexts, histories, ecologies, and these engender different forms and meanings of labor. Fair trade's concept of justice-as-fairness obscures these differences and disassociates tea from the means of its production and its oppressive colonial roots and postcolonial realities. But fair trade is not a wholly consumer-driven movement. Institutions like Fair Trade USA and Fairtrade Labelling Organizations International (FLO) set the terms of an alternative moral economy.[3] The plantation sits tenuously on the margins of market forces. To be successful, fair trade needs to remain humble in the face of history, and to ask if there are already ways to make workers' lives better: to ask if fair trade is really necessary or possible on plantations. If anything, a movement as broad and powerful as fair trade can help call attention to those existing state structures, like the PLA, that ensure stable livelihoods for workers.

GI can similarly strengthen its claims to represent workers as uniquely skilled craftspeople if it acknowledges the historical conditions under which those skills were developed. Why not make Darjeeling a place to teach consumers about the history of food production, warts and all, rather than a place to proffer romantic ideas about timeless, unchanging "ecological heritage"? To my mind, attention to the partly unsavory history of food production through the GI label can promote geographical distinction, and it may attract the kind of engaged consumer base that seeks fair-trade products.

Finally, the cause of Gorkhaland is understandable and even justifiable, but the failure of the movement's leaders to meaningfully engage with issues of class and labor signal a wider failure of Indian politics over the last few decades. The state of West Bengal, long a bastion of the socialist left in India, has, even at the zenith of Communist power, consistently failed to address the plight of Gorkha workers. It is telling that by the end of the 2007 to 2011 agitation, Gorkhaland politicians' strongest political allies came from the Bharatiya Janata Party (BJP), a hard-line, fundamentalist, right-wing Hindu nationalist organization whose vision of India's future hinges on the formation of small states. At the time of this writing, West Bengal's Communist Party has fallen, and as India's central government opens the country to free trade and global finance capital, smallholders and agricultural laborers are being further marginalized, pushed off of their land in favor of high-rise office buildings, housing developments, and factories. Darjeeling's plantations persist amid these changes, and like the plantation, dreams of Gorkhaland do not seem to be going away. Labor was almost a non-issue in the first Gorkhaland agitation, but it played something of a larger role in the second. It seems very possible that Gorkhaland will reemerge again, and perhaps laborers' struggles will play an even larger role than they did this time.

"INHERITING THE PAST THICKLY"

My conversation with Jamuna, Maya, and Som took place outside. We were enjoying the spring sunshine after a cold winter, sitting in a semicircle in the flat dirt yard in front of their houses. We spread out, some (including myself) seated on plastic chairs, and others squatting on wooden blocks. As our conversation wound down, I decided to ask them about the small compound of houses they occupied. I was never sure whose house was whose, but I felt it important to tease out households and their occupants. It was difficult for me, even after months in Darjeeling, to figure out where one house began and one ended. Surrounding our circle of chairs were at least three houses. One was a small bamboo structure, occupied by one of Som and Jamuna's relatives (they too were distant cousins). Next to that was a larger wooden house, clearly older, but to my eyes more structurally sound. Most plantation villages had many houses like this one, and a handful like the third house we could see from our chairs, a small concrete structure. Jamuna confirmed my guess that the wooden house, part of which she and her family occupied, was built by the company that once ran Windsor.

"The one on that side is the company's," she said, pointing ahead of her, and then, pointing to the concrete house, "And the ones on this side are built by us." Then she continued. "The one on that side is the company's, and it was given in the time of my ancestor. . . . It was given when he was working. He passed away, and his grandchild and great-grandchild are grown up but no repairing is done till now. When it's damaged it's supposed to be repaired, but no repairing is done." Jamuna was talking about Mr. Roy's legal responsibility to maintain plantation housing. "So, my brother requested repairs [from management] a while back, but we don't know when the repairs will come." Now she threw both hands up and half joked, "That repairing! It will come in the time of my great-grandchildren! They [the manager who took Jamuna's brother's request for repairs] made an entry and it was over." Jamuna's brother's request for repairs was duly noted by the plantation manager, but then ignored.

Jamuna's story led to a long discussion of plantation houses. People on tea plantations like to talk about houses. Houses, as plantation women told me, remain after you die. They are what your children inherit along with your job; at the same time, as something you inherit, they are your link to the plantation past. For workers, plantation histories were largely told through the narratives of who lived in which house, and when. Among *faciliti-haru*, houses were sacrosanct. Even in the era of *bisnis-men* like Mr. Roy, few plantation laborers I met expected that they would not have a house to leave to their children. Houses were *faciliti-haru* and thus technically a form of compensation, but workers and their families, through intergenerational labor, made them their own, painting them in bright colors and adorning them with flowers when Puja season bonuses allowed for extra decorations. As the Darjeeling district labor commissioner told me, the tea worker's house is like a bank account. The house was a symbol of stability and a container for a history of reciprocal, nonmonetary relationships of care among workers, the land, and management.

Tea workers imagined a "better" plantation past of strong moral economic relationships when they talked about their houses, but they also envisioned the future in relational terms. Reminiscences like Jamuna's about benevolent companies building quality housing were almost certainly veiled by nostalgia, but stories like these also attested to the material connections between the present and the past, over the long term. These long-term relations of care were at the center of plantation workers' visions of justice and of their suspicion of fair trade, GI, and Gorkhaland's promises of "something over nothing." Though they were relatively powerless in the era of *bisnis,* workers understood that power in a moral economic system based on nonmonetary exchange comes not from accumulating but from giving—from providing care in the right ways. They resisted Gorkhaland's calls for similar reasons. Gorkha politicians made Gorkhas' place in the landscape seem, like the place of tea labor in GI advertisements, "completely natural."

Signs of hard work and perseverance amid the inequalities of the plantation system were legible on the landscape. The plantation house, an outgrowth of the colonial "labor line," is perhaps one of the most visible of these. Workers reinhabited these "imperial ruins" with each generation.[4] For workers, facilities like these were, to paraphrase Donna Haraway, "inherited thickly."[5] In the imperial ruins of Darjeeling, Nepali workers saw the remnants of a stable moral economy and productive tea industry. Workers believed that they could revitalize these ruins, but not with fair-trade premiums or GI posters. Justice in Darjeeling depended upon a head-on engagement with the colonial past and with the legacy of the plantation, rather than with the nostalgic and superficial one promoted by the other three solutions. Workers understood that Gorkhas' connection to Darjeeling was forged not only through a history of labor, but also through relationships of care: of service and loyalty to the British, to the land, and to family.

"AGING THE FUTURE"

A history of labor, and service labor in particular, was central to tea plantation workers' senses of identity. Tea workers did not necessarily want to stop caring for tea, for plantation villages, or for plantations themselves. This observation may be unsettling, much as framings of plantation or peasant agricultural laborers' visions of justice as "moral economic" are unsettling. The breakdown of moral economies, as James Scott, Eric Wolf, and other ethnographers of plantation and peasant life have shown, may lead to revolutions and violence, but the moral economic subject is not always already a revolutionary subject. Close attention to the making and slow deterioration of moral economies, such as that which I have tried to present in this book, show that relations of exploitation based on minimal expectations of reciprocity operate over long spans of time. Tea laborers saw their houses and their jobs and their relationships to the plantation landscape as inherited. These relationships, even if they were fundamentally unequal, came to them because of care, and they owed them care in return. Tea laborers who spoke of the revitalization of plantations as a long process of re-creating *industri* therefore might look rather conservative.

But their tolerance for the failure of owners to reciprocate generations of care was not infinite. Ganga's joking expression of a willingness to "cut the throats" of lazy union bosses and plantation owners, and Jamuna's exasperation with the decay of *faciliti-haru* indicated that tea laborers may be reaching a breaking point. This is ironic, considering that Darjeeling's tea industry is in the midst of what most connoisseurs and market watchers would consider to be a revival, driven in part by fair trade and GI. Gorkhaland politicians recognize this, too, and despite some early moves, they have no plans to upset the system. Workers' looming sense of a final, irrevocable breakdown in the plantation moral economy is even more frustrating when we consider that the very programs aimed at helping plantation workers couch their projects as movements for "justice." This book has been about the deep disconnect between national (GI), global (fair trade), and regional (Gorkhaland) calls for justice, and the lives and work of the very people in whose names those calls have gone forth. In calling for justice, these strategies have attempted to reinvent the plantation as a garden, as a farm, or as an ethnic homeland: to make it palatable in an age of global "ethical consumption" and a rising tide of regional self-determination in India. But workers are keenly aware that in the market for justice, the plantation is not going anywhere.

NOTES

INTRODUCTION

1. *Planter* is a term that has been used since the British colonial era for tea plantation managers and assistant managers. In recent years, plantation owners have also begun using this term to describe themselves. Therefore, throughout the book, I often use "planter" to describe both plantation managers and owners as a group. Though, in certain contexts, I disaggregate the two when I discuss plantation owners directly.

2. *Vāstu* is also a concept that Indian plantation managers, tea buyers, and tea tasters alike use to explain why certain valleys or plantations in Darjeeling have better tea or are generally more successful than others.

3. As a district, Darjeeling is composed of four subdivisions: Darjeeling, Kurseong, Kalimpong, and Siliguri.

4. Guthman (2011: 19). See also Freidberg (2004); Lyon (2011); and West (2012).

5. Hoheneggar (2007: 9–11). See also Griffiths (1967: 3–13) for an early history of tea consumption in East Asia.

6. See Hoheneggar (2007: 11); Macfarlane and MacFarlane (2003).

7. See Bhadra (2005); Lutgendorf (2009).

8. For an overview of the early trade in spices and other exotic stimulants see Schivelbusch (1992).

9. Hohenegger (2007: 85–87).

10. See Chatterjee (2001: 38–50).

11. Hohenegger (2007: 87–88).

12. MacFarlane and MacFarlane (2003: 110).

13. Eventually, sugar consumption literally fuelled sugar production: it was a staple "food" for Puerto Rican cane workers by the time Mintz began studying Puerto Rican sugarcane production in the 1950s (Mintz 1985, 1960).

14. Mintz (1985: 121).

15. See DuPuis (2002) for a study of milk, the third element of tea's consumptive triad.

16. Mintz (1985: 109).

17. For more on the Opium Wars and British tea trade with China, see Chaudhuri (1978); Chung (1974); and Pettigrew (2001).

18. MacFarlane and MacFarlane (2003: 38–39).

19. Many of these studies, such as Sidney Mintz's foundational *Worker in the Cane* (1960), focus on banana, sugar, and coffee plantations in Latin America and the Caribbean. See also Scheper-Hughes (1992) for a description of Brazilian sugarcane plantations, and Bourgois (1989); Moberg (1997); and Striffler (2002) for a discussion of life and labor on banana plantations in Latin America. Other scholars have bridged anthropology and history, examining the plantation as lived and experienced in the colonial era rather than in the contemporary period (Daniel 2008; Daniel, Bernstein, and Brass 1992; and Stoler 1985). Closer to Darjeeling tea plantations, Piya Chatterjee's (2001) examination of the lives of women tea workers on a Dooars plantation, nestled in the Bengal plains between Darjeeling and Kolkata, is guided by feminist theory, ethnographic reflexivity, and subaltern studies. Chatterjee explores the forms of structural oppression that envelop female tea laborers.

20. See Edelman (1998); Kearney (1996); Mintz (1973); Redfield (1956); Scott (1976); and Wolf (1969, 1966); see also the classic work of A. V. Chayanov (1986 [1966]).

21. See Kearney (1996) and Silverman (1979) for reviews of the concept of the peasantry in anthropology.

22. Scott (1976: 157).

23. See Holmes (2013) and Minkoff-Zern and Getz (2011) for discussions of migrant farmworker insecurity.

24. See Kearney (1996) for a discussion of the genealogy and potential futures of "peasant studies." Kearney highlights how evoking the concept of "the peasant" is problematic in the context of globalization.

25. MacFarlane and MacFarlane (2003: 41).

26. The tea from certain Darjeeling plantations is deemed more desirable according to the direction they face, the valley they are in, or their general *vāstu*.

27. The rupee fluctuated quite a bit during the period of my fieldwork. The average rupee-dollar conversion rates were: 43.6 rupees to the dollar in 2008; 48.4 rupees in 2009; 45.7 rupees in 2010; 46.8 rupees in 2011; and 53.4 rupees in 2012. In later chapters, I discuss wage agreements and year-by-year incremental increases. In 2010, the wage was sixty-three rupees a day. In 2008 the daily wage was fifty-three rupees. In 2009 it was fifty-eight rupees. In 2011 it was sixty-seven rupees. The 2011 wage talks yielded an increase to ninety rupees from 2011 to 2014.

28. Government of India (1973). The Foreign Exchange Management Act (FEMA) replaced the 1973 law in 2000. FEMA liberalized trade in India, but multinational interests have not returned to Darjeeling tea plantations.

29. See also Yardley (2012).

30. See Guthman (2004) for a discussion of the agrarian imaginary in California organic agriculture.

31. Bourdieu (1984).

32. See Appadurai (1986); Clifford (1997); Kirshenblatt-Gimblett (1998); Marcus and Myers (1995); Miller (1998a, 1998b); and Steiner (1994).

33. Bourdieu (1984: 231).

34. See Freidberg (2004); Guthman (2004); Paxson (2012); and Trubek (2008).

35. Marx (1976 [1867]); Mauss (2000 [1950]).

36. Simmel (1978), quoted in Appadurai (1986: 3–4).

37. Appadurai (1986: 4).

38. Myers (2001: 6).

39. Myers (2001: 6). See also Henderson (2013) for a further analysis of Marx's concept of value.

40. Thompson (1963: 63).

41. Scott (1976).

42. There are certainly parallels between what I am calling a "moral economy" on Darjeeling tea plantations and the *jajmani* system, which is a village-based system of exchange in Nepal and Indian villages in which low-caste (usually landless or land-poor) individuals (e.g., blacksmiths, carpenters, sweepers, washermen) are forced through economic need to provide services to high-caste land owning elites, or *jajmans*. *Jajmans* pay low-caste individuals in kind in grains, clothing, agricultural implements, or foodstuffs. In this system, too, the lower castes often exchange services with one another. The *jajmani* system is a nonmonetized form of exchange (see Beidelman 1959; Breman 1993 [1973]; Dumont 1980; and Kolendra 1963). Mary Cameron (1998) also describes the *jajmani* system in Nepal, where it is know as *riti-bhāgya* (literally this means customary fortune; *riti* can be translated as "custom" or "customary," while *bhāgya* can be translated as "fortune," "portion," or "share").

43. Rhodes and Rhodes (2006).

44. After the Sino-Indian War of 1962, the Nepali-speaking independent kingdom of Sikkim, which sits on the India-China border, became a significant geopolitical entity. In 1979, Sikkim became an Indian state. And since its inclusion, Sikkim has received a large amount of development support from India's central government.

45. *Janmukti* is a compound of "person" (*janā*) and "salvation" or "liberation" (*mukti*) and *morchā* is a military term meaning "front." Gorkha Janmukti Morcha, then, translates as "Gorkha People's Liberation Front," but I will not use this translation in the text.

46. See, for example, Checker (2005); Guthman (2011); and Harrison (2011).

47. Tsing (2005: 9).

48. Marx (1976 [1867]).

49. Jill Harrison's *Pesticide Drift and the Pursuit of Environmental Justice* (2011) describes exposure to pesticides in industrial agriculture as an environmental justice issue, rather than an economic one, for both workers and for the poor and marginalized communities into which these toxic agro-chemicals drift. Harrison explains that governmental regulators, public health officials, and community members in California all voice different, and often conflicting, conceptualizations of what justice means.

50. Each of these visions reflects and engages different philosophical theories of justice, self-possession, and the nature of rights. GI's vision of property rights as justice integrates Locke's foundational view of the relationship between property and labor with libertarian philosophical principles. For libertarian political philosophers, the job of law and the government is to protect property rights. Market transactions, according to this view, are

predicated on the recognition of property rights over time. Provided that the law protects property rights, free markets require little else to function. Importantly for libertarian philosophy, rights to property can be transferred and inherited. Simply putting work into something does not make it marketable property. The law must recognize the product's transferability (Kymlicka 2002: 110–16; Nozick 1974).

The debate over the extension of fair trade to plantations demonstrates the limitations of a model of justice rooted in utilitarian principles of distribution: doing the greatest "good" for the greatest number of people. Utilitarianism, elaborated by philosophers Jeremy Bentham and John Stuart Mill, is one perspective on distributive justice (Kymlicka 2002: 10–48). This philosophy is rather simple, but nonetheless evocative. Bentham, in his discussions of justice and societal reform, emphasized "utility," the capacity to bring happiness and pleasure of a given action or policy. Actions with the greatest utility for the greatest number of people brought the most good to society and thus these actions were the most "just." In Bentham's formulation of justice, the categorical morality of an action itself is not important—the results that action brings are the focus. Fair trade adopts this utilitarian ethic of justice, in which consumption is a value-neutral action in itself—it is the benefits, the utility, that a consumptive act yields that is important.

In fair-trade discourse, this utilitarian ethic melds with a liberal view of justice. In the liberal conception of justice, elaborated by the philosopher John Rawls (1971), social goods should be distributed equally, unless the unequal distribution of goods favors the least advantaged. Rawls envisioned justice as "fairness," with fairness as socially necessary inequality. In a liberal view of justice, advantaged *individuals* must act to the benefit of disadvantaged *individuals*. The extension of fair-trade certification to more plantations aims to "do the right thing" for the greatest number of people, through individualized acts of consumption, even if its vision of the "right thing" elides the forms of structural oppression that agricultural workers face. Fair trade's liberal view of justice assumes that all the actors involved in fair-trade plantation production will behave in a similarly "fair" manner, choosing to distribute goods in a way that always benefits the least advantaged.

In terms of political philosophy, Gorkhaland was a "communitarian" antidote to the libertarian and liberal visions of justice. One version of communitarian justice holds that visions of rights come not from individuals and their decisions but from established social groups (nations, ethnic groups, towns, etc.) (Kymlicka 2002: 284–87).

51. See Paxson (2012) and Weiss (2011) for similar discussions of the links between place, taste, production practices, and feeling.

52. Many Assam and the majority of Dooars plantations specialize in CTC ["cut-tear-curl"]-grade teas for making *chiyā*. CTC production contrasts with "orthodox" tea production, in which tea leaves are rolled during processing. CTC leaves, instead of being rolled, are put through a different machine that cuts, tears, and curls them. CTC and orthodox teas are auctioned in centers across the country. In the case of Darjeeling, all grades and gardens are tasted, valued, and auctioned in Kolkata, the capital of West Bengal and the center of the Indian tea trade.

53. Kloppenburg, Hendrickson, and Stevenson (1996: 34).

54. Colman (2008: 37–67).

55. Other agricultural products now governed by Indian GI legislation include Basmati rice and Alphanso mangoes. The 1999 legislation also protects a large number of handi-

crafts, such as Kullu shawls and Kancheepuram silk (Government of India 1999). For a complete list of India GIs, see the Intellectual Property India Geographical Registrations Registry, http://ipindia.nic.in/girindia (accessed March 21, 2012).

56. The Darjeeling tea logo is available in the Darjeeling Tea Association's media kit: http://darjeelingtea.com/files/media.asp.htm (accessed February 4, 2013). The Darjeeling tea logo and the media that carry it are symbols of bureaucratic authority, which stand in for people. In actuality, people in Darjeeling have little power in the GI system. Bureaucrats and lawyers in the Kolkata offices of the Tea Board of India do most of the work of GI. See Herzfeld (1992); Hetherington (2011); and Hull (2012) for anthropological discussions of bureaucracy.

57. Rao (2005).

58. Many social scientists and scholar-activists have described the monopolization of plant genetic resources, often focusing on Monsanto's transgenic cotton in India. See Herring (2005); Shiva (2000); and Stone (2004).

59. Similarly, other products have found market stability with GI legislation. The extension of GI to non-Western contexts (and beyond wines, liquors, and cheeses) is a new phenomenon, and relatively few scholars have explored these products and processes (particularly as they relate to WTO governance). In one of the few studies of GIs in non-Western contexts, sociologist Sarah Bowen (2010) evaluates GI regulation as a form of "development from within," in which "local actors" are given the legal tools to sustainably manage their crop, but she concludes that GIs in the developing world face distinct challenges. In the case of Mexican tequila production, small agave farmers did not benefit from the tequila GI. Instead, large tequila-distilling companies benefited the most from the brand protection. There are multiple parties and interests along the tequila commodity chain that are all enveloped by the tequila GI. Despite appeals to development, distilleries retain immense power over agave farmers (see also Bowen and Zapata 2009).

60. This vision of justice is in line with John Locke's (1980 [1690]) treatises on property. For Locke, the blending of human labor with material things renders those things the property of the person or persons who put the work into them.

61. For simplicity, throughout this book, I used Fairtrade Labelling Organizations International and its acronym FLO, not the organization's truncated name, Fair Trade International. Both titles refer to the same Bonn-based fair-trade institution.

62. See www.fairtrade.net/products.html (accessed March 21, 2012). For details about FLO's Hired Labor Standards or Hired Labor Standards in Tea see FLO (2011a and 2011b).

63. See Jaffee (2007) in Mexico; Luetchford (2008) in Costa Rica; Lyon (2011) in Guatemala. In recent years, scholars have begun to look beyond coffee cooperatives to explore the lived experiences of fair-trade certification. See Frundt (2009); Moberg (2008); and Shreck (2005) on banana cooperatives; Dolan (2010); Dolan and Blowfield (2010); and Sen (2009) on cooperative tea production; Besky (2010, 2008) and Makita (2012) on tea plantation production; Ziegler (2010) on plantation-based flower production; and Prieto-Carron (2006) on "ethical sourcing" from Chiquita banana plantations.

64. Bacon (2010, 2005); Jaffee (2007); Lyon (2007); Murray, Raynolds, and Taylor (2006); Renard (2003); Rice (2000); and Smith (2007).

65. Political economist Karl Polanyi (1944) formulated the thesis of market embeddedness, and contemporary fair-trade scholars have used his ideas to analyze and critique fair

trade's attempts to materially and discursively link the production of goods back to the production of communities and persons (Lyon 2006; Guthman 2007; Jaffee 2007; Reichman 2011; and West 2012).

66. Fridell (2007).

67. FLO's pricing database is available at www.fairtrade.net/793.html (accessed on February 4, 2013).

68. There are inequities in the premium system on cooperatives, too; see Lyon (2011).

69. See Meehan (2007) for a discussion of non-fair-trade-certified "direct trade" programs with particular attention to Intelligentsia Coffee.

70. Jaffee (2007: 1).

71. See http://fairtradeforall.com/vision/innovate-the-model/ (Accessed March 21, 2012). "Every Purchase Matters" is also a keystone to Fair Trade USA's marketing campaign.

72. Despite their commitment to small farmers, Equal Exchange buys tea from Darjeeling cooperative tea farmers that must process their tea at large plantations. The plantation form is pervasive and hard to escape in the world of tea.

73. See a press release from Equal Exchange entitled "Why Is Equal Exchange for co-ops and against plantations? (http://equalexchange.coop/about/fair-trade/faqs/why-equal-exchange-co-ops-and-against-plantations-fair-trade-system [accessed February 15, 2013]). They sum up the argument as follows: "Simply put, it is the right thing to do." But even Equal Exchange has a hard time completely eliminating the plantation from their supply chain. The cooperative tea that they sell may have been *grown* on a cooperative, but it is *processed* in a tea plantation factory.

74. Neuman (2011).

75. Soule and Piper (1992), quoted in Guthman (2004: 2).

76. Guthman (2004: 9–12).

77. Jefferson (1999 [1785]).

78. This vision of rural agricultural life certainly resonates with Raymond Williams's (1973) observations in *The Country and the City* of the mythical characterization of rural life and landscapes as simple, natural, and pristine as well as John Urry's (1995, 1990) discussion of British countryside tourism.

79. See Paxson (2012) for a similar discussion of "good food."

80. See Sawyer and Agrawal (2000) for a similar discussion of what they call "environmental orientalism."

81. DTA (n.d.).

82. See Wright (2006: 88–90) for a similar discussion of value, fetish, and the hands and fingers of female laborers in Mexican *maquiladoras*.

83. Chatterjee (2001: 48–43).

84. See Doane (2007); Krech (1999); and Nadasdy (2005).

85. Taussig (1993).

86. Scott (1976: 3).

87. Scott (1976: 2–3).

88. Scott (1976: 158).

89. Scott (1976: 160).

90. Scott (1976: 32).

91. Scott (1976: 32).

92. With very few exceptions, all persons' names in this book are pseudonyms. I have also changed the names of plantations. The exceptions are public political figures, such as Subhash Ghisingh, Bimal Gurung, and Madan Tamang.

1. DARJEELING

1. See also Flueckiger (2006: 14).

2. It important to note that Nepal and Tibet were not directly colonized by a European empire. James Fisher, in his introduction to the now classic *Himalayan Anthropology: The Indo-Tibetan Interface* (1978), encourages scholars to think of the Himalayan region as a liminal space, betwixt and between different cultural traditions.

3. Stoler (2008).

4. Stoler (2008: 196).

5. Stoler (2008: 194).

6. Ingold (2000: 153–287).

7. Keith Basso (1996) describes "place-making" as a "tool of the historical imagination":

> What is remembered about a particular place—including, prominently, visual and verbal accounts of what has transpired there—guides and constrains how it will be imagined by delimiting a field of workable possibilities. . . . Instances of place-making consist of an adventitious fleshing out of particular historical material that culminates in a posited state of affairs, a particular universe of objects and events—in short, a *place-world*—wherein portions of the past are brought into being (Basso 1996: 5–6).

Along with Basso and Stoler, I am concerned with the interface between the imaginative and material aspects of place (see also West 2006). A related area of scholarship in geography examines similar questions (see, for example, Mitchell 2003, 1996).

8. Stoler (2008: 197).

9. See Stoler (1985) for an example of her earlier work on plantations.

10. Deleuze and Guattari (1987). See also Ogden (2011).

11. Stoler (2008).

12. The capital of British India moved from Calcutta to Delhi in 1911.

13. Colonial officials, doctors, and settlers all used climate-based theories of health as a justification for the establishment and development of hill stations in India. For retrospective reviews and justifications of these climatic theories, see Campbell (1867); Clarke (1881); Fayrer (1900); and Spencer and Thomas (1948).

14. Lama (2009: 51–52); Pinn (1986: 1).

15. Newman and Company (1900: 13).

16. O'Malley (1985 [1907]: 20).

17. Some people I talked to cite the fact that Darjeeling was forcibly annexed from Sikkim as a reason why Darjeeling should join the contemporary Indian state of Sikkim. This was a less popular position during the time of my fieldwork. The Akhil Bharatiya Gorkha League (ABGL), the primary opposition party to the Gorkha Janmukti Morcha (GJMM), advocated this position.

18. Biswas and Roka (2007: 3).

19. Lama (2009: 58–71); Pinn (1986: 1–3).

20. Bhanja (1943: 12).

21. Lama (2009: 59).

22. Lloyd quoted in Lama (2009: 59).

23. Waddell quoted in Kennedy (1996: 69).

24. Po'dar and Subba (1991) have more recently explored how Lepchas and other Himalayan people engage in what they call "home-grown Orientalism," in which Indians and "the other" actively re-create Orientalist discourses that highlight the primitiveness and naturalness of hill people. The Lepcha and Sikkim have long been the interest of storytellers and ethnographers, Western and Indian, colonial and postcolonial. These writings date back to the work of the superintendent of Darjeeling, Archibald Campbell (1869) in the *Journal of the Ethnological Society of London,* and Geoffrey Gorer's *Himalayan Village* (1938 [2005]). See also Lama (1994); Sinha (2008); Tamlong (2008); L. Tamsang (2008); and K. P. Tamsang (1983).

25. Darjeeling's wasteland leases are different than the practices in colonial Assam and Bengal. The provincial governments of Assam and Bengal also instituted Wasteland Rules similar to Darjeeling, but for much larger tracts of land of one hundred acres at the least. Applicants had to possess capital or stock worth at least Rs. 3 per acre. While this did not explicitly prohibit native elites from applying, the capital requirements greatly deterred them. In the rare cases when a local did have that kind of capital, they were rejected for obscure infractions. J. Sharma (2011: 34); see also Gidwani (1992).

26. Darjeeling was given this classification prior to the annexation of Bhutan, but the dates recorded in secondary historical sources are contradictory.

27. The term "nonregulated area" was changed to "scheduled district" in 1874 and again to "backward tract" in 1919. Darjeeling was also a "partially excluded area" from 1935 until 1947. And briefly, in the late 1860s, the district was a "regulated area," but not *part of* the Bengal Presidency. For more on the administrative history of Bengal and Darjeeling, see Chatterji (2007: 117–118); Samanta (1996: 77–84); and Tamang (2011).

28. In the case of Himalayan hill stations, administrators also constructed these settlements with an eye to developing overland trade route between Calcutta and Tibet (Kennedy 1996: 22–26). Hill stations were also sites for army cantonments. In Darjeeling, the army presence served to monitor the Gorkha Empire on the other side of the Mechi River.

29. Kennedy (1996: 117–46).

30. See Dewan (1991).

31. Kennedy (1996: 1–6).

32. Grove (2002); Kennedy (1990); and Kenny (1995).

33. See Hutt (1997).

34. See K. Pradhan (1991) and Whelpton (2005) for detailed histories of Nepal with particular care given to monarchial ascensions.

35. Hutt (1997: 110).

36. Whelpton (2005: 35–60).

37. Directly after the Anglo-Bhutanese War of 1864, the King of Bhutan invited "industrious Nepalis" to the southern foothills of the Himalayas bordering India to look for cultivatable land. See Nath (2005) and Hutt (2003).

38. See (K. Pradhan 1991).

39. Caplan (1970); English (1982); and Forbes (1999).

40. Burghart (1984: 101).

41. Whelpton (2005: 42–45).

42. Metcalf quoted in K. L. Pradhan (2004: 57).

43. This annexation was codified by the Treaty of Sugauli in 1815. See Moktan (2004: 4).

44. This annexation was codified by the Treaty of Titalia in 1817. See Moktan (2004: 8).

45. "Gurkha" is generally regarded as a mispronunciation of "Gorkha." Today, the Nepali regiments in both the British and Indian armies are still referred to as "Gurkha" regiments.

46. Dozey (1922: 91–92).

47. Gardening too, framed gendered visions of the imperial landscape. Judith Roberts (1998) highlights that women's garden cultivation created a familiar space and was crucial the psychological and physical well-being of colonists. Eugenia Herbert (2011) argues that British gardening practice was more political than simple nostalgia for home. Gardens and bungalows served to mark space as British and embed in the landscape distinct ideas about domesticity. Similarly, Alison Blunt (1999, 1997) suggests that the domestic spaces of women in British India were not separate from those of empire. Instead, based on her analysis of household guides on subjects ranging from keeping servants to choosing a school for an India-born child (guides aimed at the wives of British civil servants, planters, and army officers), she argues that the political significance of imperial domesticity extended beyond the boundaries of the home.

48. Blunt (1999).

49. See Kennedy (1996). Lloyd Botanical Gardens was one that Capability Brown would recognize. Capability Brown was a British landscape architect who developed over 170 public and private gardens across England. See Brown (2011).

50. Bishop (1989); Dodin and Rather (2001).

51. The purpose of the romantic constructions of local people, according to Kennedy (1996: 87), was to "fashion an image of these people as the noble guardians of Edenic sanctuaries." These images of Himalayan people were perhaps made most iconic in James Hilton's description of Shangri-la in *Lost Horizon* (1933). Shangri-la is a spiritually and physically pure place without sickness, aging, or death, located in a valley of the Himalayas.

52. Said (1978: 49–73).

53. See the work of environmental historians Arnold (2006); Beinart and Hughes (2007); Rajan (2006); and Sivaramakrishnan (1999) on environment and empire.

54. According to Richard Grove (1995), the establishment of botanical gardens by colonial scientists was an attempt at paternalistic conservation, or "green imperialism." Environmental historian Donald Worster (1977) suggested that environmental destruction has at its root an imperialist attitude toward the environment, but Grove refutes this thesis. Instead, he calls for scholars to challenge monolithic theories of ecological imperialism because, as he argues, they arise out of a misunderstanding of the heterogeneous and ambivalent nature of the early colonial state (Grove 1995: 6–7; Worster 1977: 29–55). Grove explains that modern environmentalism has its roots in both Orientalist discourse and ideas of Eden-like purity. The botanical garden became a metaphor of the purity of nature as well as human control over it (see Prest 1981). In botanical gardens, as Grove and Prest

argue, an imperial "improvement" discourse and an Edenic vision of untrammeled "nature" blended. Both the natural world and the colonial state were heterogeneous, contradictory, and ambivalent. See also Arnold (2005) for a discussion of colonial agricultural improvement in India.

55. Kennedy (1996: 39–48).

56. Metcalf (1995: 28); see also J. Sharma (2011: 14) for a discussion of this ideological shift in colonial Assam.

57. Brockway (1979: 3).

58. Brockway (1979); Drayton (2000); and Prest (1981).

59. Grove (1995: 8).

60. Brockway (1979: 4–11).

61. Brockway (1979: 5).

62. Chatterjee (2001: 7); Kar (2002); and J. Sharma (2011: 30–31).

63. Griffith (1840).

64. Chatterjee (2001: 79).

65. J. Sharma (2011: 30–40, and 2006).

66. J. Sharma (2011: 29).

67. Axelby (2008); Kar (2011).

68. See Rose (2009) for a recent biography of Robert Fortune and his expeditions to take tea from China to plant in the Himalayas.

69. See J. Sharma (2011: 30) for a brief description of indigenous tea consumption in the Northeast. Tea consumption in India developed much later and as the result of marketing campaigns aimed at middle-and working-class Indians. See Bhadra (2005) and Lutgendorf (2009) for a study of Indian tea culture and consumption.

70. J. Sharma (2011: 32).

71. Jayeeta Sharma's *Empire's Garden: Assam and the Making of Modern India* (2011: 31–36) provides a detailed examination of the role of Chinese labor in the development of the Assam tea industry. See also J. Sharma (2006).

72. J. Sharma (2006).

73. I should note the extensive writings from the 1830s to the 1860s on the relative merits of China and India (Assam) *jāts*. Planters debated with each other about which *jāt* was more productive and more flavorful. Others argued about which variety represented the empire better. Planters published widely about the superiority (and authenticity) of the Assam *jāt* in an attempt to boost consumption in the United Kingdom and expand plantation cultivation in Indian tea-growing districts, particularly those identified with being "Indian:" Assam, Cachar, and the Dooars. For an example, see Mann (1918).

74. Mintz (1985).

75. Dash (1947: 113); Pinn (2003).

76. Darjeeling's first tea plantations were Aloobari, which sloped down from the north side of town, and Steinthal, which rested underneath the bazaar and botanical gardens on the south side of town. Early plantations also included those in the Lebong spur, a sunny valley below town where army officers had their cantonment.

77. Quoted in Fox (1993: 34).

78. *Duppi* trees (*Cryptomeria japonica*) were introduced in the Azores as well and contributed to depleted bird populations and environmental degradation (Ramos 1996; and

Silva and Smith 2006). The soil underneath *Cryptomeria* trees is so acidic that other plant life cannot grow. Despite this, Darjeeling tea workers and townspeople have an ambivalent relationship to this invasive plant. *Duppi* was central to the industrialization of the Darjeeling landscape, but it also a key symbol in its regeneration. Darjeeling town residents in particular see *duppi,* and its yearlong greenness, to be a source of pride, an iconic symbol of the Darjeeling hills.

79. Alternatively *godown* or *godām* is used more often to connote goods storage, as in a store's warehouse. *Karkhāna,* the Nepali word used in Nepal for a factory was rarely used.

80. See Kling (1976: 94–121).

81. Ukers (1935: 465–490).

82. The first cinchona plantations were planted beginning in 1869, which also attracted Nepali migrant laborers.

83. For the British, the Lepcha became a "dying race," in danger of being displaced by the floods of immigrating Nepali laborers. See Kennedy (1996: 78, 188–90).

84. See Sivaramakrishnan (1999) for a discussion of the Bengal Tenancy Act, and McGowan (1860) for a discussion of land tenure and tea production in the Northwest.

85. *The Tea Cyclopaedia* (1882: 238).

86. O'Malley (1985 [1907]: 150–53).

87. See Lees (1867) for a review of Wasteland Rules, native rights, and the imperative of "improvement."

88. Baildon (1882: 20–34).

89. J. Sharma (2011: 38–40).

90. Bodhisattva Kar (2002) describes how East India Company and Assam Company officials tried to cope with surpluses in opium by paying Chinese labor in opium. They were able to control their opium-eating workforce more efficiently than "wild" native laborers. See also J. Sharma (2011: 38–40).

91. Scholars of labor in India have paid particular attention to issues of *adivāsi* treatment on plantations in Northeast India as well as the role labor recruiters, not only in the procurement of labor, but also in their manipulation. See Behal and Mohapatra (1992); Bhadra (1997); Bhadra and Bhadra (1997); Chakravorty (1997); Chatterjee (2001); Karotemprel and Roy (1990); Phukan (1984); and Sarkar (1998).

92. Bates and Carter (1992); Das Gupta (1994).

93. *Papers on the Tea Factories* (1854).

94. Chamney (1930: 43–45).

95. Baildon (1882: 30–34). Hand rolling tea is still practiced on Darjeeling plantations. Many women that I worked with sneaked leaf home and dried it over their home fires, hand rolling it, to use for their own consumption. This supply of tea supplemented their small ration of three hundred fifty grams of broken-leaf tea.

96. After retiring from the army, the British encouraged Gorkhas to settle on the frontier of Northeast India. In 1872, Colonel Lewin recommended the establishment of a permanent settlement of Gorkhas in the hills of Northeast India, on the frontier between the hills and the plains. He hoped this would properly demarcate a boundary and separate British India from Southeast Asia. Lewin's idea was "to establish . . . good stockade villages of courageous stiff necked people of Gorkha who would serve as a buffer between the Mong Raja's territories and independent Lushias to the East" (K. L. Pradhan 2004: 59).

97. Sivaramakrishnan (1999: 192–97).

98. Sivaramakrishnan (1999: 192–97).

99. Golay (2006: 28–33).

100. Other scholarly accounts of the concept of the "coolie" in colonial Asia have emphasized how it melds racial, class, gendered, and even sexual categories. See Breman (1989); Daniel (2008); Daniel, Bernstein, and Brass (1992); and Stoler (1995, 1985).

101. Chatterjee (2001: 75–77).

102. Though Des Chene (1991) explains that the British recruited Gurung and Tamang men into the Gurkha regiments, I observed that this was far from an exclusive classification. Not only were there many Gorkha men who maintained their ethnic affiliations, many others saw ethnic classifications for the army as malleable and fluid. These individuals had paperwork drawn up that stated that they were Gurungs, to gain access to Gurkha regiments. See also Caplan (1995, 1991).

103. Newman and Company (1900: 81).

104. Husain (1970: 234). There is a vast literature on Gurkha soldiers, from accounts written by British and Nepali soldiers (Marks 1974; Tucker 1957; Khanduri 1997; and Muktan 2002) to anthropologists and historians who explored the role Gurkhas played in the British Empire (Caplan 1995, 1991; Des Chene 1991; and Gould 1999). By 1887, the British Army had established two large recruiting centers, Gorakhpur, the headquarters to the south, and Ghoom (in Darjeeling), to the east. The Sikhs also recruited Nepalis into their armies. In fact, the Nepali word for a soldier in a foreign army is *lāhur*, after the Northern Indian, Urdu-speaking city of Lahore, which was the Sikhs' central recruiting center (see Seddon, Adhikari, and Gurung 2002: 19, and 2001). The British brought in Gurkha regiments to put down mutinies across the empire, as they did not bring use local armies on such occasions. The Gurkhas worked to maintain the empire. Many Darjeeling residents told me that such labor tied them to India but also ensured that they would never be fully included in it.

105. Baildon (1882: 145–227); *Notes on Darjeeling* (1888: 70–79).

106. *Notes on Darjeeling* (1888: 73–74).

107. Griffiths (1967: 86).

108. Dash (1947: 113–14).

109. See Bhadra (2005); Lutgendorf (2009).

2. PLANTATION

1. These are lines from a popular Nepali folk song. "(My heart is) fluttering like a silk scarf (*resham*) flapping in the air [*phiriri* is an idiophone for the sound of fluttering fabric]. I am a donkey, you are a monkey."

2. *Budho* is a masculine human qualifier, whereas *purano*, also meaning "old," is used for (nongendered) inanimate objects.

3. Wolf and Mintz (1957) described a seemingly similar transition in Puerto Rican sugar production—one from the hacienda to the plantation. This transition requires material transformations in the modes of production and acquisition of labor. The shift from "industry" to "business" is also materially experienced (e.g., in the actualization of facilities), but the mode of production and status of laborers—intensive plantation-based production—remains the same.

4. These words come from Donna Haraway's David Schneider lecture at the 2010 Society for Cultural Anthropology meeting in Santa Fe, New Mexico (Haraway 2010).

5. See di Leonardo (1987); Lamphere (1985).

6. In *Manufacturing Consent: Changes in the Labor Process under Monopoly Capitalism* (1979), Michael Burawoy ethnographically explores why factory workers in Chicago agree— or "consent"—to participate in an exploitative industrial labor process. See also Willis (1977).

7. See Hardt (1999); Hardt and Negri (2000); McElhinny (2010); and Muehlebach (2011) for a discussion of immaterial and affective labor.

8. Tsing (2012: 148 ff.). In this article, Tsing more directly unpacks the difference between mushroom foraging and sugar plantation cultivation. Tsing also elaborated the comparison between swidden and plantation can in her 2010 lecture, "Nonhumans and Globalization: On Multispecies Storytelling," at the Institute for Research on the Humanities at the University of Wisconsin-Madison.

9. Mintz (1960: 20–21).

10. Tsing (2012: 148 ff.). See also Tsing (2010).

11. Tsing (2012: 148).

12. See Kirksey and Helmreich (2010); Matsutake Worlds Research Group (2010).

13. Deleuze and Guattari(1987). See also Kirskey and Helmreich (2010); Nading (2012). Following a multispecies perspective, Laura Ogden, in her ethnography of the Florida Everglades, examines how human-being "is constituted through changing relations with other animals, plants, material objects, and the like" (Ogden 2011: 2).

14. Ogden (2011).

15. Mauss (2000 [1950]). Nadasdy (2007) makes a similar argument in his analysis of Kluane relationships with the animals they hunt. Nadasdy argues that hunter-quarry relationships, in Kluane conception, are unequal but nonetheless emotionally significant moments of exchange.

16. Scott (1976); Thompson (1971, 1963).

17. Ingold (2011: 51–62).

18. It is significant that labor supervisors are *kākā*, "father's younger brother," not *māmā*, or "mother's brother." *Kākā* would be important and dominant male figures in a women's *māiti ghar*.

19. For a linguistic anthropological analysis of the uses of "uncle" in Nepali, see Turin (2001).

20. Most field and factory terms related to tea manufacture were used in English.

21. In an article on the process by which men are increasingly performing the painstaking manual cross-pollination of cotton varieties in Andhra Pradesh—a task known as "women's work"—Priti Ramamurthy suggests that the feminization of agricultural labor is an "index for the changing relation between labor and capital" (2010: 418). She explains that feminization (i.e., men and children adopting typically female roles) reflects of the business strategies of the multinational corporations that dominate cotton production in India. In a context in which the global agricultural labor force has become increasingly feminized, it is important to understand "how and why laborers . . . feminize their own labor in ways that are significant to them" (2010: 399).

22. "Coolie" is a word that has crept into contemporary vernaculars in South Asia to refer to porters or other manual laborers. It is a colonial term that was used to describe a

range of laborers and is generally thought to be derived from the Tamil word for wage, *kuli* (J. Sharma 2011: 73).

23. Unlike planters in the Northwest and Assam, Darjeeling tea planters neither relied upon imported Chinese "skill" to develop their tea gardens (see J. Sharma 2011), nor did they recruit from famine-ridden areas of the plains of Chotanagpur and pay a per-head price for "coolies."

24. Griffiths (1967: 350).

25. Dash (1947: 49).

26. Quoted in Griffiths (1967: 86), emphasis added.

27. The *sardār* system was not unique to Darjeeling. The British often turned to such middlemen to recruit or indenture laborers. *Sardār* is generally translated as "headman," as in lineage or village headman. In Darjeeling and other plantation enclaves in the Northeast, *sardār* (alternatively, *sirdār* or *sirdāri* system) refers to a labor recruiter: someone who brings laborers from one location to another to work. I will use the Nepali pronunciation, *sardār*.

28. Middleton (2013b).

29. Griffiths (1967: 274).

30. For example, Bimal Gurung, the GJMM leader, was raised on Tukvar, a Gurung-dominated plantation.

31. The 1947 Darjeeling district gazetteer (Dash 1947: 118–19) explains that *sardārs* were paid three to five rupees for every recruit they obtained that worked for one year on the garden, while Nepali recruits were given a small settlement allowance of five to ten rupees.

32. My archival research, including planter diaries and Indian Tea Association archives, reveals that Darjeeling labor practices were unique because there was no district-wide recruiting system, as in Assam and the Dooars. Early planters could not effectively indenture local populations to work; instead, planters saw recruitment of the type I describe here as much more effective for maintaining a quality labor force.

33. English (1982: 264). Verena Stolcke (1988) described a similar phenomenon of family employment in Brazilian coffee.

34. Griffiths (1967: 102).

35. Griffiths (1967: 518–19). The Darjeeling Planters Association (DPA) was renamed the Darjeeling Tea Association (DTA) in the late 1980s. The location of the organization is still called the Darjeeling Planters Club, or simply "The Club."

36. Griffiths (1967: 274).

37. A Darjeeling field worker in 1947 made five annas if he was male, four annas if she was female, and three annas if he or she was a child (an anna was one-sixteenth of a rupee), while factory workers, almost always men, made upward of eight annas a day. Workers were given a per-piece incentive of six pies (there are 192 pies in a rupee) per seer (about two pounds) of green-leaf tea. These payments were perceived to be more of a "task rate" than an actual wage, since parts of this were withheld and paid as bonuses for showing up for five consecutive days (Dash 1947: 119).

38. Subba (1992: 59–60).

39. Dash (1947: 119).

40. ITA (1942: 46).

41. ITA (1942: 46).

42. Griffiths (1967: 113).

43. Dash (1947: 118–19).

44. Plantations closer to Siliguri sometimes hired temporary labor from nonplantation villages to staff monsoonal demand.

45. When referring to management, workers generally say "the company." Less frequently, they used *sahib* (master) or the name of the manager, assistant manager, or owner, accompanied by *sahib*.

46. Also known as the All India Gorkha League (AIGL).

47. Subba (1992: 90).

48. Both the ABGL and the CPI(M) agitated for the rights of workers, but the Congress-backed ABGL took a generally less antagonistic stance toward the planters and the British. The Indian National Trade Union Congress (INTUC) and Congress Party–backed unions, while prominent in other tea growing regions in the Northeast of India, were not a large presence in Darjeeling.

49. Rai (2000: 28). See also K. Sharma (2009: 60–61) for a discussion of the introduction of the bonus. In this book, Sharma also outlines other post-independence legislation for plantation reform.

50. ITA (1948: 147–49). The ITA bulletin for 1947 includes separate rules for Darjeeling houses. Plantation housing in Darjeeling could be smaller and closer together than in other parts of India, the bulletin said, because of the "extremely low temperatures" in Darjeeling, and the "constant movement of air up-hill in they day time and down-hill at night" (ITA 1942: 149).

51. Griffiths (1967: 394).

52. Griffiths (1967: 320).

53. Griffiths (1967: 320).

54. Stoler (2008).

55. Haraway (2010).

56. See Bennett (1978).

57. Plantation labor law also required that planters provide space for schools. Owners had to provide land and a building, while the state provided teachers.

58. Planters have to build new houses for workers, but while the cost of building materials has gone up since 1951, when labor laws were drafted, the fines for noncompliance have stayed the same.

59. Haraway (2010).

60. See Willis (1977) for a discussion of youth and working-class factory labor in Britain. In this ethnography, Willis addresses the structural forces that compel working class youth to participate in working-class labor, while exploring how these young laborers articulate the meaning of their work and their motivations for participating in low-wage labor.

61. Stoler (2008: 194).

62. Scott (1976); Thompson (1971, 1963).

63. The United Nations World Commission on Environment and Development's (or Brundtland Commission) 1987 report "Our Common Future" coined and defined the term "sustainable development" as "development that meets the needs of the present without compromising the ability of future generations to meet their own needs" (WCED 1987: 43). Social scientists have critiqued the implications of the report's prescriptions. For example,

Michael Kearney levies the following critique: "Official support of sustainable development and appropriate technology [is] a de facto recognition that rural poverty in the Third World is not going to be developed out of existence. All peoples will not be brought up to the comfort level of the affluent classes and must therefore adapt to conditions of persistent poverty in ways that are not ecologically, environmentally, or politically disruptive. 'They' must therefore learn to use solar cookers instead of cooking with gas, to use organic compost instead of expensive chemical fertilizer, and so on. . . . [This] project . . . is to sustain existing relations of inequality" (1996: 107). See also Sachs (1992) and Escobar (1995) for critiques of sustainability and international development.

    64. Chatterjee (2001: 6).

    65. Haraway (2010); Ingold (2000).

    66. McWilliams (1935).

    67. Tsing (2012).

3. PROPERTY

    1. After years of cajoling from the government of India and the Tea Board, the EU recognized Darjeeling tea as a Geographical Indication in 2011.

    2. Pierre Boisard (2003 [1992]), in his examination of Camembert, what he calls "the odorous emblem of France" (2003 [1992]: xi) and a recognizable *terroir*-based product, argues that this product, *naturally* associated with Frenchness, is actually embedded in "national myths" about the French nation-state. Similarly, Kolleen Guy (2003) in her study of Champagne, another comestible symbol of the French nation-state, describes how the production of uniquely French wines was tied up in rural populations' integration into the nation. Though France can be most readily identified with discussions of the taste and its relationship to place, *terroir* has become a global commentary on the values, histories, and characteristics of certain foods, as consumers become more aware about the origins of their food (Trubek and Bowen 2008: 24).

    3. Ortiz (1999: 1–2); Roseberry, Gudmundson, and Kutschbach (1995).

    4. Guthman (2007).

    5. "Estate" is another euphemism for the plantation, used as an alternative to "garden."

    6. Following Indian independence in 1947 and the end of the Kingdom of Nepal's century-long isolation, the two governments signed the 1950 Peace and Friendship Treaty (Government of India 1950). The treaty grants citizens of Nepal and India the same rights in the opposite country. Citizens of India can own property, hold a job, and live without any restrictions in Nepal. The same holds true for Nepali citizens in India (Subedi 1994).

    7. Heath and Meneley (2007); Trubek (2008: 10–12).

    8. Ulin (1995). See Wilson (1998) for an extended discussion of the geological and climatic basis for *terroir*.

    9. Hobsbawm and Ranger (1983: 1), emphasis added.

    10. Paxson (2012, 2010, 2006).

    11. Bourdieu (1984). See also Roseberry (1996) and Guthman (2003) for a discussion of class distinctions in food consumption and labeling.

    12. Weiss (2011: 446).

    13. Weiss (2011: 452).

14. These passages appear in a brochure entitled *Overwhelm Your Senses* which was coproduced by the Tea Board of India and the Darjeeling Tea Association (Darjeeling Tea Association n.d.: 3–4).

15. Paige West (2012) has discussed a similar process in the marketing of Papua New Guinean coffee. Images of Papua New Guinean coffee farmers as "primitive" and "poor" helped sell coffee even as they obscured and undermined the attempts of New Guineans to integrate themselves into a modern global market.

16. Paxson (2012); Weiss (2011).

17. Tea Board of India (2003).

18. This echoes the definition of Geographical Indication in article 22, paragraph 1 of the TRIPS agreement, which reads "Geographical indications are . . . indications which identify a good as originating in the territory of a Member, or a region or locality in that territory, where a given quality, reputation or other characteristic of the good is *essentially attributable* to its geographical origin" (Government of India 1999). See www.wto.org/english/docs_e/legal_e/27-trips_04b_e.htm (accessed May 30, 2012; emphasis added).

19. See Bair and Werner (2011).

20. See Paxson (2012); West (2010). Though this assertion and commodification of difference is familiar to scholars of fair trade (Goodman 2004; West 2012).

21. Ecosystem theories in anthropology were inspired by Eugene Odum's *Fundamentals of Ecology* (1979 [1953]), which highlighted the ecosystem as the basic unit of analysis in ecology. The goal of the ecosystem approach was to understand macrolevel organization, function, and interdependence in natural systems (Moran 1984: 6). Odum refers to an ecosystem as the set of all things in a given habitat and the relationships between these things. This conceptualization also assumes that nature tends toward order, harmony, and diversity. Species in an ecosystem evolve together in sets of symbiotic relationships. Increased development of these symbiotic relationships enables the ecosystem to become more stable. Ian Scoones (1999) has described the problems with homeostatic visions of nature and also why they have appeal for public policy.

22. World Intellectual Property Rights Organization (2011).

23. The Tea Board of India does not always win the lawsuits it raises against parties it deems to be misappropriating the Darjeeling name. In 2011, the Tea Board took the hotel chain ITC (owner of several Sonar-labeled hotels across India) to court. The ITC Sonar Bangla Hotel in Kolkata operates a teashop within the hotel, called the Darjeeling Lounge. The High Court ruled that "Darjeeling" was not the sole property of the Tea Board of India (whose offices are just across town from the hotel) and that the hotel could continue to run the teashop under the name. See Spicy IP website, http://spicyipindia.blogspot.com (accessed June 29, 2013) for a discussion of this debate.

24. Ray (1962).

25. W. Anderson (2007).

26. Gross (2007).

27. Mather (2010: 16). The *Jewel in the Crown* was a 1984 British television serial about the last days of the Raj.

28. Blackburn (2006: 70).

29. Tumsong Chiabari: Tea Retreat website, www.chiabari.com/locations.html (accessed July 9, 2013).

30. B. Anderson (1983), quoted in Handler and Saxton (1988: 242).

31. Examining the tequila GI in Mexico, sociologist Sarah Bowen (2010) critically unpacks the potentials for GI as a strategy for "development from within." She explains that national and international intellectual-property-rights law might theoretically protect not only products but also those who produce them, but finds that it may benefit large liquor producers much more than small agave farmers.

32. Guthman (2007) describes how food labels—fair trade, GI, and so on—can each be seen as protecting land, labor, and natural resources from being cheapened or destroyed by the market.

33. Guthman (2007: 473).

34. See Baudrillard (1994); Eco (1995 [1986]); and Benjamin (1968), for postmodern theory on authenticity, simulacra, and representation.

4. FAIRNESS

1. All fair-trade certified plantations were also organic certified, and the majority of these plantations were also "biodynamic," another international certification scheme attesting to sustainable operation.

2. Into this narrative, I weave in work conducted on other fair-trade certified plantations. In Darjeeling, nearly one-third of plantations have been fair-trade certified or were fair-trade certified in 2012. The four plantation owners best associated with fair-trade production in Darjeeling operated twenty-three of these fair-trade plantations.

3. Bryant and Goodman (2004) argue that the reenvisioning of production and consumption linkages through fair trade creates a "solidarity-seeking" commodity culture, in which the products themselves tell stories (what they call "political ecology narratives") about the means of their production. Molly Doane (2010) calls this consumption practice that of purchasing "relationship coffees." This self-narrating product stands in opposition to the "disembedded," personless and placeless commodities that characterize global capitalism (see Kloppenburg, Hendrickson, and Stevenson 1996).

4. West and Carrier (2004) highlight that the ecotourism experience, despite being marketed as something "authentic" and outside of capitalist flows of consumption, is very much a capitalist act that fetishizes poor people and the "natures" in which they live.

5. Fair Trade USA website, http://fairtradeusa.org/what-is-fair-trade (accessed June 12, 2013).

6. Fair Trade USA website, http://fairtradeusa.org/what-is-fair-trade (YouTube video, accessed January 23, 2013; emphasis added).

7. See Reichman (2011) for a discussion of fair trade as postmodern social movement.

8. See Rawls (1971) for an example of liberal political philosophy in which he elaborates a theory of "justice as fairness."

9. Government of India (1951).

10. See Besky (2010).

11. Fair Trade USA website, www.fairtradeusa.org/certification/producers/tea (accessed June 28, 2013).

12. Fairtrade Labelling Organizations International (2011b: 3); see also Besky (2010) for a discussion of the exemptions FLO has made for Darjeeling tea.

13. There are inequities in this system, too; see, for example, Lyon (2011).

14. Fairtrade Labelling Organizations International (2007: 4).

15. Rie Makita (2012) analyzes the material and quantifiable benefits of fair trade on certified plantations in Darjeeling, but conflates fair-trade certification with a Tazo-Starbucks corporate social responsibility project (CHAI). Furthermore, she does not problematize *who* were the recipients of these materials (e.g., medicine, food, transportation, biogas projects), and *whether* these materials were making a difference in plantation residents' lives.

16. See Dolan (2010); Lyon (2010); and Moberg (2010).

17. Forest Department regulations also prohibit owners from logging plantation forests to provide firewood (a ration guaranteed by the Plantations Labour Act).

18. These agreements usually mandate incremental wage increases over the three-year period. The 2008 wage talks resulted in incremental raises between 2008 and 2011—from fifty-three rupees (2008) to fifty-eight rupees (2009) to sixty-three rupees (2010) to sixty-seven rupees (2011). There were wage talks again in 2011, and after a GJMM-led agitation during the talks, the wage was raised to ninety rupees from 2011 to 2014.

19. I use *Pujas* to describe the autumn Hindu festival season, which includes significant festivals such as Dashain, Tihar, and Dashera.

20. Depending on the "grade" of her home plantation, a worker could expect a higher or lower percentage of the annual output to be paid to her as a "bonus." Since the colonial era, tea plantations have been graded. There are, in descending order, "A," "B," "C," and "D" gardens. These grades are based upon the historical prominence of particular tea companies as well as the geographical locations of the plantation.

21. FLO mandates that unions collectively bargain for wages and equitable treatment. On Indian plantations, no single union represents all laborers. Instead, unions are affiliated with political parties, so there can be a few contending unions on any one plantation.

22. Fair Trade USA website, http://fairtradeusa.org/certification/producers/tea (accessed January 23, 2013).

23. Fair Trade USA website, www.fairtradeusa.org/products-partners/tea (accessed June 12, 2013).

24. Fair Trade USA website, www.fairtradeusa.org/certification/producers/tea (accessed June 28, 2013).

25. Source: Indian Associated News Service. Article available online: http://twocircles.net/node/99592 (accessed March 21, 2012). The DTA president made this statement (as did many planters and DTA officials) after the wage meetings in 2008.

26. Scott (1976).

27. I thank Sarah Lyon for this astute comment.

28. Bryant and Goodman (2004).

29. Ferguson (1994) describes the discourses and practices of development agencies in Lesotho as an "antipolitics machine," which obscures the historical political economic realities of the locations in which "development" occurs.

30. Fridell (2007).

31. Kamat (2004: 164).

32. Reichman (2011).

5. SOVEREIGNTY

1. See K. Sharma (2003) for a case study of Temi Tea Estate in nearby Sikkim, which—like Meghma—does not enjoy the benefits of Darjeeling GI status despite sharing similar climatic conditions.

2. The anthropology of labor and migration in South Asia has been an important area of inquiry; see Biao (2007); De Neve (2003); Gardner (1995, 1991); Gardner and Osella (2003); Gidwani and Sivaramakrishnan (2003); Parry (2003); Osella and Osella (2003); and Shah (2006).

3. People in present-day Nepal and India have long traded with each other, primarily through Kalimpong. See Shneiderman (2005).

4. For ethnographic accounts of the Maoist insurgency, see Hutt (2004).

5. Subedi (1994).

6. Ong (1999). The Peace and Friendship Treaty reads:

> Each government undertakes, in token of neighborly friendship between India and Nepal, to give the nationals of the other, in its territory, national treatment with regard to participation in industrial and economic development of such territory and to the grant of concessions and contracts relating to such development. . . . The Government of India and Nepal agree to grant, on a reciprocal basis, to the nationals of one country in the territories of the other the save privileges in the matter of residence, ownership of property, participation in trade and commerce, movement and other privileges of similar nature. (Moktan 2004: 44–46)

7. Scholars have explored how Nepali migration to India is an important source of revenue for communities in Nepal (see Hitchcock 1961; Seddon 2005; and Seddon, Adhikari, and Gurung 2002, 2001). Since the start of the civil war in Nepal in 1999, migration is often the only option for many Nepali villagers. Seddon (2005) found that in 2004 India employed 700,000 Nepalis; 400,000 of whom worked in the private sector, 250,000 in the public sectors, and 50,000 in the Indian Army, specifically in the "Gurkha Rifles."

8. Subba (2002: 131).

9. Middleton (2013a).

10. There are interesting parallels between Guneratne's (2002) study of the Tharu and my fieldwork with Gorkhas. Both groups have only recently come to identify themselves as one people. Gorkhas, like Tharu, also identify with smaller linguistically distinct tribal and ethnic identities.

11. Hutt (1997: 102). See also Middleton (2013b), for an extended discussion of the politics of "anxiety" in the Darjeeling Nepali "identity crisis."

12. Nepali intellectuals in Darjeeling organized and founded the Nepali Sahitya Sammelan (Nepali Literature Association) in 1924, which was the first institution to use the term *Nepali* to identify people who spoke the language but lived outside the kingdom of Nepal. In the inaugural meeting of the Nepali Sahitya Sammelan in 1924, the association's chairman said: "The Darjeeling Nepalis have become a *jāti* (ethnic group) that is bound together by the thread of common experience, shared sentiments, and a single language" (Hutt 1997: 117). By the 1930s, the word Nepali had crept into the vernacular and catalyzed the construc-

tion of a cohesive "Nepali" identity (Hutt 1997: 114). The Nepali language remains one basis for being Nepali outside of Nepal (Chalmers 2007: 97; Hutt 2003, 1997). Hutt explains that there are problems with using the concept of diaspora to describe Indian Nepalis, because the consolidation of Nepali identity occurred after the formation of the contemporary kingdom of Nepal (Hutt 1997: 103). Gorkhas, like Sikkimese and Nepalis living in Bhutan before 1992, did not think of themselves as part of a diaspora. They were Nepalis, but not *of* Nepal. Gorkhas thought of themselves as part of India.

At the turn of the century, Nepalis in Darjeeling began to organize and work toward the attainment of greater rights within India. The Hillmen's Association, the Darjeeling-based political party representing Nepali and Tibetan interests, submitted two different memoranda to the central government demanding a "separate administrative setup" for Darjeeling in 1907 and 1917 (Subba 1992: 76–77). That the party adopted the colonial moniker of "hillmen" for their party speaks to a long history of embodiment of British cultural taxonomies. The Hillmen's Association petitioned various councils and commissions for political autonomy, in 1929, 1930, and 1941. A GJMM Central Committee pamphlet (2009) provides and elaborated timeline of the various attempts by different Gorkha-led parties in Darjeeling for autonomy. Perhaps more importantly, the party advocated for the collective interests of all Nepali, Bhutia, and Lepcha peoples living in Darjeeling (Hutt 1997: 127). Even after the death of the Hillmen's Association's charismatic leader, S. W. Laden La (and the folding of the Hillmen's Association into a interregional Nepali party, the Akhil Bharatiya Gorkha League [ABGL]), the idea of regional autonomy for all Nepali speakers remained an evocative force in Darjeeling life (Rhodes and Rhodes 2006). In the postcolonial era, leaders of the Nepali Bhasha Andolan (Nepali Language Movement) built upon the foundation laid by the Hillmen's Association, fighting a long-term battle for language recognition on both state and local stages. Though Bengali was made the official language of West Bengal in 1958, in 1971, Nepali was added as an additional language for the Darjeeling district. In 1992, Nepali was added to the Eighth Schedule of the Indian constitution, making it an officially recognized language in the state of West Bengal (Hutt 1997: 125–26).

13. See Hutt (2003, 1997). In the early 1990s, Bhutan had set in motion the final stages the expulsion of over one hundred thousand Bhutanese Nepalis. The king of Bhutan recruited agriculturalist Nepalis to the fertile fields of southern Bhutan at the same time their relatives were coming to Darjeeling. By the 1980s, Nepalis constituted one-third of Bhutan's population.

14. Ong (1999).

15. J. Sharma (2011); Chatterjee (2001). See also Breman (1989); Daniel (2008); Daniel, Bernstein, and Brass (1992). The condensation of labor and identity has even made it into popular historical fiction. Amitav Ghosh's fictional depiction of the plantation economies of opium and sugar in *Sea of Poppies* (2008) and *River of Smoke* (2011), describe a similar homogenization of class, caste, and regional identity in West Bengal and Mauritius.

16. Lopez (2012) and Patterson (2012) have identified a similar association between aptitude for affective service labor and Filipinos.

17. Tamang disbanded the Pranta Parishad in 1990, forming the Gorkha Democratic Front. In 2001, the Democratic front merged with the ABGL, with Tamang as president.

18. Middleton (2013b).

19. For an overview of the 1986–88 movement, see Subba (1992).

20. Banerjie, Bagchi, and Mitra (1988: 17).

21. Banerjie, Bagchi and Mitra (1988: 18–19); Samanta (1996: 148); and Subba (1992: 136–40).

22. For a detailed description of the violence on tea plantations in the mid-1980s; see Subba (1992: 125–42). And for a case study of Darjeeling plantation life after the first Gorkhaland agitation and under GNLF labor unions, see K. Sharma (2000).

23. The CPI(M) was the only party that outwardly opposed the GNLF, see Subba (1992: 125–27), though arguably the more devastating violence took place between the GNLF and the CRPF (and other members of state and national security forces dispatched to Darjeeling).

24. By the end of the first Gorkhaland agitation in 1988, GNLF politicians and planters had succeeded in marginalizing the power the Communist Party had in Darjeeling. GNLF unions marginalized CPRM unions. These new unions were not accountable to any larger regional or national political structure. While the Congress and Communist Parties maintained a nominal presence on plantations after 1988, after the end of the first Gorkhaland agitation, the GNLF unions have comprised the overwhelming majority.

25. See Middleton (2013c).

26. See Shneiderman (2009b) and Shneiderman and Turin (2006) for a discussion of samāj-based Thangmi ethnic activism in India and Nepal. This use of samāj should not be confused with a plantation samāj, or village-level (or multiple village) organizations on individual plantations.

27. See Middleton (2011); See also Shneiderman (2009).

28. See Middleton (2011) for a discussion of Indian Idol and the early days of the Gorkhaland agitation.

29. Note the three symbols: the sun, mountains (Kanchenjunga) and the crossed khukuris. These three things symbolize the strength (mountains), longevity (sun), and bravery (khukuri) of the Gorkha people. The khukuri symbolism was alternatively described to me as a reminder of the "capabilities" of the Gorkhas.

30. For an example of primordialist claims in subnationalism in Assam, another tea-growing district of India, through "the soil," see Nag (2002).

31. See Hutt (1998) for a discussion of Nepali migration to India and Bhutan in Nepali-language literature.

32. See Middleton (2013a) for a discussion of the roots of this form of legitimacy and belonging.

33. I use "Pujas" as colloquial shorthand for the autumn Hindu festival season.

34. The seventh days of October and November were significant to Gurung. He was something of a numerologist, and the dates and times of Gorkhaland events frequently appeared to him in dreams.

35. C.f. B. Anderson (1983); Foucault (1995 [1977]).

36. See also Ortner (1999).

37. See Boellstorff (2004); Bourgois (2002); Ewing (2008); Gill (1997); Gutmann (1996); and Hansen (1996) for anthropological discussions of masculinity.

38. Bhūmī is a politically charged word, borrowed from Hindi (bas bhūmī, literally translated as "sat upon land"). I translate it here as "land," or "place" (in congruence with Basso's [1996] descriptions of places as made through stories and human interactions).

Bhūmī is evoked in subnationalists and other political movements across India. That *bhūmī* (a key concept in movements for autonomy in India) accompanies *māto* (a Nepali word associated with farming) in this chant is significant. *Māto* connotes actual, physical dirt and soil. That Gorkhas are calling for the return of both conceptualizations of land—in its *bhūmī* (political) aspects and its *māto* (material) aspects, speaks to the significance of agricultural life and labor in the movement for Gorkhaland. *Jamin* is also frequently used to connote "land."

39. See Bourgois (1989, 1988); Moberg (1997, 1996)

40. See Chatterjee (2001); J. Sharma (2011).

41. Stoler (2008).

CONCLUSION

1. Tsing (2005).

2. See Escobar (1995); Ferguson (1994); W. Fisher (1997); and Gupta (1998) for discussions of the anthropology of development.

3. See Goodman (2004); Luetchford (2008).

4. Stoler (2008).

5. Haraway (2010).

BIBLIOGRAPHY

Anderson, Benedict. 1983. *Imagined Communities: Reflections on the Origin and Spread of Nationalism.* New York: Verso.

Anderson, Wes. 2007. *The Darjeeling Limited.* Film. Los Angeles: Fox Searchlight Pictures.

Appadurai, Arjun. 1986. "Commodities and the Politics of Value." Introduction to *The Social Life of Things: Commodities in Cultural Perspective,* ed. Arjun Appadurai, 3–63. Cambridge: Cambridge University Press.

Arnold, David. 2006. *The Tropics and the Traveling Gaze: India, Landscape, and Science, 1800–1856.* Seattle: University of Washington Press.

———. 2005. "Agriculture and 'Improvement' in Early Colonial India: A Pre-History of Development." *Journal of Agrarian Change* 5(4): 505–25.

Axelby, Richard. 2008. "Calcutta Botanic Garden and the Colonial Re-ordering of the Indian Environment." *Archives of Natural History* 35(1): 150–63.

Bacon, Christopher. 2010. "Who Decides What Is Fair in Fair Trade? The Agri-Environmental Governance of Standards, Access, and Price." *Journal of Peasant Studies* 37(1): 111–47.

———. 2005. "Confronting the Coffee Crisis: Can Fair Trade, Organic, and Specialty Coffees Reduce Small-Scale Farmer Vulnerability in Northern Nicaragua?" *World Development* 33(3): 497–511.

Baildon, Samuel. 1882. *The Tea Industry in India: A Review of Finance and Labour and a Guide for Capitalists.* London: W. H. Allen.

Bair, Jennifer, and Marion Werner. 2011. "Commodity Chains and the Uneven Geographies of Global Capitalism: A Disarticulations Perspective." *Environment and Planning A* 43(5): 988–97.

Banerjie, Indranil, Rajiv Bagchi, and Nirmal Mitra. 1988. "Peace in the Hills?" *Sunday* (Calcutta: Ananda Bazar) 15(34): 14–21.

Basso, Keith. 1996. *Wisdom Sits in Places.* Albuquerque: University of New Mexico Press.

Bates, Crispin, and Marina Carter. 1992. "Tribal Migration in India and Beyond." In *The World of the Rural Labourer in Colonial India*, ed. Gyan Prakash, 205–48. Delhi: Oxford University Press.

Baudrillard, Jean. 1994. *Simulacra and Simulation*. Trans. Sheila Faria Glaser. Ann Arbor: University of Michigan Press.

Behal, Rana, and Prabhu Mohapatra. 1992. "'Tea and Money Versus Human Life': The Rise and Fall of the Indenture System in the Assam Tea Plantations, 1840–1908." Special issue: *Plantations, Proletarians, and Peasants in Colonial Asia. Journal of Peasant Studies* 19(3–4): 142–72.

Beidelman, Thomas. 1959. *A Comparative Analysis of the Jajmani System*. Monographs of the Association for Asian Studies, no. 8. New York: J. J. Augustin.

Beinart, William, and Lotte Hughes. 2007. *Environment and Empire*. Oxford: Oxford University Press.

Benjamin, Walter. 1968. *Illuminations*. Ed., with an introduction by Hannah Arendt. Trans. Harry Zohn. New York: Schocken Books.

Bennett, Lynn. 1978. "Maiti Ghar: The Dual Role of High Caste Women in Nepal. In *Himalayan Anthropology: The Indo-Tibetan Interface*, ed. James Fisher, 121–40. The Hague: Mouton Publishers.

Besky, Sarah. 2010. "Colonial Pasts and Fair Trade Futures: Changing Modes of Production and Regulation on Darjeeling Tea Plantations." In *Fair Trade and Social Justice: Global Ethnographies*, ed. Sarah Lyon and Mark Moberg, 97–122. New York: New York University Press.

———. 2008. "Can a Plantation be Fair? Paradoxes and Possibilities in Fair Trade Darjeeling Tea Production." *Anthropology of Work Review* 29(1): 1–9.

Bhadra, Gautam. 2005. *From Imperial Product to a National Drink: The Culture of Tea Consumption in Modern India*. Kolkata: Tea Board India.

Bhadra R. K. 1997. *Social Dimension of Health of Tea Plantation Workers in India*. Dibrugarh: N.L. Publishers.

Bhadra, R. K., and M. Bhadra. 1997. *Plantation Labours of North-east India*. Dibrugarh: N.L. Publishers.

Bhanja, K. C. 1943. *Wonders of Darjeeling and Sikkim Himalaya: All Accounts Authentic*. Darjeeling: Gilbert.

Biao, Xiang. 2007. *Global Body Shopping: An Indian Labor System in the Information Technology Industry*. Princeton, NJ: Princeton University Press.

Bishop, Peter. 1989. *The Myth of Shangri-la: Tibet, Travel Writing, and the Creation of Sacred Landscape*. Berkeley: University of California Press.

Biswas, Sanjay, and Sameer Roka. 2007. *Darjeeling: Truth and Beyond*. Darjeeling: Systematic Computerised Offset Printers.

Blackburn, Janice. 2006. "The Perfect Tea Break." *Condé Nast Traveller*, August 2006, 69–70.

Blunt, Alison. 1999. "Imperial Geographies of Home: British Domesticity in India, 1886–1925." *Transactions of the Institute of British Geographers*, n.s., 24(4): 421–40.

———. 1997. "Travelling Home and Empire: British Women in India, 1857–1939." Ph.D. diss., Department of Geography, University of British Columbia.

Boellstorff, Tom. 2004. "The Emergence of Political Homophobia in Indonesia: Masculinity and National Belonging." *Ethnos* 69(4): 465–86.

Boisard, Pierre. 2003 [1992]. *Camembert: A National Myth*. Trans. Richard Miller. Berkeley: University of California Press.

Bourdieu, Pierre. 1984. *Distinction: A Social Critique of the Judgment of Taste*. Trans. R. Nice. London: Routledge.

Bourgois, Philippe. 2002. *In Search of Respect: Selling Crack in El Barrio*. 2nd ed. New York: Cambridge University Press.

———. 1989. *Ethnicity at Work: Divided Labor on a Central American Banana Plantation*. Baltimore: Johns Hopkins University Press.

———. 1988. "Conjugated Oppression: Class and Ethnicity among Guaymi and Kuna Banana Workers." *American Ethnologist* 15(2): 328–48.

Bowen, Sarah. 2010. "Development from Within? The Potential for Geographic Indications in the Global South." *Journal of World Intellectual Property* 13(2): 231–52.

Bowen, Sarah, and Ana Valenzuela Zapata. 2009. "Geographical Indications, *Terroir*, and Socioeconomic and Ecological Sustainability: The Case of Tequila." *Journal of Rural Studies* 25: 108–19.

Breman, Jan. 1993 [1973]. *Beyond Patronage and Exploitation: Changing Agrarian Relations in South Gujarat*. 2nd ed. Delhi: Oxford University Press.

———. 1989. *Taming the Coolie Beast: Plantation Society and the Colonial Order in Southeast Asia*. Oxford: Oxford University Press.

Brockway, Lucille. 1979. *Science and Colonialism: The Role of the British Royal Botanical Gardens in Empire-Building*. New Haven, CT: Yale University Press.

Brown, Jane. 2011. *The Omnipotent Magician: Lancelot "Capability" Brown, 1716–1783*. London: Chatto and Windus.

Bryant, Raymond, and Michael Goodman. 2004. "Consuming Narratives: The Political Ecology of 'Alternative' Consumption." *Transactions of the Institute of British Geographers*, n.s., 29(3): 344–66.

Burawoy, Michael. 1979. *Manufacturing Consent: Changes in the Labor Process under Monopoly Capitalism*. Chicago: University of Chicago Press.

Burghart, Richard. 1984. "Formation of a Concept of the Nation-State in Nepal." *Journal of Asian Studies* 1: 101–25.

Cameron, Mary. 1998. *On the Edge of the Auspicious: Gender and Caste in Nepal*. Urbana: University of Illinois Press.

Campbell, Archibald. 1869. "On Lepchas." *Journal of the Ethnological Society of London* 1(2): 143–57.

Campbell, George. 1867. "On the Geography and Climate of India, in Reference to the Best Site for a Capital." *Proceedings of the Royal Geographical Society of London* 11(2): 54–77.

Caplan, Lionel. 1995. *Warrior Gentlemen: "Gurkhas" in the Western Imagination*. Providence, RI: Berghahn Books.

———. 1991. "'Bravest of the Brave': Representation of 'The Gurkha' in British Military Writings." *Modern Asian Studies* 25(3): 571–97.

———. 1970. *Land and Social Change in East Nepal: A Study of Hindu-Tribal Relations*. Kathmandu: Himal Books.

Chakravorty, R. N. 1997. *Socio-Economic Development of Plantation Workers in North East India*. Dibrugarh: N.L. Publishers.

Chalmers, Rhoderick. 2007. "Nepal and the Eastern Himalayas." In *Language and National Identity in Asia*, ed. Andrew Simpson, 84–99. Oxford: Oxford University Press.

Chamney, Montfort. 1930. *The Story of the Tea Leaf*. Calcutta: New India Press.

Chatterjee, Piya. 2001. *A Time for Tea: Women, Labor, and Post/colonial Politics on an Indian Plantation*. Durham, NC: Duke University Press.

Chatterji, Aditi. 2007. *Contested Landscapes: The Story of Darjeeling*. Calcutta: Indian National Trust for Art and Cultural Heritage (INTACH).

Caturvedi, Madendra, and Bhola N. Tiwari. 1970. *A Practical Hindi-English Dictionary*. New Delhi: National Publication House.

Chaudhuri, K. N. 1978. *The Trading World of Asia and the English East India Company, 1660–1760*. Cambridge: Cambridge University Press.

Chayanov, A. V. 1986 [1966]. *The Theory of the Peasant Economy*. Madison: University of Wisconsin Press.

Checker, Melissa. 2005. *Polluted Promises: Environmental Racism and the Search for Justice in a Southern Town*. New York: New York University Press.

Chung, Tan. 1974. "The British-China-India Trade Triangle (1771–1840)." *Indian Economic and Social History Review*. 6(4): 411–31.

Clarke, Hyde. 1881. "The English Stations in the Hill Regions of India: Their Value and Importance, with Some Statistics of Their Products and Trade." *Journal of the Statistical Society of London* 44(3): 528–73.

Clifford, James. 1997. *Routes: Travel and Translation in the Late Twentieth Century*. Cambridge, MA: Harvard University Press.

Colman, Tyler. 2008. *Wine Politics: How Governments, Environmentalists, Mobsters, and Critics Influence the Wines We Drink*. Berkeley: University of California Press.

Daniel, E. Valentine. 2008. "The Coolie." *Cultural Anthropology* 23(2): 254—78.

Daniel, E. Valentine, Henry Bernstein, and Thomas Brass, eds. 1992. *Plantations, Proletarians, and Peasants in Colonial Asia*. London: Frank Cass.

Darjeeling Tea Association (DTA). N.d. *Overwhelm Your Senses*. Kolkata: Darjeeling Tea Association. Author's personal collection.

Das Gupta, Ranajit. 1994. *Labour and Working Class in Eastern India*. Calcutta: K. P. Bagchi.

Dash, Arthur. 1947. *Bengal District Gazetteers: Darjeeling*. Alipore: Bengal Government Press.

Deleuze, Gilles, and Felix Guattari. 1987. *A Thousand Plateaus: Capitalism and Schizophrenia*. Minneapolis: University of Minnesota Press.

De Neve, Geert. 2003. "Expectations and Rewards of Modernity: Commitment and Mobility among Rural Migrants in Tirupur, Tamil Nadu." *Contributions to Indian Sociology* 37: 251–80.

Des Chene, Mary. 1991. "Relics of Empire: A Cultural History of the Gurkhas, 1815–1987." Ph.D. diss., Department of Anthropology, Stanford University.

Desai, Kiran. 2006. *The Inheritance of Loss*. New York: Grove Press.

Dewan, Dick. 1991. *Education in the Darjeeling Hills: An Historical Survey, 1835–1985*. New Delhi: Indus Publishing.

di Leonardo, Michaela. 1987. "The Female World of Cards and Holidays: Women, Families, and the Work of Kinship." *Signs* 12(3): 440–53.

Doane, Molly. 2010. "Relationship Coffees: Structure and Agency in the Fair Trade System." In *Fair Trade and Social Justice: Global Ethnographies*, ed. Sarah Lyon and Mark Moberg, 229–57. New York: New York University Press.

———. 2007. "The Political Economy of the Ecological Native." *American Anthropologist* 109(3): 452–62.

Dodin, Thierry, and Heinz Rather, eds. 2001. *Imagining Tibet: Perceptions, Projections, Fantasies*. Boston: Wisdom Publications.

Dolan, Catherine. 2010. "Fractured Ties: The Business of Development in Kenyan Fair Trade Tea." In *Fair Trade and Social Justice: Global Ethnographies*, ed. Sarah Lyon and Mark Moberg, 147–75. New York: New York University Press.

Dolan, Catherine, and Michael Blowfield. 2010. "Fairtrade Facts and Fancies: What Kenyan Fair Trade Tea Tells Us about Business' Role as Development Agent." *Journal of Business Ethics* 93, supp. 1: 143–62.

Dozey, E. C. 1922. *A Concise History of the Darjeeling District since 1835*. Calcutta: R. N. Mukherjee.

Drayton, Richard. 2000. *Nature's Government: Science, Imperial Britain, and the "Improvement" of the World*. New Haven, CT: Yale University Press.

Dumont, Louis. 1980. *Homo Hierarchicus: An Essay on the Caste System*. Trans. Willard Sainsbury. Chicago: University of Chicago Press.

DuPuis, E. Melanie. 2002. *Nature's Perfect Food: How Milk Became America's Drink*. New York: New York University Press.

Eco, Umberto. 1995 [1986]. *Faith in Fakes: Travels in Hyperreality*. London: Minerva.

Edelman, Marc. 1998. "Transnational Peasant Politics in Central America." *Latin American Research Review* 33(3): 49–86.

English, Richard. 1982. "Gorkhali and Kiranti: Political Economy in the Eastern Hills of Nepal." Ph.D. diss., Department of Anthropology, New School for Social Research.

Escobar, Arturo. 1995. *Encountering Development: The Making and Unmaking of the Third World*. Princeton, NJ: Princeton University Press.

Ewing, Katherine Pratt. 2008. *Stolen Honor: Stigmatizing Muslim Men in Berlin*. Stanford, CA: Stanford University Press.

Fairtrade Labelling Organizations International (FLO) 2011a. *Fairtrade Standard for Hired Labour (May 1, 2011)*. Bonn, Germany: FLO.

———. 2011b. *Fairtrade Standards for Tea for Hired Labour (May 1, 2011)*. Bonn, Germany: FLO.

———. 2007. *Explanatory Document for the Fair Trade Premium and Join Bodies in Hired Labour Situations (December 17, 2007)*. Bonn, Germany: FLO.

Fayrer, Joseph. 1900. "An Address on Hill Stations of India as Health Resorts." *British Medical Journal* 1(2058): 1393–97.

Ferguson, James. 1994. *The Anti-Politics Machine: "Development," Depoliticization, and Bureaucratic Power in Lesotho*. Minneapolis: University of Minnesota Press.

Fisher, James. 1978. Introduction to *Himalayan Anthropology: The Indo-Tibetan Interface*, ed. James Fisher, 1–3. The Hauge: Mouton Publishers.

Fisher, William. 1997. "Doing Good: The Politics and Antipolitics of NGO Practices." *Annual Review of Anthropology* 26: 439–64.

Flueckiger, Joyce. 2006. *In Amma's Healing Room: Gender and Vernacular Islam in South India*. Bloomington: Indiana University Press.

Forbes, Ann Armbrecht. 1999. "Mapping Power: Disputing Claims to Kipat Lands in North-eastern Nepal." *American Ethnologist* 26(1): 114–38.

Foucault, Michel. 1995 [1977]. *Discipline and Punish: The Birth of the Prison*. New York: Vintage Books.

Fox, Jennifer. 1993. *In the Shade of Kanchenjunga*. London: British Association for Cemeteries in South Asia.

Freidberg, Susanne. 2004. *French Beans and Food Scares: Culture and Commerce in an Anxious Age*. Oxford: Oxford University Press.

Fridell, Gavin. 2007. *Fair Trade Coffee: The Prospects and Pitfalls of Market-Driven Social Justice*. Toronto: University of Toronto Press.

Frundt, Henry. 2009. *Fair Bananas: Farmers, Workers, and Consumers Strive to Change an Industry*. Tucson: University of Arizona Press.

Ganguly, Rajat. 2005. "Poverty, Malgovernance, and Ethnopolitical Mobilization: Gorkha Nationalism and the Gorkhaland Agitation in India." *Nationalism and Ethnic Politics* 11: 467–502.

Gardner, Katy. 1995. *Global Migrants, Local Lives: Travel and Transformation in Rural Bangladesh*. Oxford: Clarendon Press.

———. 1991. *Songs at the Rivers Edge: Stories from a Bangladeshi Village*. London: Verso.

Gardner, Katy, and Filippo Osella. 2003. "Migration, Modernity, and Social Transformation in South Asia: An Overview." *Contributions to Indian Sociology* 37: v–xxviii.

Ghosh, Amitav. 2011. *River of Smoke*. New Delhi: Penguin India.

———. 2008. *Sea of Poppies*. New Delhi: Penguin India.

Gidwani, Vinay. 1992. "'Waste' and the Permanent Settlement in Bengal." *Economic and Political Weekly* 27(4) (January 25, 1992): PE39–PE46.

Gidwani, Vinay, and K. Sivaramakrishnan. 2003. "Circular Migration and Rural Cosmopolitanism in India." *Contributions to Indian Sociology* 37: 339–67.

Gill, Lesley. 1997. "Creating Citizens, Making Men: The Military and Masculinity in Bolivia." *Cultural Anthropology* 12(4): 527–50.

Golay, Bidhan. 2006. "Rethinking Gorkha Identity: Outside the Imperium of Discourse, Hegemony, and History." *Peace and Democracy in South Asia* 2(1–2): 23–49.

Goodman, Michael. 2004. "Reading Fair Trade: Political Ecological Imaginary and the Moral Economy of Fair Trade Foods." *Political Geography* 23(7): 891–915.

Gorer, Geoffrey. 1938 [2005]. *Himalayan Village: An Account of the Lepchas of Sikkim*. Varnasi: Pilgrims Publishing.

Gorkha Janamukti Morcha Central Committee. 2009. *Why Gorkhaland?* Darjeeling: Gorkha Janamukti Morcha Central Committee. Author's personal collection.

Gould, Tony. 1999. *Imperial Warriors: Britain and the Gurkhas*. London: Grata Books.

Government of India. 1999. *The Geographical Indications of Goods (Registration and Protection) Act, 1999*. No. 48 of 1,999. New Delhi: Ministry of Law, Justice, and Company Affairs (Legislative Department).

———. 1973. *The Foreign Exchange Regulation Act*. No. 46 of 1973. Amended, no. 29 of 1993. New Delhi.

———. 1951. *The Plantations Labour Act, 1951*. No. 69 of 1951, November 2, 1951. New Delhi.

———. 1950. *Treaty of Peace and Friendship between the Government of India and the Government of Nepal*. July 31, 1950. Kathmandu, Nepal.

Griffith, William. 1840. *Report on the Tea Plant of Upper Assam.* Originally published in *British Parliamentary Papers,* 1839. National Library Papers, Calcutta.

Griffiths, Percival. 1967. *The History of the British Tea Industry.* London: Weidenfeld and Nicolson.

Gross, Matthew. 2007. "High Tea, India Style." *New York Times,* October 14, 2007.

Grove, Richard. 2002. "Climatic Fears: Colonialism and the History of Environmentalism." *Harvard International Review* 23(4): 50–55.

———. 1995. *Green Imperialism: Colonial Expansion, Tropical Island Edens, and the Origins of Environmentalism, 1600–1860.* Cambridge: Cambridge University Press.

Guneratne, Arjun. 2002. *Many Tongues, One People: The Making of Tharu Identity in Nepal.* Ithaca, NY: Cornell University Press.

Gupta, Akhil. 1998. *Postcolonial Developments: Agriculture and the Making of Modern India.* Durham, NC: Duke University Press.

Guthman, Julie. 2011. *Weighing In: Obesity, Food Justice, and the Limits of Capitalism.* Berkeley: University of California Press.

———. 2007. "The Polanyian Way? Voluntary Food Labels as Neoliberal Governance." *Antipode* 39(3): 456–478.

———. 2004. *Agrarian Dreams: The Paradox of Organic Farming in California.* Berkeley: University of California Press.

———. 2003. "Fast Food/Organic Food: Reflexive Tastes and the Making of 'Yuppie Chow.'" *Journal of Social and Cultural Geography* 4(1): 43–56.

Gutmann, Matthew. 1996. *The Meanings of Macho: Being a Man in Mexico City.* Berkeley: University of California Press.

Guy, Kolleen. 2003. *When Champagne Became French.* Baltimore: Johns Hopkins University Press.

Handler, Richard, and William Saxton. 1988. "Dyssimulation: Reflexivity, Narrative, and the Quest for Authenticity in 'Living History.'" *Cultural Anthropology* 3(3): 242–60.

Hansen, Thomas Blom. 1996. "Recuperating Masculinity: Hindu Nationalism, Violence, and the Exorcism of the Muslim 'Other.'" *Critique of Anthropology* 16(2): 137–72.

Haraway, Donna. 2010. "Staying with the Trouble: Xenoecologies of Home for Companions in the Contested Zones." David Schneider Lecture, Society for Cultural Anthropology (SCA) meeting, May 7, 2010. Santa Fe, NM.

Hardt, Michael. 1999. "Affective Labor." *boundary* 26(2): 89–100.

Hardt, Michael, and Antonio Negri. 2000. *Empire.* Cambridge, MA: Harvard University Press.

Harrison, Jill. 2011. *Pesticide Drift and the Pursuit of Environmental Justice.* Cambridge, MA: MIT Press.

Heath, Deborah, and Anne Meneley. 2007. "Techne, Technoscience, and the Circulation of Comestible Commodities: An Introduction." *American Anthropologist* 109(4): 593–602.

Henderson, George. 2013. *Value in Marx: The Persistence of Value in a More-Than-Capitalist World.* Minneapolis: University of Minnesota Press.

Herbert, Eugenia. 2011. *Flora's Empire: British Gardens in India.* Philadelphia: University of Pennsylvania Press.

Herring, Ronald. 2005. "Miracle Seeds, Suicide Seeds, and the Poor: GMOs, NGOs, Farmers, and the State." In *Social Movements in India: Poverty, Power, and Politics,* ed. Raka Ray and Mary Katzenstein, 203–32. New Delhi: Oxford University Press.

Hetherington, Kregg. 2011. *Guerilla Auditors: The Politics of Transparency in Neoliberal Paraguay.* Durham, NC: Duke University Press.

Herzfeld, Michael. 1992. *The Social Production of Indifference: Exploring the Symbolic Roots of Western Bureaucracy.* Chicago: University of Chicago Press.

Hilton, James. 1933. *Lost Horizon.* New York: Grosset and Dunlap.

Hitchcock, John. 1961. "A Nepalese Hill Village and Indian Employment." *Asian Survey* 1(9): 15–20.

Hobsbawm, Eric, and Terence Ranger, eds. 1983. *The Invention of Tradition.* Cambridge: Cambridge University Press.

Hoheneggar, Beatrice. 2007. *Liquid Jade: The Story of Tea from East to West.* New York: St. Martin's Press.

Holmes, Seth. 2013. *Fresh Fruit, Broken Bodies: Migrant Farm Workers in the United States.* Berkeley: University of California Press.

Hull, Matthew. 2012. *Government of Paper: The Materiality of Bureaucracy in Urban Pakistan.* Berkeley: University of California Press.

Husain, Asad. 1970. *British India's Relations with the Kingdom of Nepal, 1857–1947: A Diplomatic History of Nepal.* London: George Allen and Unwin.

Hutt, Michael, ed. 2004. *Himalayan People's War: Nepal's Maoist Rebellion.* Bloomington: Indiana University Press.

———. 2003. *Unbecoming Citizens: Culture, Nationhood, and the Flight of Refugees from Bhutan.* New York: Oxford University Press.

———. 1998. "Going to Mugulan: Nepali Literary Representations of Migration to India and Bhutan." *South Asia Research* 18(2): 195–214.

———. 1997. "Being Nepali without Nepal: Reflections on a South Asian Diaspora." In *Nationalism and Ethnicity in a Hindu Kingdom: The Politics of Culture in Contemporary Nepal,* ed. David N. Gellner, Joanna Pfaff-Czarnecka, John Whelpton, 101–44. Amsterdam: Harwood.

Ingold, Tim. 2011. *Being Alive: Essays on Movement, Knowledge, and Description.* London: Routledge.

———. 2000. *The Perception of the Environment: Essays on Livelihood, Dwelling, and Skill.* London: Routledge.

ITA. 1948. *Detailed Report of the General Committee of the Indian Tea Association for the Year 1947, Including a List of Tea Estates Members of the Association, Corrected to 30th June 1948, with Proceedings of the Sixty-Seventh Annual General Meeting Held on the 12th March 1948.* Calcutta: Indian Tea Association.

———. 1942. *Detailed Report of the General Committee of the Indian Tea Association for the Year 1941, Including a List of Tea Estates Members of the Association, Corrected to 31st May 1942, with Proceedings of the Sixty-First Annual General Meeting Held on the 6th March 1942.* Calcutta: Indian Tea Association.

Jaffee, Daniel. 2007. *Brewing Justice: Fair Trade Coffee, Sustainability, and Survival.* Berkeley: University of California Press.

Jefferson, Thomas. 1999 [1785]. *Notes on the State of Virginia.* New York: Penguin Classics.

Kamat, Sangeeta. 2004. "The Privatization of Public Interest: Theorizing NGO Discourse in a Neoliberal Era." *Review of International Political Economy* 11(1): 155–76.

Kar, Bodhisattva. 2011. "Frontier, Collected: Nathaniel Wallich in the North-Eastern Frontier of India." Lecture at Natural History Museum, London, December 6, 2011.

———. 2002. "Energizing Tea, Enervating Opium: Culture of Commodities in Colonial Assam." In *Space, Sexuality, and Postcolonial Cultures: Papers from the Cultural Studies Workshop.* ENRECA Papers Series, ed. Manas Ray, 27–53. Calcutta: Centre for Studies in Social Sciences.

Karotemprel, Sebastain, and B. Dutta Roy. 1990. *Tea Garden Labourers of North East India: A Multidimensional Study on Adivasis of the Tea Gardens of North East India.* Shillong: Vendrame Institute.

Kearney, Michael. 1996. *Reconceptualizing the Peasantry: Anthropology in Global Perspective.* Boulder: Westview Press.

Kennedy, Dane. 1996. *The Magic Mountains: Hill Stations and the British Raj.* Berkeley: University of California Press.

———. 1990. "The Perils of the Midday Sun: Climatic Anxieties in the Colonial Tropics." In *Imperialism and the Natural World,* ed. John MacKenzie, 118–40. Manchester: Manchester University Press.

Kenny, Judith. 1995. "Climate, Race, and Imperial Authority: The Symbolic Landscape of the British Hill Station in India." *Annals of the Association of American Geographers* 85(4): 694–714.

Khanduri, C. 1997. *A Re-discovered History of the Gorkhas.* Delhi: Gyan Sagar Publications.

Kirksey, Eben, and Stefan Helmreich. 2010. "The Emergence of Multispecies Ethnography." *Cultural Anthropology* 25(4): 545–76.

Kirshenblatt-Gimblett, Barbara. 1998. *Destination Culture: Tourism, Museums, and Heritage.* Berkeley: University of California Press.

Kling, Blair. 1976. *Partner in Empire: Dwarkanath Tagore and the Age of Enterprise in Eastern India.* Berkeley: University of California Press.

Kloppenburg, Jack, John Hendrickson, and George Stevenson. 1996. "Coming into the Foodshed." *Agriculture and Human Values* 13(3): 33–42.

Kolenda, Pauline. 1963. "Towards a Model of the Hindu *Jajmani* System." *Human Organization* 22(1): 11–39.

Krech, Shepard. 1999. *The Ecological Indian: Myth and History.* New York: W. W. Norton.

Kymlicka, Will. 2002. *Contemporary Political Philosophy: An Introduction.* 2nd ed. Oxford: Oxford University Press.

Lama, Basant. 2009. *Through the Mists of Time: The Story of Darjeeling, the Land of Indian Gorkha.* Kurseong: Bhawani Offset Printing and Publication.

Lama, Mahendra, ed. 1994. *Sikkim: Society, Polity, Economy, and Environment.* New Delhi: Indus Publishing.

Lamphere, Louise. 1985. "Bringing the Family Home to Work: Women's Culture on the Shop Floor." *Feminist Studies* 11: 519–40.

Lees, W. Nassau. 1867. *The Land and Labour of India: A Review.* London: Williams and Norgate.

Locke, John. 1980 [1690]. *Second Treatise of Government.* Ed. C. B. Macpherson. Indianapolis: Hackett Publishing.

Lopez, Mario. 2012. "Reconstituting the Affective Labour of Filipinos as Care Workers in Japan." *Global Networks* 12(2): 252–68.

Luetchford, Peter. 2008. *Fair Trade and a Global Commodity: Coffee in Costa Rica.* London: Pluto Press.

Lutgendorf, Peter. 2009. "Chai Why? The Triumph of Tea in India as Documented in the Priya Paul Collection." Tasveer Ghar: A Digital Archive of South Asian Popular Visual Culture website, www.tasveerghar.net/cmsdesk/essay/89/ (accessed April 19, 2012).

Lyon, Sarah. 2011. *Coffee and Community: Maya Farmers and Fair Trade Markets*. Boulder: University of Colorado Press.

———. 2010. "A Market of Our Own: Women's Livelihoods and Fair Trade Markets." In *Fair Trade and Social Justice: Global Ethnographies*, ed. Sarah Lyon and Mark Moberg, 125–46. New York: New York University Press.

———. 2007. "Maya Coffee Farmers and Fair Trade: Assessing the Benefits and Limitations of Alternative Markets." *Culture and Agriculture* 29(2): 110–12.

———. 2006. "Just Java: Roasting Fair Trade Coffee." In *Fast Food / Slow Food: The Cultural Economy of the Global Food System*, 241–58. New York: AltaMira Press.

Lyon, Sarah, and Mark Moberg, eds. 2010. *Fair Trade and Social Justice: Global Ethnographies*. New York: New York University Press.

MacFarlane, Alan, and Iris MacFarlane. 2003. *Green Gold: The Empire of Tea*. London: Ebury.

Makita, Rie. 2012. "Fair Trade Certification: The Case of Plantation Workers in India." *Development Policy Review* 30(1): 87–107.

Mann, Harold. 1918. *The Early History of the Tea Industry in North-east India*. Reprinted from *Bengal Economic Journal*. Calcutta: D. L. Monro.

Marcus, George, and Fred R. Myers. 1995. *The Traffic in Culture: Refiguring Art and Anthropology*. Berkeley: University of California Press.

Marks, James. 1974. *Ayo Gurkha!* Oxford: Oxford University Press.

Mather, Victoria. 2010. "Best List." *Vanity Fair on Travel*, April 2010, 15–16.

Matsutake Worlds Research Group. 2010. "A New Form of Collaboration in Cultural Anthropology." *American Ethnologist* 36(2): 380–403.

Marx, Karl. 1976 [1867]. *Capital*. Vol. 1. New York: Penguin Books.

Mauss, Marcel. 2000 [1950]. *The Gift: The Form and Reason for Exchange in Archaic Societies*. Trans. W. D. Halls. New York: W. W. Norton.

McElhinny, Bonnie. 2010. "The Audacity of Affect: Gender, Race, and History in Linguistic Accounts of Legitimacy and Belonging." *Annual Review of Anthropology* 39: 309–28.

McGowan, Alexander. 1860. *Tea Planting in the Outer Himalayah*. London: Smith, Elder.

McWilliams, Carey. 1935. *Factories in the Field: The Story of Migratory Farm Labor in California*. Berkeley: University of California Press.

Meehan, Peter. 2007. "To Burundi and Beyond for Coffee's Holy Grail." *New York Times*, September 12.

Merry, Sally Engle. 2000. *Colonizing Hawaii: The Cultural Power of Law*. Princeton, NJ: Princeton University Press.

Metcalf, Thomas. 1995. *Ideologies of the Raj*. Cambridge: Cambridge University Press.

Middleton, Townsend. 2013a. "States of Difference: Refiguring Ethnicity and Its 'Crisis' at India's Borders." *Political Geography* 35: 14–24.

———. 2013b. "Anxious Belongings: Anxiety and Politics of Belonging in Subnationalist Darjeeling." *American Anthropologist* 115(4).

———. 2013c. "Scheduling Tribes: A View from Inside India's Ethnographic State." *Focaal* 65: 13–22.

———. 2011. "Across the Interface of State Ethnography: Rethinking Ethnology and its Subjects in Multicultural India." *American Ethnologist* 38(2): 249–66.

Miller, Daniel. 1998a. *A Theory of Shopping*. Ithaca, NY: Cornell University Press.

———, ed. 1998b. *Material Cultures: Why Some Things Matter*. Chicago: University of Chicago Press.

Minkoff-Zern, Laura-Anne, and Christy Getz. 2011. "Bringing Farmworkers in Food Justice." *Race, Poverty, and the Environment* 18(1): 17-19.

Mintz, Sidney. 1985. *Sweetness and Power: The Place of Sugar in Modern History*. New York: Penguin Books.

———. 1973. "A Note on the Definition of Peasantries." *Journal of Peasant Studies* 1(3): 291–325.

———. 1960. *Worker in the Cane: A Puerto Rican Life History*. New Haven, CT: Yale University Press.

Mitchell, Don. 2003. "Cultural Landscapes: Just Landscapes or Landscapes of Justice?" *Progress in Human Geography* 27(6): 787–96.

———. 1996. *The Lie of the Land: Migrant Workers and the California Landscape*. Minneapolis: University of Minnesota Press.

Moberg, Mark. 2010. "A New World? Neoliberalism and Fair Trade Farming in the Eastern Caribbean." In *Fair Trade and Social Justice: Global Ethnographies*, ed. Sarah Lyon and Mark Moberg, 47–71. New York: New York University Press.

———. 2008. *Slipping Away: Banana Politics and Fair Trade in the Eastern Caribbean*. Brooklyn, NY: Berghahn Books.

———. 1997. *Myths of Ethnicity and Nation: Immigration, Work, and Identity in the Belize Banana Industry*. Knoxville: University of Tennessee Press.

———. 1996. "Myths That Divide: Immigrant Labor and Class Segmentation in the Belizean Banana Industry." *American Ethnologist* 23(2): 311–30.

Moktan, R., ed. 2004. *Sikkim, Darjeeling: Compendium of Documents*. Varnasi: Gopal Press.

Moore, Sally Falk, ed. 2005. *Law and Anthropology: A Reader*. Malden, MA: Blackwell.

Moran, Emilio. 1984. "Limitations and Advances in Ecosystems Research." In *The Ecosystem Concept in Anthropology*, 3–32. Boulder: Westview Press.

Muehlebach, Andrea. 2011. "On Affective Labor in Post-Fordist Italy." *Cultural Anthropology*. 26(1): 59–82.

Muktan, K. K. 2002. *The Legendary Gorkhas*. Guwahati: Spectrum Publications.

Murray, Douglas, Laura Raynolds, and Peter Taylor. 2006. "The Future of Fair Trade Coffee: Dilemmas Facing Latin America's Small-Scale Producers." *Development in Practice* 16(2): 179–92.

Myers, Fred. 2001. "The Empire of Things." Introduction to *The Empire of Things: Regimes of Value and Material Culture*, ed. Fred Myers, 3–61. Santa Fe, NM: School for Advanced Research Press.

Nadasdy, Paul. 2007. "The Gift in the Animal: The Ontology of Hunting and Human-Animal Sociality." *American Ethnologist* 34 (1): 25–43.

———. 2005. "Transcending the Debate over the Ecologically Noble Indian: Indigenous Peoples and Environmentalism." *Ethnohistory* 52(2): 291–331.

Nading, Alex. 2012. "'Dengue Mosquitoes are Single Mothers:' Biopolitics Meets Ecological Aesthetics in Nicaraguan Community Health Work." *Cultural Anthropology* 27(4): 572–96.

Nag, Sajal. 2002. *Contesting Marginality: Ethnicity, Insurgency, and Subnationalism in North-East India.* Delhi: Manohar.

Nath, Lopita. 2005. "Migrants in Flight: Conflict Induced Internal Displacement of Nepalis in Northeast India." *Peace and Democracy in South Asia* 1(1): 57–72.

Neuman, William. 2011. "A Question of Fairness." *New York Times,* November 23.

Newman and Company. 1900. *Newman's Guide to Darjeeling and Its Surroundings, Historical and Descriptive, with Some Account of the Manners and Customs of the Neighbouring Hill Tribes.* London: W. H. Allen.

Notes on Darjeeling by a Planter. 1888. Calcutta: Military Orphan Press.

Nozick, Robert. 1974. *Anarchy, State, and Utopia.* New York: Basic Books.

Odum, Eugene. 1979 [1953]. *Fundamentals of Ecology.* 3rd ed. Philadelphia: Saunders.

Ogden, Laura. 2011. *Swamplife: People, Gators, and Mangroves Entangled in the Everglades.* Minneapolis: University of Minnesota Press.

O'Malley, L. S. S. 1985 [1907]. *Bengal District Gazetteer: Darjeeling.* New Delhi: Logos Press.

Ong, Aihwa. 1999. *Flexible Citizenship: the Cultural Logics of Transnationality.* Durham, NC: Duke University Press.

Ortiz, Sutti. 1999. *Harvesting Coffee, Bargaining Wages: Rural Labor Markets in Columbia.* Ann Arbor: University of Michigan Press.

Ortner, Sherry. 1999. *Life and Death on Mt. Everest: Sherpas and Himalayan Mountaineering.* Princeton, NJ: Princeton University Press.

Osella, Filippo, and Caroline Osella. 2003. "Migration and the Commoditisation of Ritual: Sacrifice, Spectacle and Contestations in Kerala, India." *Contributions to Indian Sociology* 37: 109–39.

Papers on the Tea Factories and Plantations in Kumaon and Gurhwal. 1854. Agra: Secundra Orphan Press. Bound with other documents in *Boodhism and Cave Temples in India,* National Library, Calcutta.

Parry, Jonathan. 2003. "Nehru's Dream and the Village 'Waiting Room': Long-Distance Labour Migrants to a Central Indian Steel Town." *Contributions to Indian Sociology* 37: 217–49.

Patterson, Christopher B. 2012. "Cosmopolitanism, Ethnic Belonging, and Affective Labor: Han Ong's Fixer Chao and the Disinherited." *Journal of Labor and Society* 15: 87–102.

Paxson, Heather. 2012. *The Life of Cheese: Crafting Food and Value in America.* Berkeley: University of California.

———. 2010. Locating Value in Artisan Cheese: Reverse Engineering *Terroir* for New-World Landscapes. *American Anthropologist* 112(3): 444–57.

———. 2006. "Artisanal Cheese and Economies of Sentiment in New England." In *Fast Food/Slow Food: The Cultural Economy of the Global Food System,* ed. Richard Wilk, 201–18. Lanham, MD: AltaMira Press.

Pettigrew, Jane. 2001. *A Social History of Tea.* London: National Trust Enterprises.

Phukan, Umananda. 1984. *The Ex-Tea Garden Labour Population in Assam.* Delhi: B.R. Publishing.

Pinn, Fred. 2003. *Darjeeling Pioneers: The Wernicke-Stölke Story.* Somerset, England: Pagoda Tree Press.

———. 1986. *The Road of Destiny: Darjeeling Letters, 1839.* Calcutta: Oxford University Press.

Po'dar, Preym, and Tanka B. Subba. 1991. "Demystifying Some Ethnographic Texts on the Himalayas." *Social Scientist* 19(8–9): 78–84.

Polanyi, Karl. 1944. *The Great Transformation: the Political and Economic Origins of Our Time.* Boston: Beacon Press.

Pradhan, K. L. 2004. "Settlement of Gorkhas." In *Cross-Border Migration: Mizoram Cross-Border Migration: Mizoram*, ed. Sangkima. Delhi: Shipra Publications.

Pradhan, Kumar. 1991. *The Gorkha Conquests: The Process and Consequences of the Unification of Nepal, with Particular Reference to Eastern Nepal.* Oxford: Oxford University Press.

Prest, John. 1981. *The Garden of Eden: The Botanical Garden and the Recreation of Paradise.* New Haven, CT: Yale University Press.

Prieto-Carron, Marina. 2006. "Central American Banana Production: Women Workers and Chiquita's Ethical Sourcing from Plantations." In *Ethical Sourcing in the Global Food System*, ed. Sarah Barrientos and Catherine Dolan, 97–114. London: Earthscan.

Rai, R. B. 2000. *Hamro Basbhūmimā Chiyābāri Majdūr Āndolanko Pahilo Charan: Pheri Nayā Charan.* Darjeeling: Compuset Centre.

Rajan, S. Ravi. 2006. *Modernizing Nature: Forestry and Imperial Eco-Development, 1800–1950.* Oxford: Oxford University Press.

Ramamurthy, Priti. 2010. "Why Are Men Doing Floral Sex Work? Gender, Cultural Reproduction, and the Feminization of Agriculture." *Signs* 35(2): 397–424.

Ramos, Jaime. 1996. "Introduction of Exotic Tree Species as a Threat to Azores Bullfinch Population." *Journal of Applied Ecology* 33(4): 710–22.

Rao, C. Niranjan. 2005. "Geographical Indications in Indian Context: A Case Study of Darjeeling Tea." *Economic and Political Weekly*, October 15, 4545–50.

Rawls, John. 1971. *A Theory of Justice.* Cambridge, MA: Harvard University Press.

Ray, Satyajit. 2004 [1962]. *Kanchenjunga.* Film. Kolkata: Angel Video.

Redfield, Robert. 1956. *The Little Community.* Chicago: University of Chicago Press.

Reichman, Daniel. 2011. *The Broken Village: Coffee, Migration, and Globalization in Honduras.* Ithaca, NY: Cornell University Press.

Renard, Marie-Christine. 2003. "Fair Trade: Quality, Markets and Conventions." *Journal of Rural Studies* 19: 87–97.

Rhodes, Nicholas, and Deki Rhodes. 2006. *A Man of the Frontier: S. W. Laden La (1876–1936), His Life, and Times in Darjeeling and Tibet.* Kolkata: Library of Numismatic Studies.

Rice, Robert. 2000. "Noble Goals and Challenging Terrain: Organic and Fair Trade Coffee Movements in the Global Marketplace." *Journal of Agricultural and Environmental Ethics* (14)1: 39–66.

Roberts, Judith. 1998. "English Gardens in India." *Garden History* 26(2): 115–35.

Rose, Sarah. 2009. *For All the Tea in China: How England Stole the World's Favorite Drink and Changed History.* New York: Viking Press.

Roseberry, William. 1996. "The Rise of Yuppie Coffees and the Reimagination of Class in the United States." *American Anthropologist* 94(4): 762–75.

Roseberry, William, Lowell Gudmundson, and Mario Samper Kutschbach, eds. 1995. *Coffee, Society, and Power in Latin America.* Baltimore: Johns Hopkins University Press.

Rosen, Lawrence. 1989. *The Anthropology of Justice: Law as Culture in Islamic Society.* Cambridge: Cambridge University Press.

Sachs, Wolfgang. 1992. "Environment." In *The Development Dictionary: A Guide to Knowledge as Power,* ed. Wolfgang Sachs. London: Zed Books.

Said, Edward. 1978. *Orientalism.* New York: Vintage Books.

Samanta, Amiya, 1996. *Gorkhaland: A Study in Ethnic Separatism.* New Delhi: Khama Publishers.

Sarkar, R. L. 1998. *Christian Tea Garden Workers of Tribal Origin.* Delhi: Christian Institute for the Study of Religion and Society.

Sawyer, Suzana, and Arun Agrawal. 2000. "Environmental Orientalisms." *Cultural Critique* 45: 71–108.

Scheper-Hughes, Nancy. 1992. *Death without Weeping: The Violence of Everyday Life in Brazil.* Berkeley: University of California Press.

Schivelbusch, Wolfgang. 1992. *Tastes of Paradise: A Social History of Spices, Stimulants, and Intoxicants.* New York: Vintage Books.

Schmidt, Ruth Laila. 1993. *A Practical Dictionary of Modern Nepali.* Delhi: Ratna Sagar.

Scoones, Ian. 1999. "New Ecology and the Social Sciences: What Prospects for a Fruitful Engagement?" *Annual Review of Anthropology* 28: 479–507.

Scott, James. 1976. *The Moral Economy of the Peasant: Rebellion and Subsistence in Southeast Asia.* New Haven, CT: Yale University Press.

Seddon, David. 2005. "Nepal's Dependence on Exporting Labor." *Migration Information Source.* Migration Policy Institute, www.migrationinformation.org/Profiles/print.cfm?ID = 277 (accessed March 21, 2012).

Seddon, David, Jagannath Adhikari, and Ganesh Gurung. 2002. "Foreign Labor Migration and the Remittance Economy of Nepal." *Critical Asian Studies* 34(1): 19–40.

———. 2001. *The New Lahures: Foreign Employment and Remittance Economy of Nepal.* Kathmandu: Nepal Institute of Development Studies.

Sen, Debarati. 2009. "From Illegal to Organic: Fair Trade-Organic Tea Production and Women's Political Futures in Darjeeling, India." Ph.D. diss., Department of Anthropology, Rutgers University.

Shah, Apla. 2006. "The Labor of Love: Seasonal Migration from Jharkand to the Brick Kilns of Other States in India." *Contributions to Indian Sociology* 40(1): 91–118.

Sharma, Jayeeta. 2011. *Empire's Garden: Assam and the Making of Modern India.* Durham, NC: Duke University Press.

———. 2006. "British Science, Chinese Skill, and Assam Tea: Making Empire's Garden." *Indian Economic and Social History Review* 43(4): 429–55.

Sharma, Khemraj. 2009. *Globalization and Tea Plantation Workers in North-East India.* Delhi: Kalpaz Publications.

———. 2003. *Tea Plantation Workers in a Himalayan Region.* New Delhi: Mittal Publications.

———. 2000. The Himalayan Tea Plantation Workers. Dibrugarh: N.L. Publishers.

Shiva, Vandana. 2000. *Stolen Harvest: The Hijacking of the Global Food Supply.* Cambridge: South End Press.

Shneiderman, Sara. 2009a. "Rituals of Ethnicity: Migration, Mixture, and the Making of Thangmi Identity across Himalayan Borders." PhD diss., Department of Anthropology, Cornell University.

————. 2009b. "Ethnic (P)reservations: Comparing Thangmi Ethnic Activism in Nepal and India." In *Ethnic Activism and Civil Society in South Asia*, ed. David Gellner, 115–41. Delhi: Sage Publications.

————. 2005. "The Other Nepali Politics: Darjeeling." *Nation Weekly* 1(42): 27–29.

Shneiderman, Sarah, and Mark Turin. 2006. "Seeking the Tribe: Ethno-Politics in Darjeeling and Sikkim." *Himāl South Asian* 18(5): 54-58.

Shreck, Aimee. 2005. "Resistance, Redistribution, and Power in the Fair trade Banana Initiative." *Agriculture and Human Values* 22: 17–29.

Silva, Luís, and Clifford Smith. 2006. "A Quantitative Approach to the Study of Non-Indigenous Plants: An Example from the Azores Archipelago." *Biodiversity and Conservation* 15(5): 1661–79.

Silverman, Sydel. 1979. "The Peasant Concept in Anthropology." *Journal of Peasant Studies* 7(1): 49–69.

Simmel, Georg. 1978. *The Philosophy of Money*. Trans. David Frisby. New York: Routledge, Kegan, and Paul.

Sinha, A. C. 2008. *Sikkim: Feudal and Democratic*. New Delhi: Indus Publishing.

Sivaramakrishnan, K. 1999. *Modern Forests: Statemaking and Environmental Change in Colonial Eastern India*. Stanford, CA: Stanford University Press.

Smith, Julia. 2007. "The Search for Sustainable Markets: The Promise and Failures of Fair Trade." *Culture and Agriculture* 29(2): 89–99.

Soule, Judith, and Jon Piper. 1992. *Farming in Nature's Image: An Ecological Approach to Agriculture*. Washington DC: Island Press.

Spencer, J. E., and W. L. Thomas. 1948. "The Hill Stations and Summer Resorts of the Orient." *Geographical Review* 38(4): 637–51.

Steiner, Christopher. 1994. *African Art in Transit*. New York: Cambridge University Press.

Stolcke, Verena. 1988. *Coffee Planters, Workers, and Wives: Class Conflict and Gender Relations on São Paulo Plantations, 1850–1980*. New York: St. Martin's Press.

Stoler, Ann Laura. 2008. "Imperial Debris: Reflections on Ruins and Ruinations." *Cultural Anthropology* 23(2): 191–219.

————. 1995. *Race and the Education of Desire: Foucault's "History of Sexuality" and the Colonial Order of Things*. Durham, NC: Duke University Press.

————. 1985. *Capitalism and Confrontation in Sumatra's Plantation Belt, 1870–1979*. Ann Arbor: University of Michigan Press.

Stone, Glenn Davis. 2004. "Biotechnology and the Political Ecology of Information in India." *Human Organization* 63: 127–40.

Striffler, Steve. 2002. *In the Shadows of State and Capital: The United Fruit Company, Popular Struggle, and Agrarian Restructuring in Ecuador, 1900–1995*. Durham, NC: Duke University Press.

Subba, Tanka B. 2002. "Nepal and the Indian Nepalis." In *State of Nepal*, ed. Kanak Mani Dixit and Shastri Ramachandran, 119–36. Lalitpur: Himal Books.

————. 1992. *Ethnicity, State, and Development: A Case Study in the Gorkhaland Movement*. New Delhi: Vikas Publishing House.

Subedi, Surya. 1994. "India-Nepal Security Relations and the 1950 Treaty: Time for New Perspectives." *Asian Survey* 34(3): 273–84.

Tamang, Sudha. 2011. "Darjeeling; British Sikkim, Scheduled District, and Separate Administrative Set-Up." *Darjeeling Times*, July 23.

Tamlong, D. T. 2008. *Mayel Lyang and The Lepchas*. Darjeeling: Mani Printing Press.

Tamsang, K. P. 1983. *The Unknown and Untold Reality of the Lepchas*. Kalimpong: Mani Printing Press.

Tamsang, Lyangsong. 2008. *Lepcha Folklore and Folk Songs*. New Delhi: Sahitya Academi.

Taussig, Michael. 1993. *Mimesis and Alterity: A Particular History of the Senses*. New York: Routledge, Chapman, and Hall.

Tea Board of India. 2003. *Darjeeling Tea: A Geographical Indication*. Promotional video. Author's personal collection.

The Tea Cyclopaedia: Articles on Tea, Tea Science, Blights, Soils and Manures, Cultivation, Buildings, Manufacture, &c. with Tea Statistics. 1882. Compiled by the editor of the *Indian Tea Gazette*. London: W. B. Whittingham.

Thompson, E. P. 1971. "The Moral Economy of the English Crowd in the Eighteenth Century." *Past and Present* 50: 76–136.

———. 1963. *The Making of the English Working Class*. New York: Pantheon Books.

Trubek, Amy. 2008. *The Taste of Place: A Cultural Journey into Terroir*. Berkeley: University of California Press.

Trubek, Amy, and Sarah Bowen. 2008. "Creating the Taste of Place in the United States: Can We Learn from the French?" *GeoJournal* 73: 23–30.

Tsing, Anna. 2012. "Unruly Edges: Mushrooms as Companion Species." *Environmental Humanities* 1: 141–54.

———. 2010. "Nonhumans and Globalization: On Multispecies Storytelling." Institute for Research on the Humanities, University of Wisconsin-Madison, February 27.

———. 2005. *Friction: An Ethnography of Global Connection*. Princeton, NJ: Princeton University Press.

Tucker, Francis. 1957. *Gorkha: The Story of the Gurkhas of Nepal*. London: Constable.

Turin, Mark. 2001. "Call Me Uncle: An Outsider's Experience of Nepali Kinship." *Contributions to Nepalese Studies* 28(2): 277–83.

Turner, Ralph Lilley. 1997 [1931]. *A Comparative Entomological Dictionary of the Nepali Language*. New Delhi: Allied Publishers.

Ukers, William. 1935. *All about Tea*. Vol. 1. New York: Tea and Coffee Trade Journal Company.

Ulin, Robert. 1995. "Invention and Representation as Cultural Capital: Southwest French Winegrowing History." *American Anthropologist* 97(3): 519–27.

Urry, John. 1995. *Consuming Places*. London: Routledge.

———. 1990. *The Tourist Gaze: Leisure and Travel in Contemporary Societies*. London: Sage Publications.

Weiss, Brad. 2011. "Making Pigs Local: Discerning the Sensory Character of Place." *Cultural Anthropology* 26(3): 438–61.

West, Paige. 2012. *From Modern Production to Imagined Primitive: The Social World of Coffee from Papua New Guinea*. Durham, NC: Duke University Press.

———. 2010. "Making the Market: Specialty Coffee, Generational Pitches, and Papua New Guinea. *Antipode* 42(3): 690–718.

———. 2006. *Conservation Is Our Government Now: The Politics of Ecology in Papua New Guinea*. Durham, NC: Duke University Press.

West, Paige, and James Carrier. 2004. "Ecotourism and Authenticity: Getting Away from it All?" *Current Anthropology* 45(5): 483–98.

Whelpton, John. 2005. *A History of Nepal.* Cambridge: Cambridge University Press.

Williams, Raymond. 1973. *The Country and the City.* Oxford: Oxford University Press.

Willis, Paul. 1977. *Learning to Labour: How Working Class Kids Get Working Class Jobs.* New York: Columbia University Press.

Wilson, James. 1998. Terroir: *The Role of Geology, Climate, and Culture in the Making of French Wines.* Berkeley: University of California Press.

Wright, Melissa. 2006. *Disposable Women and Other Myths of Global Capitalism.* New York: Routledge.

Wolf, Eric. 1969. *Peasant Wars of the Twentieth Century.* New York: Harper and Row.

———. 1966. *Peasants.* Englewood Cliffs, NJ: Prentice-Hall.

Wolf, Eric, and Sidney Mintz. 1957. "Haciendas and Plantations in Middle America and the Antilles." *Social and Economic Studies* 6(3): 380–412.

World Commission on Environment and Development (WCED). 1987. *Our Common Future.* Oxford: Oxford University Press.

World Intellectual Property Rights Organization (WIPO). 2011. "Managing the Challenges of the Protection and Enforcement of Intellectual Property Rights: Darjeeling Tea." WIPO website, www.wipo.int/ipadvantage/en/details.jsp?id = 2540 (accessed February 23, 2012).

Worster, Donald. 1977. *Nature's Economy: A History of Ecological Ideas.* San Francisco: Sierra Club Books.

Yardley, Jim. 2012. "Good Name Is Restored in Terrain Known for Tea." *New York Times,* December 16.

Ziegler, Catherine. 2010. "Fair Flowers: Environmental and Social Labelling in the Global Cut Flower Industry." In *Fair Trade and Social Justice: Global Ethnographies,* ed. Sarah Lyon and Mark Moberg, 72–. New York: New York University Press.

INDEX

ABGL (Akhil Bharatiya Gorkha League): founding and activities, 77–78, 167, 187n17, 195n48, 200–201n12; Tamang's presidency and murder, 141–42, 167–68, 201n17
adivāsi labor, 50, 54–55, 56, 58*fig.*, 191n91, 194n23
agave production, 185n59, 198n31
Agrarian Dreams (Guthman), 29, 31. *See also* Guthman, Julie
agrarian imaginary, 29–30. *See also* Third World agrarian imaginary
agro-environment. *See* land and landscape; tea cultivation; tea plants
Akhil Bharatiya Gorkha League. *See* ABGL; Tamang, Madan
Aloobari estate, 190n76
Anglo-Nepal Wars, 41, 42, 47
antipolitics, 133, 199n29
Appadurai, Arjun, 16
appellation of origin protections. *See* GI status
Assam Agricultural University, 117, 158
Assam and Assam tea industry, 83, 129; Assam teas, 8, 50, 51, 52, 104, 130, 184n52, 190n73; Cherrapunji hill station, 42; development and labor recruitment, 50, 51, 53, 54–55, 73, 74, 75, 194nn23,32; wasteland leases, 188n25
Assam Company, 51

Basso, Keith, 187n7
Bentham, Jeremy, 184–85n50
Bentinck, Lord, 50

Bhanubhakta Acharya statue, 44–45, 46*fig.*
Bharatiya Janata Party (BJP), 166–67, 177
bhūmī, 202–3n38
Bhutan, xxii*map*, 139, 188nn25,26,37, 200–201n12, 201n13
biodynamic certification, 115, 198n1
Birla Tea Management School, 34–35, 159
bisnis, 36–37, 61–63, 84, 124; unions and, 80, 175; workers' critiques of, 61–62, 63, 80, 85, 134–35, 171–72, 173
BJP (Bharatiya Janata Party), 166–67, 177
blended teas, 21, 24, 101, 103
Blunt, Alison, 189n47
Boisard, Pierre, 196n2
botanical gardens, 48–50, 52
Bourdieu, Pierre, 15, 96
Bowen, Sarah, 185n59, 198n31
Britannia (equipment manufacturer), 53
British East India Company, 4–6, 41, 47, 191n90; plantation labor issues, 54–56. *See also* British India
British India: Anglo-Nepal Wars, 41, 42, 47; China tea trade and, 4–5; gardening in, 189n47; Gurkha soldiers in the British Army, 18, 47, 55, 67, 76, 78, 144, 148, 189n45, 192nn102,104; hill stations, 41–44, 45, 106, 188n28; independence movements, 76, 77–78; indigenous tea consumption, 3, 51, 190n69; opium cultivation, 4; reimaginings/remakings of landscape and peoples, 49–50; tea cultivation, 3, 5–6.